BLACK SHAKESPEARE

Race may dominate everyday speech, media headlines, and public policy, still questions of racialized blackness and whiteness in Shakespeare are resisted. In his compelling new book, Ian Smith addresses the influence of systemic whiteness on the interpretation of Shakespeare's plays. This far-reaching study shows that significant parts of Shakespeare's texts have been elided, misconstrued, or otherwise rendered invisible by readers who have ignored the presence of race in early modern England. Bringing the Black American intellectual tradition into fruitful dialogue with European thought, this urgent interdisciplinary work offers a deep, revealing, and incisive analysis of individual plays, including *Othello*, *The Merchant of Venice*, and *Hamlet*. Demonstrating how racial illiteracy inhibits critical practice, Ian Smith provides a necessary antiracist alternative that will transform the way you read Shakespeare.

IAN SMITH is the Richard H., Jr. '60 and Joan K. Sell Professor in the Humanities at Lafayette College. He is the author of *Race and Rhetoric in the Renaissance: Barbarian Errors* (2009) and collaborator on *Othello Re-imagined in Sepia* (2012). He has held several fellowships including the *Los Angeles Times* Distinguished Fellowship in the History and Culture of the Americas. He is currently Vice President of the Shakespeare Association of America.

"*Black Shakespeare* is an important and timely study of how race affects reading and interpretation. Smith not only illuminates various functions of whiteness within Shakespeare's plays, but also demonstrates that whiteness has shaped the idea of Shakespeare in Shakespeare Studies. Beyond the brilliant insights that it offers about Shakespeare, *Black Shakespeare* requires literary scholars to reckon with how white supremacy is perpetuated through interpretive practices."

Dennis Britton, The University of British Columbia

"In *Black Shakespeare,* Ian Smith trenchantly demonstrates how white epistemology and systemic whiteness cause readers to sanitize, distort, and elide key parts of Shakespeare's texts. Theoretically and historically grounded, *Black Shakespeare* also deploys dazzling acts of close reading to show exactly what a white reading practice misses or gets wrong. Throughout, Smith makes the stakes of his argument clear: readers must acquire an expanded racial literacy both to read Shakespeare well and also to become citizens fit for the demands of a democratic polity."

Jean E. Howard, Columbia University

"Ian Smith delivers an indisputable, learned, and earth-shattering intervention into our habits and practices of reading the works of William Shakespeare. If Smith is right that Shakespeare's plays are read, taught, and interpreted on stage overwhelmingly through the lens of whiteness, then racial illiteracy informs our relationship with the Bard. To read Shakespeare rigorously, thoroughly, and with intention is to acknowledge what Smith calls our 'racial blindspots.' Smith's novel readings of Shakespeare's tragedies are unflinching as he asks us to confront what is actually before our eyes. *Black Shakespeare* is essential reading for all those studying, teaching, and performing these works."

Farah Karim-Cooper, Shakespeare's Globe and King's College London

"Ian Smith's *Black Shakespeare* begins by asserting that lingering contemporary resistance to the evidence that people in the early modern world believed that race was real and that it mattered participates in a larger denial of the kinds of work that race performs in our own time. In a series of subtle and revelatory readings – I am thinking particularly of the dazzling chapter on *Hamlet* – Smith implicitly argues that learning to recognize race's subtle and extensive operations in Shakespeare can be an important first step toward our own achievement of what he calls 'racial literacy.' To see and to know, Smith believes, is to begin to be able to recognize and resist white supremacy's purchase in our field, and in the culture that shapes it. Persuasively argued and deeply ethically engaged throughout, *Black Shakespeare* is the work of a mature scholar who believes that Shakespeare matters, and who calls on us both to embrace and to question the conditions under which he has achieved his place in our world."

Joyce MacDonald, University of Kentucky

"*Black Shakespeare* is revelatory, stunning, and arresting! Crafting a disorienting tour de force, Ian Smith has written an essential book for all readers of Shakespeare that demonstrates not only how we have misread the plays, but also how we might rectify readings in the future. A requisite read!"

Ayanna Thompson, Arizona State University

"In an argument that is both elegant and forceful, Smith makes the obvious but heretofore underappreciated point that the act of 'reading historically' is itself saturated with a racial history that must be a subject of analysis. For putting this argument on the table, and for its convincing reappraisal of some of Shakespeare's best-known plays, Smith's study is destined to be a landmark in a field that continues to pose powerful, searching questions in the humanities."

Michael Witmore, Folger Shakespeare Library

BLACK SHAKESPEARE

Reading and Misreading Race

IAN SMITH
Lafayette College

CAMBRIDGE
UNIVERSITY PRESS

Shaftesbury Road, Cambridge CB2 8EA, United Kingdom

One Liberty Plaza, 20th Floor, New York, NY 10006, USA

477 Williamstown Road, Port Melbourne, VIC 3207, Australia

314–321, 3rd Floor, Plot 3, Splendor Forum, Jasola District Centre, New Delhi – 110025, India

103 Penang Road, #05–06/07, Visioncrest Commercial, Singapore 238467

Cambridge University Press is part of Cambridge University Press & Assessment, a department of the University of Cambridge.

We share the University's mission to contribute to society through the pursuit of education, learning and research at the highest international levels of excellence.

www.cambridge.org
Information on this title: www.cambridge.org/ 9781009224093

DOI: 10.1017/9781009224116

First published 2022
First paperback edition 2025

A catalogue record for this publication is available from the British Library

ISBN 978-1-009-22408-6 Hardback
ISBN 978-1-009-22409-3 Paperback

Contents

Acknowledgments

I am grateful to Lafayette College for granting me a period of research leave to work on this book. For their time reading chapters, I express my deepest thanks to Pat Donahue and Erik Mathews; their generosity and encouragement in providing feedback galvanized my efforts. I had occasion to share some of my thinking as work-in-progress and recognize especially the Renaissance Literature Seminar at the Huntington Library and the Shakespeare Association of America for providing venues where conversations with participants and interlocutors gave me the confidence to pursue the line of inquiry that has resulted in this book. From the beginning of the project to its completion, Jean E. Howard has been an unwavering source of support. Finally, the vigilance of family, Joy Franklin, Mary Gray, and Grace Henry, has sustained me throughout the process.

Introduction
Toward Racial Literacy

The Fact of Early Modern Race

Grappling with reading and misreading Shakespeare goes back as far as the publication of his collected works. Addressed "To the Great Variety of Readers," the Preface to Shakespeare's 1623 First Folio ties book sales to potential consumers' "diuers capacities," meaning the diversity or variety in reading skills or literacy.[1] The Folio's editors, John Heminge and Henry Condell, emphasized literacy as central to an effective marketing strategy, and Folio sales, they argued, relied on a literate, readership who would publicize the virtues of Shakespeare's collected works. Literacy as reading competence had a commercial value in popularizing the works and would, in hindsight, prove canonically consequential to the author's legacy. Today, however, a markedly different learned capacity – a *racial literacy* – is demanded of scholars and critics who, as modern readers and stewards of the maintenance and growth of the Shakespeare industry, are confronted with a racially different research scenario and perception of texts.

We now know that the early modern theater manifested a global awareness of blackness through the multiple African characters in works by several writers, including William Shakespeare, George Peele, George Chapman, Ben Jonson, John Webster, Thomas Middleton, and Richard Brome.[2] The textual encoding of blackness sets in relief the moment in early modern history when the presence of blackness, in the form and person of Africans, entered the lives of white Europeans – whether through trade, travel and exploration, immigration, and, perhaps most widely, through readings of various texts and the staged encounters of theatrical representation.[3] Transported enslaved Africans, black household servants, royal musicians, weavers, porters, mariners, and other laborers among the varied professions populate the historical and literary archives; imported goods and fashionable items rehearse the black presence in the residual cultural traces of their foreign affiliations.[4] Accounts of English national and political culture now reflect reconsiderations of religion, gender, language, civility, kinship, trade, commerce, and imperialism as deeply embedded categories and vectors of race.[5] Making visible this black corporal and textual presence, early modern race research has altered the demographic landscape of traditional scholarship over the last thirty years.[6]

This study posits, therefore, that the fact of blackness in Shakespeare's world and work is sufficient to claim his considerable investment in race is more far-reaching and complex than we have historically been prepared to acknowledge. The crucial question thus remains: How have scholars, as readers, adjusted to the evidence of Shakespeare's racial interests? Despite the explicit attention early modern theatrical texts and audiences paid to signs and sights of blackness,[7] Francesca T. Royster's observations from the late 1990s concerning early modern studies as an "'unraced' enterprise" remains true today, albeit in more nuanced forms.[8] In his review of early modern scholarship for 2017, Henry S. Turner laments the paucity of only two race monographs being published, the majority of publications being devoted to ecocriticism, with a focus on animal studies.[9] Turner observes: "Put most sharply, we might wonder: how has it come to pass that the creaturely life of sheep, oranges, and yeast seem more significant than the life of Caliban, say – the lives of slaves and persons of color?"[10] I read Turner's critique not as a dismissal of any specific research agenda, but instead as an attempt to call attention to particular scholarly acts of deferral and displacement. The intense, legitimate interest in "creaturely life" can work to suspend discussions of race, in effect, urging us to look away from the uneasy questions of injustice to fellow humans and the role of whiteness in the historical arc of that display of inhumanity. As a response to this longstanding disciplinary pattern and practice, in 2020 the RaceB4Race Executive Board delivered a polemic against institutional gatekeeping by journals whose editorial boards profess inclusion despite an actual record of meager publications of premodern race scholarship.[11] Admittedly, gatekeeping has always been a part of any professional and academic effort to set and maintain standards of scholarship and practice. I understand the Executive Board's call, however, as an attempt to redress the inconsistency between editorial boards' stated purpose and action.

What began as a groundswell of skepticism toward so-called unhistorical methods in the 1990s has endured, though bereft of the historical cudgel.[12] Even after "more than twenty years of scholarship in early modern studies," Peter Erickson and Kim F. Hall remark in a 2016 special issue of *Shakespeare Quarterly*, "we can only conclude that these acts of refusal are also due to a pathological averseness to thinking about race under the guise of protecting historical difference."[13] Importantly, I would add, early modern race studies initiated a revolution that challenged the pre-existing methodological and hermeneutic status quo, expanded the range and substance of investigatory inquiry, rendered explicit the political stakes of critical representation, and effected a reorientation of intellectual perspective in Shakespeare and premodern texts.[14] What has become increasingly clear in hindsight is that the opposition to early modern race studies betrayed a profound understanding of the challenges to established practices that were slow to change. More tellingly, the resistance constituted a political response to the calling out of the dominant white epistemology that was the unstated coin of the critical realm.

Traditional reading and interpretive habits have left us unprepared, therefore, to fully appreciate Shakespeare's persistent appeal to notions of race through textual evidence in his works that is often passed over or misrecognized. More than anything, race unsettles the epistemological status quo and disturbs long-held intellectual positions that have become normalized so that the response to the question, "How have scholars adjusted to the evidence of Shakespeare's racial interests?" can be stated briefly: the playwright's investment has been subject to resistance. However, rather than simply remark on this opposition, as many have done, *Black Shakespeare: Reading and Misreading Race* shifts the focus to the cause and purpose and locates resistance to race in the historical conditions that shape readers, inform their epistemologies, and influence their reading practices. This book argues that the tension between the textual signs of blackness and the modern scholar–reader's blindness to this racial evidence derives from a cultural conditioning, intellectual formation, and epistemological predisposition identified in this study as *systemic whiteness*, the derivative of institutional and structural norms that have created white privilege, preference, and bias.

Reading, as explicitly evoked in the book's subtitle, refers primarily to the kinds of textual engagements that are central to the production of scholarship and criticism. Related to that definition is the work of interpretation, evaluation, and debating that includes the range of dialogue and exchange from the classroom, the academic symposium, and the work of editors and publishers, to the textual interactions of theater directors, actors, and audiences. Race, as typically invoked and understood, describes otherness, concerns people of color and, more often than not, as Patricia J. Williams maintains, "permits whites to entertain the notion that race lives 'over there' on the other side of the tracks, in the black bodies and inner-city neighborhoods, in the dark netherworld where whites are not involved."[15] A complicating factor is "race obliviousness," since for most whites, Harlon Dalton argues, whiteness as race "is simply part of the unseen, unproblematic background."[16] Thus, to discuss reading Shakespeare is not just to recognize, concede, or confront the culturally learned slippages and maneuvers of avoiding race, but also to locate whiteness within the enterprise and to understand whiteness itself as a source of racial blindness. To discuss reading Shakespeare is to admit that reading as a culturally embedded activity is informed by complex social pressures implied in the paradigm of seeing and not seeing race, accounting or not accounting for whiteness.

Moreover, while the advent of early modern race studies substantially changed the dialogue in Shakespeare scholarship and criticism, it has not, to date, likewise addressed the specific questions concerning the reader.[17] In this study, the reader is situated at the juncture of the fact of early modern blackness and critical denial. Ayanna Thompson asserts in *Passing Strange* that "race is the giant elephant in the room," at once a confirmation of the intensive, fruitful advance in race scholarship as well as an open question about early modern scholars' reaction to the impact of race in Shakespeare studies, with more than a hint at residual skepticism and discomfort in the field.[18] The matter of response takes us directly to the critic as reader. To revisit Thompson's provocative metaphor, one must ask today whether the *racialized reader* is the elephant in the room of Shakespeare and early modern studies. The answer bears significantly on the protocols and practice of literary criticism, where the reader, ranging from student and dramaturg to professional scholar and critic, sits at a nexus of considerable privilege. Such a reader is the focus of *Black Shakespeare: Reading and Misreading Race.*

Finding the Reader

Literary criticism, involving acts of reading and the interpretation of texts, has been instrumental to the sustained growth of Shakespeare as a body of work with immense cultural and intellectual influence. While different literary movements and schools of theory have exerted their influence on the practice of criticism, the reader has remained a curiously "underprivileged" category of attention.[19] Gregory Castle observes that the "importance of the reader in literary theory has long been acknowledged, but the reader's role has typically been subordinated."[20] Reception or reader-response theory is a notable exception, positing reading as a dynamic process requiring the reader to actualize the text's verbal codes in the construction of meaning.[21] To fulfill this function, "the reader will bring to the work certain 'pre-understandings,' a dim context of beliefs and expectations within which the work's various features will be assessed."[22] Even such a promising acknowledgment is insufficiently cognizant of the reader's material grounding in the historical matrix of race that in today's cultural environment powerfully informs the critic–reader's "pre-understandings." Moreover, if, as Terry Eagleton explains, the importance of reading for Wolfgang Iser "is that it brings us into deeper self-consciousness [and] catalyzes a more critical view of our identities,"[23] the modern profusion of critical theories has studiously avoided the epistemological significance of the critic–reader's racial identity in producing criticism and scholarship. Referencing reader-response theory is not intended as a statement of this study's commitment to that set of critical systems. Rather, its citation is a brief measure of the distance in time since that school's emergence and the subsequent failure to fill the racial gaps and capitalize on the phenomenon of the reader embedded in history.

More recently, reading has become a phenomenon of interest beyond the remit of Shakespeare studies.[24] Focused mainly on non-dramatic works, the "methods wars"[25] have contested the various forms of close, flat, surface, distant, close but not deep, reparative, or uncritical reading; overseen the conjunction and separation of book studies and reading studies; broadened the discussion on textual materiality to include new digital forms; and attributed value to textual instability in contrast to New Criticism's preferred self-enclosed object. One must, however, distinguish between the reader and reading, the latter often used as a synonym for interpretation in literary criticism, a practice that has also come under scrutiny for being too paranoid or suspicious. More insidiously, in this growing output of theories, reading often describes an event akin to a disembodied act, one that is disinterested in the textual interlocutor, the actual human subject known as the reader. Reading in this instance becomes, in effect, a code for textuality, and abandons a full accounting of the real reader.[26] Thus, reading as commonly used among critics only implies a reading subject whose liminal existence lacks the full substance of history and culture. This study is not interested in an implied or fictional reader, to redeploy the terminology of reception theory, but has progressed to a real critic–reader historically situated in an interpretive community defined by the dynamics of race for over 400 years of United States history.

Reading involves not just words on a page, but the navigation of those words by a reader shaped by cultural habits, learned behavior, and ideologies of race. As Michel de Certeau states, "the text has a meaning only through its readers; it changes along with them; it is ordered in accord with codes of perception that it does not control. It becomes a text only in its relation to the exteriority of the reader."[27] The main task, therefore, is to identify and define that reader external to the text. De Certeau is concerned with the class-marked "social hierarchization" of a professional elite that imposes interpretive constraints on private readers.[28] In his view, the modern, "*socially* authorized professionals and intellectuals" stand between the text and the individual reader, determining patterns of reading and interpretation that follow the tastes of the dominant class they represent.[29] In this class-centered thinking, de Certeau is influenced by Pierre Bourdieu's life-long commitment to the critique of "class domination" and inequality.[30]

The external reader can also be historicized and set within another hierarchy: the racial order that has defined the history of the West. De Certeau's observation has even greater consequences when applied to the systemic racialization of readers, where whiteness assumes an elite function in the prescriptive interpretation of texts. Implicit in de Certeau's class analysis is an argument, central to this book, waiting to be extrapolated: prescriptive readings that result from the elite function of whiteness are prone to elision, avoidance, and oversight because they are inclined to follow a white racial orthodoxy. As such, my focus turns to the scholar and critic as systemically racialized readers who produce interpretive substance and content that get distributed through multiple channels. *Black Shakespeare* is, therefore, interested in foregrounding the reader – professional or private, since race, that is whiteness, cuts across class – who occupies the transit point between the inert text and the meaning produced, as the fulcrum agent whose collective interpretive substance constitutes the body of work and idea designated "Shakespeare."

Importantly, engaging race studies, whether in opposition or in supportive practice or partnership, entails a unique burden, a weight of responsibility: it necessarily implicates the scholar, professional intellectual, or editorial board member in the racial project itself. For that reason, early modern race studies is not simply a dispassionate scholarly enterprise. Because of its unique praxis, it is one that inevitably places its racialized scholar–readers under the spotlight of self-scrutiny. As a result, the resistance to race in Shakespeare and early modern studies presents itself as a defensive form of white preservation of the racial status quo. Much more is at stake, however, than a form of anxious self-protectionism. *Black Shakespeare* argues that the history of such opposition has produced racial ellipses and gaps that define and deform reading, its interpretive acts, and the literary criticism that ensues. In this view, the denial of race is more than a simple failure of acknowledgment. It represents the scholar–reader's deeply contradictory relationship to blackness that is driven by an epistemology of systemic whiteness formed over time, with its own learned patterns of exclusion and disavowal that affect how we read. I propose that the challenge to incorporate early modern race comprehensively into our teaching, scholarship, and professional lives is as deeply personal as it is political and that the personal is systemic.

The Reader Positioned as White

In her 1992 book *Playing in the Dark*, Toni Morrison makes a startling claim about readers, the significance of which has yet to be grappled with in Shakespeare and early modern studies. Mounting a powerful critique of the persistent denials in literary studies about the fact of blackness and race in United States history and culture, Morrison links this tendency to critics' intellectual formation in whiteness. These denials rest on "a certain set of assumptions conventionally accepted among literary historians and critics and circulated as 'knowledge'" that separates imaginative literature and criticism from this history.[31] "This knowledge," Morrison remarks, "holds that traditional, canonical American literature is free of, uninformed, and unshaped by the four-hundred-year-old presence of, first, Africans and then African-Americans in the United States."[32] Still, this black presence, the consequence of African slavery, stands as a reality that is never eliminated but, rather, has an antithetical structural value. It insinuates itself everywhere in the imaginary and social texture of America because of its contrastive value in defining the morals, ideas, and foundational principles of the republic. The divorce of literary discourse from the fact of blackness pretends, therefore, to lift literature above the racial fray of history to create a sanitized, purified, whiter idea of the nation, one that is not itself unrelated to the peculiar interests of a perpetrating cadre of professional critics. "Above all," Morrison writes, criticism's agenda of denial has "impoverished the literature it studies."[33]

One cannot help but be struck by the pertinence of these observations, now three decades old, to the state of contemporary early modern criticism. From attempts to delegitimize the scholarship and field of early modern race studies starting in the 1990s, with claims of unhistorical, backward projection that declare, in effect, the early modern race project a spurious fiction, to the sheer resistance to race work and the different, field-reorienting questions it raises, traditional early modern and

Shakespeare studies have reacted in the ways Morrison describes. She observes succinctly, "in matters of race silence and evasion have historically ruled literary discourse."[34] At the center of it all is the tactical denial of blackness and race that, if successful, would create a bifurcation between early modern literature and its history of a racial presence, preserve and elevate this literature from the taint of blackness to keep it white, and, ultimately, impoverish the works through repeated acts of critical erasure.

Thirty years on from Morrison's study, denial not only signifies the futile rejection of a black presence, but also the minimization of a whiteness whose repeated manifestation as violence is, as Ibram X. Kendi argues, a threat to American democracy. In recent years and months, the motivating force of whiteness in deciding the political and cultural acts that are our history has become all too evident; yet, far too often, incidents of racist calamity are met with denial: "What is the inevitable response of Americans," Kendi writes, "to tragic stories of mass murder, of extreme destitution, of gross corruption, of dangerous injustice, of political chaos, of a raw attack on democracy within the very borders of the United States, as we witnessed at the US Capitol? *This is not who we are.*" He continues: "But the denial is normal. In the aftermath of catastrophes, when have Americans commonly admitted who we are? The heartbeat of America is denial."[35]

In the current moment, when race dominates everyday speech, media headlines, and public policy, a theory of reading that pays attention to the reader's racial formation in systemic whiteness is responsive and necessary even as it works to minimize the perception of early modern studies as removed from the racial and political realities of our time.[36] I propose, therefore, a consideration of the possible consequences for systemic whiteness on reading, positing that parts of texts get elided, become invisible, or are misconstrued because of the reader's white racial formation. Since whiteness itself has been consistently performed and defined as culturally normative and, therefore, categorized as invisible, we should not be surprised – in fact, we might *expect* – that whiteness thus understood might also privilege reading habits steeped in normative strategies of invisibility: denial, erasure, and blindness that enforce the elision of certain forms of racial content. The current rising tide of white extremism has only raised the value of normal, quotidian whiteness as benignly neutral and undemanding. The practice and critique undertaken in this study contribute to making whiteness visible so that reading, and its subsequent manifestation in early modern criticism and scholarship, remains fully connected to race as the urgent social and political concern of our time.

Seen from this perspective, the pivotal moment in Morrison's text comes early in her Preface, where its single articulation risks being overlooked. To understand the critical establishment's wariness and denial of blackness and race, Morrison suggests that we look to racial formation and identity. "For reasons that should not need explanation here," she notes, "until very recently, and regardless of the race of the author, the readers of virtually all of American fiction have been positioned as white."[37] Morrison's use of the word "positioned" conveys the epistemological situatedness of the reader in the history of systemic whiteness. Woody Doane observes that in "the context of the ideology of race, 'whiteness' must be understood as a position in a specific set of social relationships."[38] "The notion of position," writes Renato Rosaldo, "refers to how life experiences both enable and inhibit particular kinds of insight."[39] Importantly, that position bears a significant historical component. Morrison's incisive phrase "positioned as white" encapsulates the reader's social, political, and cultural situatedness in the world as deriving from a history that has produced a clearly constructed social identity and recognizable racial mentality. According to Stuart Hall, "identities are the names we give to the different ways we are positioned by, and position ourselves within, the narratives of the past."[40] Such identities are culturally embedded and carry the weight, meaning, and expectation assigned through historical formation. Morrison's designation of whiteness as the reader's unique cultural and political identity is grounded in a specific locality that orients perception and knowledge. Moreover, Morrison points to "a more or less tacit agreement among literary scholars that, because American literature has been clearly the preserve of white male views, genius, and power, those views, genius, and power are without relationship to and removed from the overwhelming presence of black people in the United States."[41] Readerly whiteness is a situated identity that draws its meaning, political agency, and outlook from the historical disposition toward white racial preference that has defined the American experience.

Given Morrison's argument, the general interest in the reader paves the way to speak more specifically about scholars as readers "positioned as white" who produce, as a result of that situated identity, the impoverished literary criticism she laments. This book expands and historically reframes this notion of the reading subject "positioned as white" to propose a theory of reading that turns on the tension between an early modern black presence and the modern white reader. Recognizing the reader's epistemological, cultural, and political position opens new directions for theories of reading by concentrating on the racial formation of the white reader. Applied to Shakespeare, however, this new set of theoretical and methodological opportunities is complicated by questions of the white reader's capacity and competence to admit and process the racial content of Shakespeare's texts. Whiteness, because of its obfuscating and evasive maneuvers, struggles to contend with race. The central premise of *Black Shakespeare*, therefore, argues for a historically compelled and situated reader whose engagement with race is hampered by whiteness' inherent epistemological limitations.

Reading Through the Filters of Race

The scholarly avoidance of seeing blackness and reading race in early modern studies runs parallel to the evolution of Shakespeare as the literary avatar of English culture. Scholars have not traditionally identified blackness and read race, the process of recognizing and assigning social and political meaning to somatic and textual signs. Moreover, in the standard accounts of Shakespeare's rise to iconic status, the actual reader is often a liminal presence, even though the human work, assessment, and judgment that follow from reading are everywhere implied. The Preface to the First Folio envisaged the connection between print, literacy, and reading.[42] By the eighteenth century, scholarly editions of his works, multiple adaptations of his plays, dictionaries of Shakespearean quotations, Shakespeare biographies, and the beginning of curricular inclusion in secondary and higher education all contributed to what Michael Dobson describes as "the extensive cultural work that went into the installation of Shakespeare as England's National Poet."[43] In particular, the slew of collected editions by Nicholas Rowe (1709), Alexander Pope (1725), Lewis Theobald (1733), Thomas Hanmer (1744), Samuel Johnson (1765), and Edmond Malone (1790), created a conversation about textual accuracy even as more moderate pricing appealed to an expanded readership, so that "reading Shakespeare rather than seeing Shakespeare in performance was becoming the primary mode for experiencing his plays."[44]

Fully intertwined with the nation's political mythology, Shakespeare was pressed further into the service of imperial literacy: "Throughout the period of the Seven Years' War and its aftermath, as Britain acquired ever greater colonial dependencies in the East and the Americas, ever larger claims were made for the national poet's art, praised more and more insistently in terms of world exploration and conquest."[45] It was in this moment of British colonial expansion that the initial stages of the

American appropriation of Shakespeare invested the writer's new transatlantic home with "its own national and imperial project" in ways that justified the words of the poet Peter Markoe: "Shakespeare's bold spirit seeks our western shore."[46] The teeming, ebullient energies of the sixteenth-century playhouse were supplanted in the twentieth by the studious professionalization of an academic Shakespeare who was "destined to become the Shakespeare of the college and university, and even more the Shakespeare of private and select culture."[47] Throughout the historical accounts of Shakespeare's print and textual reception, the unraced "Great Variety" of readers was the prevailing unstated assumption.

The eighteenth-century consolidation of national Shakespeare was also the historical highpoint of the capture, ownership, and forced labor of African people within the global network of the intercontinental triangular slave trade. If the interlocking histories of Shakespeare and race were not already evident, the timing of the Enlightenment canonization of Shakespeare only confirmed this fact. As scholars of American history have come to recognize, the seeming contradiction of the declaration of freedom and inalienable rights in a slaveholding nation lay bare a stark truth: the enslavement of black Africans was the very portrait and premise of un-freedom on which the founding fathers' articulation of liberty and rights was imagined. Toni Morrison writes that the "slave population, it could be and was assumed, offered itself up as the surrogate selves for meditation on the problems of human freedom, its lure and its elusiveness."[48] The black population's social objectification, insofar as this enslaved group was denied power and absorption into the cultural mainframe, provided the requisite political foil. A similar formation of English identity follows from the intersecting projects of cultural nationalism and British colonial slavery.[49] Thus, the Enlightenment moment of English national Shakespeare requires a contrapuntal reading: What is Englishness when the very idea of national identity is being constructed in contrast to and at the expense of tortured black bodies?[50] Not coincidentally, a similarly insistent question sets the stage for Shakespeare studies today: What does it mean to be American when the very ideals of equality and democracy are deformed by the daily brutality of a seemingly endless black body count? The cultural work required of Enlightenment Shakespeare in enforcing a vision of Englishness was to push the acknowledgment of black bodies to the margins in order to build, despite its ostensible neutrality, what was in truth a white national mythology. It is thus that the portrait and premise of blackness became the necessary building block on which whiteness, Englishness' distinguishing racial feature, was constructed. As a result, Shakespeare's cooptation into both the English and American nationalist discourse means that his dramatic oeuvre had to be stripped, sanitized, and made white for that particular cultural task – a project of rhetorical segregation. It follows, therefore, that the critical tradition of Shakespeare has been unraced, that it has effectively reproduced the apparent racial disinterest of white Shakespeare.

Missing from standard accounts of the nexus of Shakespeare, English cultural nationalism, British imperial expansion, and his American appropriation is what W. J. T. Mitchell calls the racial frame, a useful concept to initiate this book's examination of the conjunction of race, culture, and reading Shakespeare. Writing in 2012, Mitchell argued fiercely "the continuing presence of racism in the world today."[51] Since then, in the United States, immigration has become an expansive code for branding people of color; white extremism is on the rise; a global pandemic exposed the racial fault lines in a culture of chronic inequality; "I can't breathe" entered the lexicon of protest against police killing of black persons; and racial vitriol in large doses was delivered routinely to the public by "America's First White President," to adopt Ta-Nehisi Coates's incisive moniker.[52] Writing in the middle of the Obama presidency, an administration helmed by an African American whose election was heralded in many quarters as a sign of the end of race, Mitchell pushed back against the premature declarations of a postracial America.[53] Confronting the racial realities that continue to define the United States, Mitchell countered postracial denialism with a proposal of racial accountability. More than "an object to be represented visually or verbally, or a thing to be depicted in a likeness or image," race is "not simply something to be seen, but itself a framework for seeing through." Race should be reimagined as "a frame, a window, a screen, or a lens," Mitchell explains, "a repertoire of cognitive and conceptual filters through which forms of human otherness are mediated."[54] The intervention made by early modern race studies has for some time, in fact, argued for such a revisionary "framework" for traditional Shakespeare studies, a scholarly industry that has remained for quite some time skeptical of race. Importantly, the stark reality of our contemporary society saturated by racial debates compels us to ponder the effects of race on our most mundane activities as well as our highly prized cultural engagements like reading Shakespeare. This book examines, therefore, the impact of racial formation on modern scholarship's reading practices. This scholarship, in turn, continues to influence Shakespeare's widest contemporary audience – students by way of classroom instruction – and is in constant dialogue with theater and film artists' readings and interpretations of Shakespeare.

In what is a profound irony, the field of Shakespeare and early modern studies has already been forged in racial terms – it has been historically a de facto white field – despite the general reluctance to grapple with that fact, submit it to analysis, and take its significance into account. Among full-time faculty, nationally, roughly 75 percent are white, with much smaller numbers for Black (5 percent) and Hispanic (4 percent) professors as reported in 2016.[55] If we use the registrant self-reporting for the 2019 Shakespeare Association of America conference as a rough gauge, the data revealed: White 79.1 percent; Black, African or African American 1.6 percent; Latinx or Hispanic 2.4 percent; Asian, South Asian, and/or Asian American 4.3 percent; Native, Indigenous, and/or Pacific Islander 0.4 percent.[56] Moreover, the field has been marked historically by hesitation and, in some instances, outright resistance to race. The tradition of Shakespeare scholarship has always engaged in the practice of seeing through race, understood in this instance as a specifically resistant white racial framework, even though reconciling to the full consequence of that admission has been held in abeyance. The Shakespeare industry's primary traditional stakeholders and gatekeepers – academics, scholars, critics, educators, teachers, book and journal publishers, theater practitioners, members of professional organizations, devotees, and donors who support programs, performances, and institutions with their dollars – have shared more than a white racial demographic; they have been the beneficiaries of a cultural and intellectual formation that, for too long, has denied the relevance of race.

During a recent roundtable hosted by black artists from the Stratford Festival, for example – all of whom I consider part of the collective reading, interpretive practice – they identified a creative environment in which their blackness was in constant retreat because of what can only be described as a culture of whiteness and institutional gaslighting.[57] Keith Hamilton Cobb's *American Moor* (2020) is a searing portrayal of white racial pressures and exclusions in the Shakespeare performance arena.[58] The difficulties expressed by these artists point to whiteness' chronic affiliation with gross inequality. AnnLouise Keating writes, "'whiteness' and its 'violent denials of difference' serve a vital function in masking social and economic inequalities of contemporary western culture."[59] According to Timothy Barnett, whiteness' veiled effects are also of considerable concern in education: English studies as a "discipline remains unable to question its own 'white ground' despite the very real gains scholars have made in coming to understand reading and writing in relation to human difference."[60] Mitchell's approach to race's function as a governing intellectual frame is germane to acts of reading and interpretation, therefore, when considered in the context of Shakespeare and the mostly unexamined presumption of the field's "white ground."[61] Conceiving of race as a filter and frame for reading shifts our attention to interrogating its salient organizing perspective; its propensity for denial and epistemological violence; and its tendency to limit seeing, comprehending, and accounting for the racial signs in Shakespeare's texts.

My goal is not to attempt a full report on the vast topic of reading, but in a study that is fundamentally concerned with the racial motives of interpreting Shakespeare, my specific theoretical interest lies in highlighting the role whiteness plays in acts of reading. Shakespeare has come to represent high art, elite culture, and intellectual cachet even when those designations go against his works' popular roots in early modern theater and have assumed a distinctly white racial cast in contemporary culture. While one might posit a cultural coordination of elite Shakespeare with demographic or class identity, more fundamental to the argument is the indisputable fact of *systemic whiteness*, the structuration of knowledge and identity, that defines American society such that no one is excluded from the claims that whiteness makes on reading subjects.[62] In my view, the country's history of systemic whiteness, related, though not exclusively, to the politics of black enslavement, enables a defective epistemology and creates *racial blind spots* that misrecognize both the signs and embodied realities of "human otherness" as well as whiteness itself. *Black Shakespeare* argues that systemic whiteness, the racial framework within which criticism and scholarship have been produced for centuries and which reproduce that system itself, inhibits and constrains the practices of reading and interpretation. Unless one believes that literary criticism is hermetically sealed off from the world in which it is produced, the current state of affairs concerning race in the United States is undeniably an issue that cannot, and should not, be avoided. Neither can we neglect accounting for the predominant whiteness of our field as a matter intricately related to the racial urgency of our time.

As such, the current state of racial foment must serve as yet another reminder and opportunity for scholarship to be accountable to its readership and commit to a practical purpose. At stake is the notion of *racial literacy*, which demands a transformational competence in understanding race – its politics, history, and epistemologies – for reading texts and to know *how to be* in relation to others to meet the demands of a modern, just, plural democracy. Racial literacy requires the acquisition of a reading competence in response to overdetermined histories of erasure, dismissal, or forgetting of racial facts, including the facts of whiteness. Racial literacy is at once textual and practical, literary and cultural, intellectual and political in exercising the practice of textual hermeneutics in the domain of everyday living. The historical demands, at this moment, cannot concede or condone racial illiteracy and the ignorance of knowing how to be *in relation to others and oneself.* Racial literacy, in this study, constitutes a responsibility facing a range of persons including teachers, editors, theater practitioners, and general readers even though my discussion will often address scholars who serve a central interpretive function in the Shakespeare industry. So, from the classroom to performance spaces, instruction must aim to better equip us all to contribute to a debating world that struggles to confront systems and structures of racial inequality that were, we cannot fail to recognize, instituted at the nation's inception. While I attend to broad structural features that affect reading, I recognize that the work of racial decoloniality operates at the local level – across diverse nations and territories, but also from within professional organizations to the geographies of individual classrooms – where the search for means toward an egalitarian society is engaged.[63] It is no longer sufficient to be not racist, as we have come to understand, but we must be actively and declaratively antiracist. The book's overall concern with racial literacy has this collaborative and antiracist project in mind, as the closing chapter and Epilogue affirm.

To be clear, whiteness is more than skin color; it is an ideology that saturates and an epistemology that creates its own fictions and ways of seeing the world and texts. Yet, somatic whiteness has become the most readily identifiable marker of white racial belonging and a powerful shorthand for a set of complex moral and intellectual processes that allows subjects all too easily to blindly assent and conform to what appears to be a set of overlapping and synonymous categorical frames. Since systemic whiteness is institutional and pervasive, it affects everyone, regardless of self-proclaimed racial identification. The deployment of Shakespeare along with other British works in the matrix of colonial education, for example, promoted mental identification – "a determination to turn blacks into whites, or Africans into Europeans" – despite a marked discontinuity in the somatic appearance of colonial subjects.[64] Still, in instances where persons of color are constantly reminded of their non-affiliation with whiteness, their racial exclusion can foster a critical consciousness of white dominance and an awareness of the insidiousness of dysfunctional white epistemologies. The black intellectual tradition has been, in major part, a frontal assault on miseducation, especially of persons of color, in order to undo the hegemonic thrall of white-dominant intellectual frameworks. Black and postcolonial studies, along with a rich conglomerate of ethnic studies emerging since the last decades of the twentieth century, have given serious thought to the decolonization of the mind and critiqued white reason.[65]

Those self-identified as white are, however, in constant danger of surrender to a deeply flawed logic that so fuses and equates somatic signification to epistemological operation that they appear seamlessly unified and one. An easy blurring of categories enables this confusing conflation: white skin, a physical trait, is equated to the process of socialization of white intellectual identity within histories of differential power and exceptionalism. Because of their fair or white skin, such persons continue to be implicated in the routines of whiteness and are more at risk of being unprepared, naïve readers whose complicity in white epistemology creates severe disadvantages for reading race. To institute change, one cannot continue to conflate white skin and the legacy of a defective white epistemology, but must break this linkage to make conscious and visible the possibilities of constructing antiracist *forms of whiteness*. Somatic identity must be dislodged from white epistemological conditioning to secure a hard-won intellectual liberation within that disjuncture. Breaking apart this nexus of conflation creates the possibilities for a new epistemological space in which to imagine and inhabit different and diverse forms of whiteness appropriate for a just, equitable antiracist practice and commitment. Faced with the racial urgency that has come to define the current state of American culture and society, readers can no longer afford to be naïve or uninvested in understanding their racial position if they aspire to justice and accountability and to have the teaching and representation of Shakespeare matter.

The Critique of Whiteness

Registering the continued growth of the field, some recent accounts of early modern race studies note with justifiable excitement the current second-wave renaissance of scholarship.[66] In the short period since Peter Erickson and Kim F. Hall's recommendations in 2016 for future directions in scholarship, encouraging signs of engagements with race are evident in published essays, special issues of journals, plenaries, symposia, and workshops dedicated to field-expanding intersections and inquiries.[67] Among the seven areas targeted by Erickson and Hall for major new research is "early modern whiteness studies. The use of the term 'race' to mean only 'black' or 'of color' is unsatisfactory even in the Renaissance.

The full complexity of the term becomes accessible when whiteness as a racial category is also examined."[68] Whiteness studies, they observe, is already a substantial subfield within critical race studies, but one whose impact has yet to be fully realized in early modern race studies.[69] "There is a growing realization," write Monica McDermott and Frank L. Samson, "that one cannot fully understand the existence of racism and racial inequality without paying close attention to the formation and maintenance of white racial identity."[70] A whiteness studies approach redirects the sole focus of attention away from the racial other to pose pertinent questions about the formation of white identity and the operations of a white epistemology in comprehending representations of others in a move that makes whiteness' reading disability and political purpose more legible.

Beginning around 1990, whiteness studies emerged in a decade marked by seminal works of which Morrison's *Playing in the Dark* is the singularly noteworthy representative in literary analysis. Other studies include David R. Roediger's *The Wages of Whiteness* (1991), Theodore W. Allen's *The Invention of the White Race, Volumes 1 and 2* (1994 and 1997), Richard Dyer's *White* (1997), and Matthew Frye Jacobson's *Whiteness of a Different Color* (1998).[71] Notably, none of these took the early modern period as its subject. As a subfield, whiteness studies envisioned an antiracist program with two overarching claims: that whiteness is a construct, that is, an ideology, and that its existence is predicated on self-perpetuating privilege.[72] Consequently, whiteness is not neutral or naïve but constitutes a highly motivated social project. "Historians working in this subfield," argues Robert P. Baird, "demonstrated the myriad ways in which the pursuit of white supremacy – like the pursuit of wealth and the subjection of women – had been one of the central forces that gave shape to Anglo-American history."[73] Roediger pressed the case of whiteness' consuming self-interest further: "it is not merely that whiteness is oppressive and false; it is that whiteness is nothing but oppressive and false."[74] Given my specific focus on the scholar of early modern studies as a white reader who interprets texts and disseminates knowledge, my intention is not to re-center such a figure but to question the epistemological tendencies and reading practices that continue to inform and give organizing shape to the field of early modern studies.[75] With the renaissance of attention to early modern critical race studies, which includes a new and growing multicultural coalition of scholar–readers, such an inquiry acquires renewed urgency to understand the specific nature of the impact and challenges of reading, now and going forward.

Whiteness studies' overlapping chronology with the substantive beginnings of early modern race studies is noteworthy for the delay in cross-fertilization over the past three decades. Faced with skepticism and outright hostility, early modern critical race studies had the ethical and intellectual responsibility to establish the disciplinary ground on which it stands. Making whiteness a central project in those earliest years, though its antithetical presence was everywhere implied, would have seemed counterintuitive, delaying further the scholarship on the cultural politics of blackness and race. Despite scholars' intent to "problematize" whiteness, at the time Margaret Talbot warned of the insidiousness of privilege: "the whole enterprise gives whites a kind of standing in the multicultural paradigm they have never before enjoyed. And it involves them, inevitably, in a journey of self-discovery in which white people's thoughts about their own whiteness acquire a portentous new legitimacy."[76] Michael Eric Dyson eyed with suspicion what he regarded as the narcissistic monopolization of institutional resources: "At the very moment when African-American studies and Asian-American studies and so on are really coming into their own, you have whiteness studies shifting the focus and maybe the resources back to white people and their perspective."[77] However, the continued expressions of white supremacy into the twenty-first century that lead Coates to declare whiteness "an existential danger to the country and the world," demand a direct, frontal critique.[78]

Black Shakespeare addresses in a timely fashion, therefore, the missing intersection of whiteness studies and early modern race studies by concentrating on one of the most paradoxically inarticulate phenomena in Shakespeare studies: the white reader as scholar whose body of critical and theoretical work sustains the political infrastructure of the Shakespeare academic and performance industry. Baird situates white silence as a convenient retreat from public discourse in the immediate aftermath of the reckoning of the 1960s: "many white people found it easier to decide that the civil rights movement had accomplished all the anti-racism work that needed doing," while continuing "to exercise the institutional and structural power that had accumulated on their behalf across the previous three centuries."[79] I examine this silence, hesitation, and refusal to name whiteness as a dispositive scholarly identity that has enormous power in the academic community. The history of silence around whiteness is one of its prodigiously effective strategies of disciplinary regulation. Simon Clarke and Steve Garner set out the key concerns: "Whiteness, as a form of ethnicity, is rarely acknowledged by its bearers, yet it has significant ramifications in terms of the construction of 'other' identities; in the creation of community; in processes of exclusion and inclusion; and discourses around 'race' and nation."[80] A whiteness studies critique in Shakespeare and early modern studies understands that the scholarly hesitations about race are rooted in an anxious defense of whiteness often fashioned in the cool language of scholarly rigor and historical precision, terms that have become effectively racialized – as if intellectual rigor were the sole prerogative of a white scholarly majority. The implication impugns both the content and intellectual quality of research produced by scholars of color specifically; it impugns the scholars of color themselves.

It follows that the historical reluctance to consider race in early modern studies is also inseparable from debates about identity politics, meaning in this instance the role racial identity plays in the scholarly projects selected. Stated baldly, persons of color research race, and the meritless questions raised about this scholarship replay the unfortunate, discriminatory racial tribalism that has riven our national history.[81] Directed at persons of color, the charge of identity politics is meant to delegitimize an intellectual position, casting it as an essentialist bias based in a reductively vague biological premise that recreates the familiar hierarchy of the mind–body split. Given their tendency toward racial self-effacement, whites might find the application of the concept to themselves surprising: "Whites' hegemonic position in the social order 'normalizes' Whiteness in ways that make it elusive to those who have it. Whites' numerical advantage in the United States further reduces the perceptual salience of White racial identity."[82] However, based on their research, the psychologists Eric D. Knowles and Christopher K. Marshburn argue "that Whites routinely engage in identity politics, acting in ways that further their interests as members of the dominant group."[83] And bell hooks decries the sidestepping of "progressive white intellectuals" who criticize identity in race scholarship but "have not focused their critiques on white identity and the way essentialism informs representations of whiteness."[84]

The self-awareness of white identity must be leveraged for antiracist purpose or recuperative work that, in the words of Dyson, "names a whiteness that doesn't want to be named, disrobes a whiteness that dresses in camouflage as humanity, unmasks a whiteness costumed as American, and fetches to center stage a whiteness that would rather hide in visible invisibility."[85] The matter is not simply that whites traffic in identity politics, too, a mere turning of the table, though the table in this metaphor has historically been set for the privileged. Rather, the acknowledgment of white identity politics breaks the silence around the white scholar as reader to examine the veiled political self-interests that, ironically, have operated in plain sight. Thus, while the implicit charge of identity politics hovers over the debates concerning early modern race studies, we must be similarly attuned to the unstated white identity politics that have governed the wider field. Looking at the hitherto largely invisible whiteness of early modern critics is a project in visibility that calls out whiteness, examines its strategies and epistemologies, and tests its stamina in the hope of ultimately effecting a more inclusive scholarship that is truer and more sensitive to the texts and the cultural histories they represent. Noting the defenses and emotions unleashed when white entitlement and privilege are challenged, Robin DiAngelo argues that "we can practice building our stamina for the critical examination of white identity – a necessary antidote to white fragility."[86] Reading, understood within a racial literacy frame, is a practice and exercise for accomplishing more than testing the fragility or resilience of whiteness by arming readers with the means to pursue personal and structural reform toward a more just and equitable society.

Black Shakespeare

The twenty-first century has witnessed the crippling encroachment of toxic whiteness on the integrity of American democratic institutions, cultural ethos, and political discourse. If there was ever a moment to address whiteness in literary and Shakespeare studies, it is now. *Black Shakespeare*, because it insists on Shakespeare's investment in issues of race, asserts the urgency of confronting myriad forms of prejudice, exclusion, and discrimination as instances of quotidian bias with the capacity to metastasize without the steadfast vigilance of an aware, responsible reader. Further delays in collective and individual accountability in Shakespeare studies only prolong the sort of erasures around whiteness that in the wider culture have allowed the destructive politics of extremism to grow. The juxtaposition of Shakespeare and racial politics is intended to highlight the prevalent insidiousness of racial ignorance that must be combated across all fronts. As a result, the book argues for the reader's social readiness, through the epistemological work of engaging with literary studies, for personal, political, and ethical reform in a culture grappling with questions of social equity and justice.

The organizational arc of the book proceeds from defining the racialized reader positioned within a culture of systemic whiteness; identifying the obstacles or blind spots whiteness poses to reading; to, ultimately, envisioning an antiracist, critical practice informed by racial literacy. Remarking on the inattention among critics about the function of the white reader, Chapter 1, "The Racialized Reader," attends to the racial formation of the American reader from a historical perspective. It argues, as a result, that the racialized reader produces acts of reading and interpretation that are inhibited by the epistemological imperatives of a conditioning culture of systemic whiteness. Chapter 2, "Racial Blind Spots: Misreading Bodies, Misreading Texts," disputes traditional arguments about the temporal emergence of white identity, extending the historical parameters of white racial formation back to Shakespeare, who is especially attentive to the impact of whiteness in producing racial blind spots that subvert the audience's racial and, hence, interpretive knowledge in *Othello*. These two opening chapters provide the historical and theoretical frame for understanding how racial blind spots have engendered acute oversights and misreadings of Shakespeare, as demonstrated in the remaining chapters. Chapter 3, "Antonio's 'Fair Flesh' and The Property of Whiteness," maintains that criticism has been blind to the racialized whiteness of Antonio's skin that is the cause of Shylock's targeted resistance to the racial oppression festering in the city state of *The Merchant of Venice*. Fomenting this tense, violent atmosphere, Antonio asserts and models the authority of the white reader who denies the role of race in textual interpretation and, thereby, rejects the hermeneutic and human validity of being made racially literate. Chapter 4, "Hamlet: Playing in the Dark," proclaims *Hamlet* a race play: scholars have been blind to Hamlet's appropriation of "black" subjectivity in the guise of the new and emergent theatrical Violent Black Man type. In his pursuit of revenge, Hamlet equivocates in his relationship toward blackness, which he, nevertheless, feels obliged to coopt for his own racial improvisation that renders black humanity a casualty of white interests. Chapter 5, "We Are Othello," concentrates on the blindness to Othello's centuries-old challenge to audiences and readers to speak of him, a black man, justly and with racial competence. This chapter extends the examination of Hamlet's personal ambivalence toward blackness to question how in telling Othello's story we can test our resilience and reliability in matters of race, seeing literary analysis as a window of accountability onto the contemporary world of racial politics. The closing chapter effects a transition to the Epilogue, "Forms of Whiteness," which concludes explicitly on the book's appeal for a self-reflective, antiracist scholarly practice and pedagogy.

I have selected three of the most popular and best-known of Shakespeare's plays, *Othello*, *The Merchant of Venice*, and *Hamlet*, which have been subjected to centuries of criticism and performance commentary, to make the point about the scholar–reader's tendency toward racial erasure even more forcefully. Even among plays so routinely studied and performed, our intellectual formation in systemic whiteness blinds us from seeing important racial content. Each chapter also incorporates an instance of antiblackness or white supremacy in US history to introduce a problematic of reading and misreading race that the chapter analyzes. These include: James Baldwin's meditation on the cultural avoidance of race in America as he traveled the South in the 1950s; the eighteenth-century antiliteracy laws that granted whites the exclusive rights to reading literacy as well as the politically fraught authority to read and determine the semantic value of corporal blackness; the refusal of an implacable nineteenth-century plantation owner to entertain the redemption of a fugitive slave's full freedom over preference for the escaped man's lifeless flesh; the 2021 US Capitol insurrection, its relation to white extremism and indebtedness to the lie of black inferiority; and the recent spate of killings of unarmed black men and women. Together these chapters simultaneously ground whiteness within the historical contexts of modernity while upending the stipulation of whiteness' post-Enlightenment appearance to posit a longer history extending back to Shakespeare's time. Together, they challenge reading orthodoxy in the book's commitment to racial literacy's capacity to sustain an attentive, renovative scholarship.

Finally, I would like to suggest that "Black Shakespeare" is both a descriptive and critical concept. "Black Shakespeare" reminds us that race has so suffused Western culture and thinking that the failure to remark on race does not leave our scholarship unmarked by race. To this end, the term "black" is also meant to invite expansive reflection and inclusion of other racial codes and identities in early modern texts typically identified as nonwhite, even as I focus in this study on the critical function of racialized blackness. Importantly, I intend the term to relate to multiple indices of race, to be generative and expansive in critical capacity, so that "Black Shakespeare" is not limited to a specific content but refers to a positionality and critical operation of destabilizing the perceptual and epistemological tendencies in Shakespeare studies in the interest of a renovative, emancipatory, inclusive practice.[87]

Notes

1 *Mr. William Shakespeare's Comedies, Histories, & Tragedies* (London: Isaac Jaggard and Edward Blount, 1623), A3r.

2 Coverage of black characters in early modern drama is undertaken by Anthony Gerard Barthelemy, *Black Face, Maligned Race: The Representation of Blacks in*

English Drama from Shakespeare to Southerne (Baton Rouge: Louisiana State University Press, 1987) and Elliot H. Tokson, *The Popular Image of the Black Man in English Drama, 1550–1688* (Boston: G. K. Hall, 1982).

3 Elizabeth Spiller, *Reading and the History of Race in the Renaissance* (Cambridge: Cambridge University Press, 2011).

4 Imtiaz Habib, *Black Lives in the English Archives, 1500–1677: Imprints of the Invisible* (Burlington: Ashgate, 2008); Ruben Espinosa and David Ruiter, eds., *Shakespeare and Immigration* (New York: Routledge, 2016); James Walvin, *The Black Presence: A Documentary History of the Negro in England 1555–1860* (New York: Schocken Books, 1971); see also T. F. Earle and K. J. P. Lowe, eds., *Black Africans in Renaissance Europe* (Cambridge: Cambridge University Press, 2005); Jonathan Spicer, ed., *Revealing the African Presence in Renaissance Europe* (Baltimore: Walters Art Museum, 2012); Ania Loomba and Jonathan Burton, eds., *Race in Early Modern England: A Documentary Companion* (New York: Palgrave Macmillan, 2007); and Paul Edwards, "The Early African Presence in the British Isles," in *Essays on the History of Blacks in Britain*, ed. Jagdish G. Gundera and Ian Duffield (Aldershot: Avebury, 1992): 9–29.

5 For a comprehensive review of the relevant scholarship, see Dennis Austin Britton, "Recent Studies in English Renaissance Literature," *English Literary Renaissance* 45.3 (2015): 459–478. I would highlight the following: Ayanna Thompson, ed., *The Cambridge Companion to Shakespeare and Race* (Cambridge: Cambridge University Press, 2021); Joyce Green MacDonald, *Shakespearean Adaptation, Race, and Memory in the New World* (New York: Palgrave, 2020); Patricia Akhimie, *Shakespeare and the Cultivation of Difference: Race and Conduct in the Early Modern World* (New York: Routledge, 2018); Matthieu Chapman, *Anti-Black Racism in Early Modern English Drama* (New York: Routledge, 2016); Dennis Austin Britton, *Becoming Christian: Race, Reformation, and Early Modern English Romance* (New York: Fordham University Press, 2014); Peter Erickson, "Invisibility Speaks: Servants and Portraits in Early Modern Visual Culture," *Journal for Early Modern Cultural Studies* 9(2009): 23–61; Ian Smith, *Race and Rhetoric in the Renaissance: Barbarian Errors* (New York: Palgrave Macmillan, 2009); Ayanna Thompson, *Performing Race and Torture on the Early Modern Stage* (New York: Routledge, 2007); Sujata Iyengar, *Shades of Difference: Mythologies of Skin Color in Early Modern England* (Philadelphia: University of Pennsylvania Press, 2004); Ania Loomba, *Shakespeare, Race, and Colonialism* (Oxford: Oxford University Press, 2002); Peter Erickson and Clark Hulse, eds., *Early Modern Visual Culture: Representation, Race, and Empire in Renaissance England* (Philadelphia: University of Pennsylvania Press, 2000); Margo Hendricks, "Race: A Renaissance Category?" in *A Companion to English Literature and Culture*, ed. Michael Hattaway (Malden: Blackwell Publishers, 2000); Arthur Little Jr., *Shakespeare Jungle Fever: National-Imperial Re-Visions of Race, Rape, and Sacrifice* (Stanford: Stanford University Press, 2000); Joyce Green MacDonald, ed., *Race, Ethnicity, and Power in the Renaissance* (Madison: Farleigh Dickinson University Press, 1997); Kim F. Hall, *Things of Darkness: Economies of Race and Gender in Early*

Modern England (Ithaca: Cornell University Press, 1995); and Margo Hendricks and Patricia Parker, eds., *Women, "Race," and Writing in Early Modern England* (New York: Routledge, 1994).

6 Contrast Michael Neil's skepticism in "'Mullatos,' 'Blacks,' and 'Indian Moors': *Othello* and Early Modern Constructions of Human Difference," *Shakespeare Quarterly* 49.4 (1998), 361–374 with Vanessa Corredera, "'Not a Moor exactly': Shakespeare, *Serial*, and Modern Constructions of Race," *Shakespeare Quarterly* 61.1 (2016), 30–50.

7 Ania Loomba addresses some critics' rejection of color consciousness in "'Delicious traffic': Racial and Religious Differences on Early Modern Stages," in *Shakespeare and Race*, ed. Catherine M. S. Alexander and Stanley Wells (Cambridge: Cambridge University Press, 2000), esp. 204.

8 Francesca T. Royster, "The 'End of Race' and the Future of Early Modern Cultural Studies," *Shakespeare Studies* 26 (1998): 59–69 (60). Matthieu Chapman's anecdotal account of his first experience at an academic conference resonates familiarly for some, in the blanket opposition to race in early modern studies delivered in the terse, uninformed indictment made by respected scholars: "There were no black people in England during Elizabeth's reign" (*Anti-Black Racism in Early Modern English Drama*, 1).

9 Henry S. Turner, "Recent Studies in Tudor and Stuart Drama," *Studies in English Literature, 1500–1900* 58.3 (2018): 473–537. He references undertakings by the Shakespeare Association of America, the Folger Shakespeare Library, and the Globe Theatre (474).

10 Turner, "Recent Studies in Tudor and Stuart Drama," 481.

11 The Executive Board, RaceB4Race, "It's Time to End the Publishing Gatekeeping!" June 11, 2020. https://medium.com/the-sundial-acmrs/its-time-to-end-the-publishing-gatekeeping-75207525f587.

12 On this ongoing, urgent debate about the place of race in early modern studies, see Peter Erickson and Kim F. Hall, "'A New Scholarly Song': Rereading Early Modern Race," *Shakespeare Quarterly* 67.1 (2016): 1–13; and Kimberly Anne Coles, Kim F. Hall, and Ayanna Thompson, "BlacKKKShakespearean: A Call to Action for Medieval and Early Modern Studies," *Profession* (Fall 2019). https://profession.mla.org/blackkkshakespearean-a-call-to-action-for-medieval-and-early-modern-studies/.

13 Erickson and Hall, "A New Scholarly Song," 2.

14 For a comprehensive review, see Britton, "Recent Studies in English Renaissance Literature."

15 Patricia J. Williams, "In Living Black and White," *Washington Post*, March 29, 1998. www.washingtonpost.com/archive/lifestyle/magazine/1998/03/29/in-living-black-and-white/929dae95-7fd3-4680-ac7b-c957f8bcef14/.

16 Harlon Dalton, "Failing to See," in *White Privilege: Essential Readings on the Other Side of Racism*, ed. Paula S. Rothenberg (New York: Worth Publishers, 2012), 17.

17 On the physiological effects of reading on the early modern reader, see Spiller, *Reading and the History of Race*.

18 Ayanna Thompson, *Passing Strange: Shakespeare, Race, and Contemporary America* (Oxford: Oxford University Press, 2011), 1.
19 Terry Eagleton, *Literary Theory: An Introduction*, 3rd ed. (Minneapolis: Minnesota University Press, 2008), 74.
20 Gregory Castle, *The Blackwell Guide to Literary Theory* (Malden: Blackwell, 2007), 174.
21 In addition to Eagleton, *Literary Theory*, 54–90 and Castle, *The Blackwell Guide to Literary Theory*, 174–180, see Wolfgang Iser, *The Implied Reader: Patterns of Communication in Prose Fiction from Bunyan to Beckett* (Baltimore: Johns Hopkins University Press, 1974); Gerald Prince, "Introduction to the Study of the Narratee," in *Reader-Response Criticism: From Formalism to Post-Structuralism*, ed. Jane Tompkins (Baltimore: Johns Hopkins University Press, 1980); and Stanley Fish, *Is There a Text in This Class?: The Authority of Interpretive Communities* (Cambridge, MA: Harvard University Press, 1980).
22 Eagleton, *Literary Theory*, 77; for an explanation of the role of the real reader's experiences as distinct from the concept of the implied reader, see Wolfgang Iser, *The Act of Reading: A Theory of Aesthetic Response* (Baltimore: Johns Hopkins University Press, 1978), esp. 27–38.
23 Eagleton, *Literary Theory*, 79.
24 The recent double issue of *PMLA* is a case in point: Evelyne Ender and Deidre Shauna Lynch, eds., Special Topic: Cultures of Reading, *PMLA* 133.5 (2018) and *PMLA* 134.1 (2019). See also Leah Price and Seth Lerer, eds. Special Topic: The History of the Book and the Idea of Literature, *PMLA* 121.1 (2006).
25 Lynch and Ender, "Time for Reading," *PMLA* 133.5 (2018), 1076.
26 Iser refers to the "real reader" to distinguish this historical subject from the "implied reader," *The Act of Reading*, 27.
27 Michel de Certeau, *The Practice of Everyday Life*, trans. Steven Rendall (Berkeley: University of California Press, 1984), 170.
28 Ibid., 172.
29 Ibid., 171.
30 John Lechte, *Fifty Key Contemporary Thinkers: From Structuralism to Post-Humanism* 2nd ed. (New York: Routledge, 2008), 66.
31 Toni Morrison, *Playing in the Dark: Whiteness and the Literary Imagination* (Cambridge, MA: Harvard University Press, 1992), 4.
32 Ibid., 4–5.
33 Ibid., 8–9.
34 Ibid., 9.
35 Ibram X. Kendi, "Denial is the Heartbeat of America," *The Atlantic*, January 11, 2021, www.theatlantic.com/ideas/archive/2021/01/denial-heartbeat-america/617631/.
36 See the use of the term "racial formation" in Michael Omi and Howard Winant, *Racial Formation in the United States: From the 1960s to the 1990s*, 2nd ed. (New York: Routledge, 1994), esp. 53–76.
37 Morrison, *Playing in the Dark*, xii.

38 Woody Doane, "Rethinking Whiteness Studies," in *Whiteout: The Continuing Significance of Racism*, edited by Ashley W Doane. and Eduardo Bonilla-Silva (New York: Routledge, 2003), 9.

39 Renato Rosaldo, *Culture and Truth: The Remaking of Social Analysis* (Boston: Beacon Press, 1993), 19. On positionality, see also Lawrence Grossberg, "Cultural Studies and/in New Worlds," *Critical Studies in Mass Communication* 10 (1993): 1–22, esp. 12–16; Ruth Frankenberg, "The Mirage of an Unmarked Whiteness," in *The Making and Unmaking of Whiteness*, edited by Birgit Brander Rasmussen et al. (Durham: Duke University Press, 2001), 72–96, where Frankenberg, referencing standpoint theory and its similar concerns of political identity and conditioned perspective, writes: "Whiteness is a 'standpoint,' a location from which to see selves, others, and national and global orders" (76).

40 Stuart Hall, "Cultural Identity and Diaspora," in *Colonial Discourse and Post-colonial Theory: A Reader*, ed. Patrick Williams and Laura Crisman (London: Harvester Wheatsheaf, 1994), 222–237 (225).

41 Morrison, *Playing in the Dark*, 5.

42 Douglas Lanier, *Shakespeare and Modern Popular Culture* (Oxford: Oxford University Press, 2002), 24. Lanier uses the term "unpopularizing Shakespeare" to describe the evolution from the Elizabethan popular theater toward print, reading, and elite consumers (21–49).

43 Michael Dobson, *The Making of the National Poet: Shakespeare, Adaptation, and Authorship, 1660–1769* (Oxford: Clarendon Press, 2001), 3. The accelerated uptick of collected editions in the eighteenth century prolonged the reflective and moralizing practices associated with individual reading. On the history of Shakespeare in print and the related theatrical intersections, see Lanier, *Shakespeare and Modern Popular Culture*, 21–49; Lawrence W. Levine, *Highbrow/Lowbrow: The Emergence of Cultural Hierarchy in America* (Cambridge, MA: Harvard University Press, 2002), 11–81.

44 Lanier, *Shakespeare and Modern Popular Culture*, 29.

45 Dobson, *The Making of the National Poet*, 227.

46 Quoted in Ibid., 229.

47 A. A. Lipscomb, "Uses of Shakespeare Off the Stage," quoted in Levine, *Highbrow/Lowbrow*, 73; see also Leah S. Marcus, *How Shakespeare Became Colonial: Editorial Tradition and the British Empire* (New York: Routledge, 2017); Terence Hawkes, "Swisser-Swatter: Making a Man of English Letters," in *Alternative Shakespeares*, ed. John Drakakis (New York: Methuen, 1985).

48 Morrison, *Playing in the Dark*, 37.

49 Susan Dwyer Amussen, *Caribbean Exchanges: Slavery and the Transformation of English Society, 1640–1700* (Chapel Hill: University of North Carolina Press, 2007).

50 See Edward Said's contrapuntal reading of the English upper middle-class and its dark side of West Indian plantation slavery in Jane Austen in *Culture and Imperialism* (New York: Vintage, 1994), esp. 84–97; and Lolita Chakrabarti, *Red Velvet* (New York: Bloomsbury Methuen Drama, 2012). The setting of the

play is 1833, on the eve of the abolition of British slavery, and the African American actor Ira Aldridge substitutes for the English actor Edmund Kean in a production of *Othello* in London.

51 W. J. T. Mitchell, *Seeing Through Race* (Cambridge, MA: Harvard University Press, 2012), xi.

52 Ta-Nehisi Coates, "The First White President," *The Atlantic*, October 2017, www.theatlantic.com/magazine/archive/2017/10/the-first-white-president-ta-nehisi-coates/537909/; Marc Lamont Hill, *Nobody: Casualties of America's War on the Vulnerable, from Ferguson to Flint and Beyond* (New York: Atria Books, 2016).

53 An important contribution to this evolution of the post-racial argument is made by Anthony Appiah, "The Uncompleted Argument: DuBois and the Illusion of Race," *Critical Quarterly* 12.1 (1985): 21–37.

54 Mitchell, *Seeing Through Race*, 13.

55 Ben Myers, "Where are the Minority Professors?" *The Chronicle of Higher Education*, February 14, 2016, www.chronicle.com/interactives/where-are-the-minority-professors. Similar results were reported in 2019; see Colleen Flaherty, "Professors Still More Likely Than Students to be White," *Inside Higher Ed*, August 1, 2019, www.insidehighered.com/quicktakes/2019/08/01/professors-still-more-likely-students-be-white.

56 I am grateful for the information shared with me by the Executive Office of the SAA on May 13, 2020.

57 "Black Like Me, Past Present, and Future: Behind the Stratford Festival Curtain," June 6, 2020, www.youtube.com/watch?v=xJK85IRtzYM.

58 Keith Hamilton Cobb, *American Moor* (New York: Methuen, 2020).

59 AnnLouise Keating, "Interrogating 'Whiteness,' (De)constructing 'Race,'" *College English* 57.8 (1995): 901–918 (902).

60 Timothy Barnett, "Reading 'Whiteness' in English Studies," *College English* 63.1 (2000): 9–37 (10).

61 The phrase comes from Sharon Stockton, "'Blacks vs. Browns': Questioning the White Ground," *College English* 57.2 (1995): 166–181.

62 On systemic racism, a related concept to what I term systemic whiteness, see Joe R. Feagin, *Racist America: Roots, Current Realities, and Reparations*, 4th ed. (New York: Routledge, 2019), 1–34.

63 On the issue of decoloniality, see Walter D. Mignolo and Catherine E. Walsh, *On Decoloniality: Concepts, Analytics, Praxis* (Durham: Duke University Press, 2018), esp. 1–2.

64 On colonial education and its racial discrepancies, see J. Edward Chamberlin, *Come Back to Me My Language: Poetry and the West Indies* (Chicago: University of Illinois Press, 1993), 73, see also 73–82; and see Ania Loomba and Martin Orkin, eds., *Post-Colonial Shakespeares* (New York: Routledge, 1998).

65 I can mention only a handful of classic and recent texts among a constantly expanding archive of criticism: W. E. B. Du Bois, *The Souls of Black Folk* (1903) (New York: Penguin, 2018); Frantz Fanon, *Black Skin, White Masks*, trans. Charles Lam Markmann (New York: Grove Press, 1967); bell hooks, *Black Looks: Race and Representation* (New York: Routledge, 2015); Charles

W. Mills, *Black Rights/White Wrongs: The Critique of Racial Liberalism* (Oxford: Oxford University Press, 2017); Achille Mbembe, *Critique of Black Reason*, trans. Laurent Dubois (Durham: Duke University Press, 2017).

66 Urvashi Chakravarty, "The Renaissance of Race and the Future of Early Modern Race Studies," Special Issue: The State of Renaissance Studies II, *English Literary Renaissance* 50.1 (2019): 17–24; and Jean E. Howard, "Renaissance Studies in a Different Time," 70–75, in the same special issue. Howard, however, sets her assessment poignantly within the larger frame of the administrative contraction that besets the profession and strategies to ensure the survival of early modern studies more broadly.

67 Among the most recent publications since 2016 covering diverse topics and approaches, see Espinosa and Ruiter, *Shakespeare and Immigration*; Chapman, *Anti-Black Racism in Early Modern English Drama*; Akhimie, *Shakespeare and the Cultivation of Difference*; MacDonald, *Shakespearean Adaptation*; Thompson, *The Cambridge Companion to Shakespeare and Race*; Catherine E. Fletcher, *The Black Prince of Florence: The Spectacular Life and Treacherous World of Alessandro de' Medici* (Oxford: Oxford University Press, 2016); Delia Jarrett-Macauley, ed., *Shakespeare, Race, and Performance: The Diverse Bard* (New York: Routledge, 2017); Cassander L. Smith, Nicholas R. Jones, and Miles P. Grier, eds., *Early Modern Black Diaspora Studies: A Critical Anthology* (New York: Palgrave, 2018); Cord J. Whitaker, *Black Metaphors: How Modern Racism Emerged from Medieval Race-Thinking* (Philadelphia: University of Pennsylvania Press, 2019); and Ruben Espinosa, *Shakespeare and the Shades of Racism* (New York: Routledge, 2021). Still others locate Shakespeare and race in larger discursive contexts; see, for example, Dennis Austin Britton and Melissa Walter, eds., *Rethinking Shakespeare Source Study* (New York: Routledge, 2018).

68 Erickson and Hall, "A New Scholarly Song," 7.

69 One should recall, however, the work on cosmetics and racial whiteness in the early modern period as presented by Kimberly Poitevin, "Inventing Whiteness: Cosmetics, Race, and Women in Early Modern England," *Journal for Early Modern Cultural Studies* 11.1 (2011): 59–89. See also Arthur Little Jr., ed., *White People in Shakespeare* (New York: Palgrave, 2022).

70 Monica McDermott and Frank L. Samson, "White Racial and Ethnic Identity in the United States," *Annual Reviews in Sociology* 31(2005): 245–261 (246).

71 David R. Roediger, *The Wages of Whiteness: Race and the Making of the American Working Class* (New York: Verso, 1991); Toni Morrison, *Playing in the Dark: Whiteness and the Literary Imagination* (Cambridge, MA: Harvard University Press, 1992); Theodore W. Allen, *The Invention of the White Race*, 2 vols (New York: Verso, 1994 and 1997); Richard Dyer, *White: Essays on Race and Culture* (New York: Routledge, 1997); and Matthew Frye Jacobson, *Whiteness of a Different Color: European Immigrants and the Alchemy of Race* (Cambridge, MA: Harvard University Press, 1998). Subsequent important contributions include Nell Irvin Painter, *The History of White People* (New York: Norton, 2010); Michael Monahan, *The Creolizing Subject: Race, Reason, and the Politics of*

Purity (New York: Fordham University Press, 2011); Veronica T. Watson, *The Souls of White Folk: African American Writers Theorize Whiteness* (Jackson: University Press of Mississippi, 2013); George Lipsitz, *The Possessive Investment in Whiteness: How White People Profit from Identity Politics* (Philadelphia: Temple University Press, 2006). See also Doane, "Rethinking Whiteness Studies," which provides an informed historical overview of the growth and emergence of the field along with an assessment of its theoretical protocols.

72 Margaret L. Andersen, "Whitewashing Race: A Critical Perspective on Whiteness," in *Whiteout: The Continuing Significance of Racism*, ed. Ashley W. Doane and Eduardo Bonilla-Silva (New York: Routledge, 2003), 21; the twentieth anniversary edition of Richard Dyer, *White* (1997) (New York: Routledge, 2017); Peter Kolchin, "Whiteness Studies: The New History of Race in America," *The Journal of American History* 89.1 (2002): 154–173; and Valerie Babb, *Whiteness Visible: The Meaning of Whiteness in American Literature and Culture* (New York: New York University Press, 1998); Ruth Frankenberg, *White Woman, Race Matters: The Social Construction of Whiteness* (Minneapolis: University of Minnesota Press, 1993); Stephen Middleton, David R. Roediger, and Donald M. Shaffer, eds., *The Construction of Whiteness: An Interdisciplinary Analysis of Race Formation and the Meaning of a White Identity* (Jackson: University Press of Mississippi, 2016); Linda Martin Alcoff, *The Future of Whiteness* (Cambridge: Polity Press, 2015).

73 Robert P. Baird, "The Invention of Whiteness: The Long History of a Very Dangerous Idea," *The Guardian*, April 20, 2021, www.theguardian.com/news/2021/apr/20/the-invention-of-whiteness-long-history-dangerous-idea.

74 Roediger, *The Wages of Whiteness*, 13.

75 Arthur Little Jr.'s focus on nostalgic critics yearning for a race-free past, who maintain that whiteness "claims for itself a racial exceptionalism even as it does racial work," bears some broad relevance to my arguments while making a strong case for a whiteness studies critique; see his "Re-Historicizing Race, White Melancholia, and Shakespearean Property," *Shakespeare Quarterly* 67.1 (2016): 84–103, esp. 95.

76 Margaret Talbot, "Getting Credit for Being White," *The New York Times Magazine*, November 20, 1997.

77 Quoted in Ibid.

78 Coates, "The First White President."

79 Baird, "The Invention of Whiteness."

80 Simon Clarke and Steve Garner, *White Identities: A Critical Sociological Approach* (New York: Pluto Press, 2010), 1.

81 For a vigorous defense of identity politics, acknowledging the productive intersection between embodied, lived experience and the knowledge produced, see Alexander G. Weheliye, *Habeas Viscus: Racializing Assemblages, Biopolitics, and Black Feminist Theories of the Human* (Durham: Duke University Press, 2014), 6–7.

82 Eric D. Knowles and Christopher K. Marshburn, "Understanding White Identity Politics Will Be Crucial to Diversity Science," *Psychological Inquiry*

21 (2010): 134–139 (135). The authors note that the current numerical advantage will contract to a plurality by 2042, according to the US Census Bureau.

83 Knowles and Marshburn, "Understanding White Identity Politics Will Be Crucial," 134.

84 bell hooks, *Black Looks*, 20.

85 Michael Eric Dyson, foreword to *White Fragility: Why It's So Hard for White People to Talk about Racism* by Robin DiAngelo (Boston: Beacon Press, 2018), x.

86 DiAngelo, *White Fragility*, xiv.

87 For a comparison to the function "queer," see David Halperin, *Saint Foucault: Towards a Gay Hagiography* (Oxford: Oxford University Press, 1997), esp. 62; and Melissa E. Sanchez, *Shakespeare and Queer Theory* (New York: Arden Shakespeare, 2019).

CHAPTER 1

The Racialized Reader

The Reader as Historical Subject

At the end of the title essay from the collection *Nobody Knows My Name*, James Baldwin delivers his verdict on Americans' unwillingness to address the country's racial history: "What it comes to, finally, is that the nation has spent a large part of its time and energy looking away from one of the principal facts of its life."[1] Baldwin's claim that Americans have expended considerable effort in "looking away from" the racial facts of American life – the Scottsboro case of nine black teens wrongfully convicted of rape in 1931; targeted attacks on returning post-WW2 black servicemen; intense white reaction to school desegregation in 1954 – suggests not only a habit of conscious avoidance, but also the studied erasure of a history of black persons so that "Nobody Knows My Name." Baldwin's critique of denial has broad cultural relevance and is uniquely pertinent to the kinds of looking away in traditional Shakespeare criticism that effectively negate a black presence. Embarking on a journey through the South in the late 1950s, Baldwin hoped to confront this invalidating American experience that consigned him to social death as both author and black man. While Baldwin's authorial identity is not in doubt, as the essay's title reasons about his deftly stated racial isolation, the racial identity of the negligent observer as reader who insists on looking away occupies an important place in the theater of cultural spectacle. We are rightfully sensitive to the racial deletion of the ignored in the dialectic of looking away; we must be equally vigilant in accounting for the negligent onlooker as racialized reader to offset the critical fate of invisibility or disappearance. In conceiving the racial import of such a reader in the equation of looking away, criticism has been woefully negligent.

In 1968, only nine years after Baldwin's essay appeared, Roland Barthes published his seminal "The Death of the Author" in which, I argue, the racial erasure or death of the reader constitutes a compelling blind spot. Barthes maintains that textual interpretation must not rely on authorial biography, leading him famously to declare the "death of the Author" for whom writing is that "obliquity into which our subject flees, the black-and-white where all identity is lost, beginning with the very identity of the body that writes."[2] A similar fate of disappearance has befallen the reader in modern criticism, which has often collapsed the distinction between the reader and reading, reader-reception theory notwithstanding. Where Barthes's author cedes ground to textuality, a hallmark of poststructuralism, the reader in criticism has been subsumed into the seemingly abstract, autonomous activity of reading in ways that have quietly eroded the singularity and significance of the historically situated reading subject. Today, theories of early modern and contemporary reading betray this common tendency to conflate the reader and reading, resulting in the near nullification of the reader as a consequential historical presence.

Barthes insists, nevertheless, that the reader, unlike the author, determines textual meaning, that "the unity of a text is not in its origin but its destination." Still, for Barthes, such a "reader is a man without history, without biography, without psychology; he is only that *someone* who holds collected into one and the same field all of the traces from which writing is constituted."[3] Barthes's reader is a history-less subject and, specifically, an unraced interpretant whose "identity of the body," in his suggestive but race-blind formulation, is supremely negligible. On the contrary, my interest resides precisely in a reader–critic situated and formed by a history of structural systems ranging from the slave economy and its social legacies to congressional legislation about immigration and racialized citizenship in the Unites States. This chapter not only addresses the missing racialized white reader within existing scholarship, but also sets out the historical and cultural parameters of that reader's formation and the environments that have fostered racial denial and elicited racial distortion.

Theories of Early Modern Reading

To define more clearly the stakes of the theory of the racialized reader I propose, I will consider two important approaches as points of differentiation and emphasis: critics on early modern reading, dedicated to retrieving the lost reader, and, in the next section, recent debates on interpretation relative to the notion of the text's hidden meaning. Theories of early modern reading have been influenced by historicist theories and methods but pursued in ways very different from the theory I propose.[4] The revolutionary turn to history in early modern studies, in the last two decades of the twentieth century, encapsulated a flashpoint that proves instructive. Stated briefly, humanism, long the bedrock of early modern studies, was critiqued for its universal and essentialist standpoint by scholars with historicist, cultural materialist, and neo-Marxist views who, despite some differences among them, placed a greater emphasis on "specific discourses and social processes" in constructions of the self.[5] Humanism's continuing universal appeal, writes Zeus Leonardo, "is quickly betrayed when, upon deconstruction, human experience appears cultural or racial (usually Eurocentric or White), and not universal."[6] Questions of race were largely ignored, however, by literary scholars engrossed in the particular late twentieth-century debate that worried about how to conceive of the human. In Jean E. Howard's characterization of the constructionist view at the height of the historicist debates, "nothing exists before the human subject is *created* by history."[7] Howard's critical assessment is correct, of course, but it sets up the following unaddressed question among scholars of the time: what about the racialized human created *in* history? The response relative to reading specifically produced a full body of work that, in effect, pursued business as usual. That is, despite the overt rejection of the universal human subject, the universal white subject was left firmly in place.

Evelyn Tribble notes that, beginning in the 1980s, scholars "increasingly located texts within the material conditions of early modern England, seeing writers as not transcending these conditions but complicatedly embedded within them."[8] In a highly influential essay, Robert Darnton describes the social life cycle of books as a "communications circuit" of production, circulation, and consumption running "from the author to the publisher (if the bookseller does not assume that role), the printer, the shipper, the bookseller, and the reader."[9] Such a focus on the material history of the book inspired interest in library inventories, customized bindings, the dynamics of the printed page, commonplace books, marginal notations, and, more generally, book use, to employ William Sherman's formulation, that implies multiple forms of human interaction with books that included reading.[10] One of the most concentrated areas of scholarship involved the reconstruction of a putative reader from the fragmentary evidence and material traces of the book's social life. Marginal comments, textual corrections, scribbled annotations, and various jottings as found in Shakespeare's First Folio, for example, constitute a record of writerly use from which human interaction and readerly activity might be intuited.[11]

After more than three decades of these developments, Stephen Orgel, in his recent *The Reader in the Book*, can still speak of the "reading revolution" that follows from the evidence left by readers in early modern texts. This is a revolution "which has involved noticing what has been unnoticeable and finding evidence in the hitherto irrelevant; so that habits of reading, manifested in various marks and marginalia, have become as central to the nature of the book as format and typography, watermarks and chain lines."[12]

Jennifer Richards and Fred Schurink observe that Darnton challenged reader-response critics like Wolfgang Iser and Hans Robert Jauss on the grounds that "what they proposed was a theory of reading not a history."[13] Iser, following Georges Poulet, excluded the "life-story of the author" as well as the "individual disposition of the reader" from his reading formula.[14] "Disposition," when taken to mean more than a unique psychological constitution and emotional temperament, can be rehabilitated to refer to the tendencies and learned intellectual habits that are shared among significant swaths of a culture. I build on the historicizing impulse, broadly speaking, with a distinctly different focus on modern readers, whether students, theater practitioners, or most often, scholars producing criticism, who maintain or recreate the field of Shakespeare studies. Where Tribble speaks of the contextually determining "material conditions of early modern England," I turn to the material conditions of race that have constitutionally altered our cultural disposition, and become the defining feature of modernity, to consider its significance for readers. Despite the impact of the material approach to theories of reading, I forego its indebtedness to the infrastructure of book history to address the modern reader in history more pointedly.

Trying to reconstruct individual early modern readers from fragmentary material evidence constitutes a return to the project of white invisibility, despite scholars' laudable efforts, and defers, seemingly endlessly, any serious discussion about the racial identity of the contemporary scholar–reader. Instead of searching for ghostly human traces in the scribbles or cup stains on book pages, I am invested in understanding the motives of modern readers for whom the heritage of whiteness requires a transformative commitment to a racial ethics in our scholarship. In contrast to Orgel, who decodes readerly presences in books through "noticing what has been unnoticeable and finding evidence in the hitherto irrelevant," I am more focused on what prevents readers from seeing in Shakespeare's texts the "unnoticeable" or "hitherto irrelevant" racial signs that are anything but insignificant. These signs are often "unnoticeable," this book argues, because of the modern mental and social disposition of whiteness to not see or read race, and this tendency toward denial is especially significant in reading Shakespeare, who has become an icon of culture, humanism, and a largely white reading industry. The persistent pattern of racial ellipses that ignores the white subject–reader has, as I have argued, diminished and unmoored theories of reading.

According to Leonardo, White humanism cannot be conceded as a generalized concept unrelated to actual persons: "Transforming an event into something 'human' when it is racial in nature has been a staple of White humanism's inability to come to terms with people of color's concrete experience."[15] Finally, therefore, this study posits that examining systemic whiteness, the political and epistemological driver of White humanism, reveals the intellectual and cognitive difficulty of white scholars and readers in navigating race, the traces of which are evident in the erasures and elisions of the scholarship produced. Shakespeare, as a major early modern figure, and one located centrally within literary humanism, must be scrutinized closely in terms of the glaring racial erasures perpetrated by a historically white-dominant critical tradition. Again, the question is: What about the racialized human created *in* history? One robust response came in the form of an emergent body of scholarship in early modern race studies that located race relative to blackness through various historicist approaches touching on religion, colonialism, networks of trade, forms of labor, language, gender, and sexuality.[16] I propose an alternative, and complementary, inquiry concerning the racialized white reader who is influenced by the institutional prerogatives of the systemic whiteness that is the informing epistemological and political practice in United States history and culture.

Interpretation: Beyond Surface Reading

As I indicated earlier, reading in literary studies often connotes modes of interpretation separate from the actual reader engaged in the interpretive enterprise. Before turning directly to discuss systemic whiteness as an epistemological formation, I would like to examine "interpretation" and the recent debate it has generated. It is a debate that focuses on the practice of unlocking secrets in texts without sufficiently unpacking the idea of the reader–interpretant as a subject in history. Once again, we must confront the issue of racial ellipsis. Deidre Shauna Lynch and Evelyne Ender offer a description of reading on which many would agree: "the one thing reading almost always entails, after all, is an encounter between a consciousness and a material object."[17] The authors, however, observe that historians of reading have consistently noted the methodological complexities that belie an assessment of an apparently straightforward activity. Recent discussion has centered on interpretation in contemporary literary and early modern criticism. According to Rita Felski, the debates around interpretation concern a particular mode of analysis, "a *thought style* that slices across differences of field and discipline," whose intellectual reflex to search out hidden truths is epitomized in Paul Ricoeur's hermeneutics of suspicion.[18] The main outlines of this current critique of interpretation are found in the 2009 article, "Surface Reading: An Introduction," by Sharon Best and Stephen Marcus. Interpretation as decoding hidden meaning, they argue, is superfluous in a media-saturated age that divests itself of secrets through overexposure. History wears its horrors and political projects openly on its sleeve, as represented in the articulate images of human torture at Abu Ghraib or the utter dispossession of African Americans in the aftermath of Hurricane Katrina left adrift by the state's racial indifference and incompetence. As a result, Best and Marcus postulate a methodological shift toward "surface reading" that only requires description: "we take surface to mean what is evident, perceptible, apprehensible in texts; what is neither hidden nor hiding." They conclude: "A surface is what insists on being looked *at* rather than what we must train ourselves to see *through*."[19]

Best and Marcus set out a project that challenges a dominant reading practice dating from the last quarter of the twentieth century among scholars "trained to equate reading with interpretation," identified specifically with uncovering concealed, coded, or latent information.[20] Dubbed "symptomatic reading," this particular "practice encompasses an interpretive method that argues that the most interesting aspect of a text is what it represses."[21] Notably, symptomatic reading singles out the critic as a heroic, unusually skilled, master decoder "who performs interpretive feats of demystification."[22] Admitting to their own earlier pleasures in this hunt for undisclosed material, Best and Marcus now eschew this particular investigatory pursuit, which they identify most closely with Fredric Jameson's *The Political Unconscious* (1981). Jameson writes: "If everything were transparent, then no ideology would be possible, and no domination either; evidently that is not our case."[23] In this passage, Jameson sets out the predicate of his reading practice, arguing that the uncovering of undisclosed meanings in texts equates to attempts to expose ideology and its political work in the name of freedom. Reading strategies that unearth covert content have, therefore, a wider, more far-reaching social purpose than any narrowly defined, local act of textual encounter, committed as reading is in Jameson's view to a grand liberatory vision. By contrast, Best and Marcus admit a retrenchment in Jameson's aspirational politics and remain "skeptical about the very possibility of radical freedom and dubious that literature or its criticism can explain our oppression or provide the keys to our liberation."[24] Their assessment of the limited "revolutionary capacities of both texts and critics" within the university have resulted in the far more modest project of surface reading.[25] But when the political stakes are as high as they are today, given the destructive purposes to which race has increasingly been put, reading, literary studies, and the role of the critics engaged in the project of racial literacy seem urgently important and capacious once again.

Best and Marcus's intervention provoked a strong response. Critics appreciate the value placed on the close attention to texts in English literary studies, where teaching students to be better, more astute readers is a priority. Whether Best and Marcus focus on "'surface reading,' 'slow reading,' 'close but not deep reading,'" writes Lisa Freeman approvingly, they have isolated and foregrounded a "renewed interest in an attentiveness to textual detail."[26] Still, Freeman notes that suspicion plays a valuable role in the archive; for example, eliciting greater self-awareness "both about what we see before us and about our own reading tendencies."[27] Elizabeth Weed welcomes the opportunity for reassessment, since "no critical practice can maintain its vitality without continually questioning its reading practices," even though she laments the authors' sense of political defeat and frustration.[28] And Crystal Bartolovich adds that the narrowly stated textual preoccupations of surface reading "mark a pointed withdrawal from politics."[29] In this political retreat, Jeffrey L. Williams sees "the shrunken expectations of academe, particularly of the humanities, and a decline in the social prestige of literary criticism."[30] Thus, the charge of "narrowness" and "blinkered vision" punctuate the criticism leveled at the overall project that displays an otherwise useful close attention to texts.[31] The challenge presents itself: to maintain textual attentiveness without loss of political import, by proposing a notion of racial literacy that impinges on the most critical concerns facing our culture today.

Notably, Best and Marcus begin by interrogating the "we" in the title of the special issue in which their essay appears, "Reading 'The Way We Read Now.'" They describe a "relatively homogeneous group of scholars who received doctoral degrees in either English or comparative literature after 1983," who are trained in theory and fluent in symptomatic reading as the mainstay of interpretation.[32] Acknowledging the constitution of the readerly community is an indispensable and welcome point of departure. Now, decades later, in light of their disavowal of earlier theoretical persuasions and the adoption of surface reading, a glaring oversight of an even more influential commonality appears: the racial homogeneity of this corpus of critics whose academic formation they describe. This "we" that Best and Marcus attribute to educational preparation must be examined further to include among its defining features the systemic whiteness within which the vast majority of academics in early modern and Shakespeare studies operate. With this acknowledgment, a significant crack in the façade of surface reading appears when attention to describing fails to admit or even look *at* "evident, perceptible, apprehensible" signs of race.

When Best and Marcus claim that "A surface is what insists on being looked *at* rather than what we must train ourselves to see *through*," they echo Peter Stallybrass and Margreta de Grazia's proposition for reading Shakespeare where stubborn material data – "old typefaces and spellings, irregular line and scene divisions, title pages and other paratextual matter" – demand to be "looked *at*, not seen *through*."[33] I contend that these arguments express an egregious oversight by looking *past* the reader who is structurally impelled by the motives of white reading. For all the renewed skepticism about hidden or repressed content, the circumvention or occlusion of the white readerly identity from the equation of reading is a spectacular example of irony. The consistent refusal among critics to acknowledge whiteness as the indelible criterion of identity in the United States is a function of the purposeful strategies of systemic whiteness: pervasive, dominant, and the wielder of power, but not the *object* of discussion or conversation that, by definition, would subvert its agential status. Other identities are raced, but whiteness exists uncontained, describing but not described so that it eludes even Best and Marcus's minimal descriptions of "we." My use of the terminology of denial and repression is meant as a response to Best and Marcus's objections, not an adoption of a psychoanalytic framework. I am, however, interested in how we read, by calling attention to the racial blind spots in criticism and the cognitive dodges employed as a consequence of systemic whiteness. Again, we recall Best and Marcus's claim: "A surface is what insists on being looked *at* rather than what we must train ourselves to see *through*." They suggest, unfortunately, that looking *at* is a much less complex venture, requiring less training for the human reader conceived as recorder of data, and much less subject to the vagaries of human input and interpretation when, in fact, one of the central arguments of this book is that looking at, especially when conditioned by race, is far from perfect, easy, or straightforward. In early modern studies, looking at, through the lens of race, is constrained by a history of ignoring race or seeing race from a jaundiced, biased perspective that leads to distortions in the critical visual field.

We can learn much from the authors' omission; their debate over interpretation constitutes a misinterpretation. First, surface reading is insufficient for the deep cultural and historical reading of race's somatic signs, bearing in mind that words, too, have a somatic racial expression. Racialized skin color, rooted in the obvious properties of surface matter, is treated, following Best and Marcus's logic, as if it is an unimportant or nonexistent historical sign when race, by definition, is a function of interpretation: the symptomatic, culture-specific interpretation of bodily signs. Let us also bear in mind Alexander Weheliye's definition of race "as a set of sociopolitical processes of differentiation and hierarchization, which are projected onto the putatively biological human body," whose materiality is required reading of the kind abjured by these critics.[34] If the reader deserves to be read, as the authors concede, then the analog of skin color to surface signs suggests the necessary disclosure and unearthing of the historical and cultural forces that constitute whiteness in American culture and shape the epistemological habits that inform our reading. The necessary and unavoidable conjunction of race and symptomatic reading posits a return to the political pertinence of literary criticism and a reaffirmation of its relevance in our time, when the urgency of history calls for a reckoning, and the academy, especially the humanities, can marshal its considerable intellectual resources in eloquent response. If symptomatic reading boasts the heroic reader, we must all be heroic in our collective efforts to recognize race, its historical reality, and deep interference in our scholarly identities and practices as a point of transformative departure.

Second, the authors' extraordinary claim of textual transparency ignores the definition stated earlier: reading as "an encounter between a consciousness and a material object," where that embodied consciousness, imprinted, constrained, and defined by the institutional imperatives of systemic whiteness, is excluded from the reading equation. Accounting for a white reading subject, therefore, leads to the following recognition: that the epistemological training (as opposed to only the educational one discussed by Best and Marcus) in cultural whiteness creates a *textual product* that is not to be confused with the text itself as a dense linguistic entity. We are, by now, used to the idea of multiple versions of a Shakespeare text due to editorial interventions of recent decades.

Similarly, the textual product of white reading, different from the actual printed words and text, connotes multiple textual variants and versions whose editorial criteria are guided by omissions, obfuscations, and oversights whose purpose is to maintain fidelity to principles of institutional whiteness and the project of racial erasure. Systemic whiteness has coopted the notion of textual and critical production and transformed – one might even say disfigured – what the very notion of reading (whether surface or deep) means.

Systemic Whiteness and Racial Formation

In the absence of a theory of a racialized reader, therefore, I attend here to the role of the cultural and racial formation of the reading subject that produces a specific mental conditioning and praxis. I build on Michael Omi and Howard Winant's definition of "*racial formation* as the sociohistorical process by which racial categories are created, inhabited, transformed, and destroyed" to foreground the epistemological effects of such a "sociohistorical process."[35] For this theory of reading, I cite the concept of pragmatics to underscore my understanding of reading, which incorporates not only the reader's interaction with the text, but also the cultural formation of the reader and its effect on the reading event.[36] If, according to Iser, texts have a repertoire, that is, the contexts and histories that inform them, I emphasize here a contextual and historical repertoire of the reader – its cultural and cognitive sources, influences, and authorizing master narratives – that in the United States is grounded in systemic whiteness.[37] Modeled on the institutional formation that produces the chronic inequalities of structural racism, systemic whiteness is inversely proportional in securing the institutional privileges created for whites in a white-dominant society.[38] Systemic whiteness is rooted in history and deeply invested in the conscious and deliberate tactics that have been deployed in securing a white-dominant framework within which United States culture operates to sustain subjects' position as white. It is a term that speaks to the cultural location of subjects shaped and informed by a history of institutional dictates and practices that have codified the nation's episteme since its founding. As a result, in a reading event, like any other social activity or practice, the cultural and epistemological formation of systematic whiteness functions as an active agent that influences how we read.

Omi and Winant describe the history of the United States as largely a "*racial dictatorship*."[39] Beginning in 1607 with the founding of

Jamestown, this racial dictatorship carried through independence from Britain to the end of the Civil War in 1865 and up to the present. Despite notations of physical difference among groups of people in the Bible or Herodotus, these authors argue that the modern idea of race began with the rise of Europe and the prosecution of conquest in the New World, that is, from the age of Shakespeare and beyond. The racial project of conquest, subjugation, and seizure initiated a history of white rule in the United States that was legitimized in its institutions and exercised with seeming impunity in every human sphere. This includes the racial hierarchization of legalized black slavery and the instauration of white supremacy; congressional declaration of white citizenship beginning in the eighteenth century; governmental manipulation of the census; exclusive immigration policies, especially since the nineteenth century; the collapse of Reconstruction and the rise of Jim Crow; racially targeted, restrictive voting rights laws; and persistent, authorized social discrimination up to the present in the judicial system, housing and labor markets, the military, and education.[40] Racial dictatorship in the United States has had three main consequences: it established whiteness as *the* defining American identity; authorized social organization along a color-line; and consolidated racial identities, such as "black," pursuant to the politics of slavery and marronage.[41]

Although historians understand that "racial disparities are older than the life of the United States," the entanglement of the nation's origins with the enslavement of Africans has left an attitudinal imprint on its character and a legacy of structural inequality.[42] The contradictions of Thomas Jefferson, founding father and proponent of freedom while a slaveholder, distill into a representative figure the hypocrisies of a nation that blindly ignored the burden of racial exclusion from its aspiration of inalienable right to liberty.[43] Ibram X. Kendi records the opposition of Jefferson Davis, the future president of the Confederacy, to a bill intended to fund black education in 1860: "'This Government was not founded by negroes nor for negroes,' but 'by white men for white men.'" For Davis, the bill's flawed intent was doomed because the essential "'inequality of the black and white races' was 'stamped from the beginning.'"[44] Douglas Blackmon's account of exploited human labor by big American companies after Emancipation up to the post-World War II period illustrates the persistent pattern of inhumanity surrendered to profiteering. The trove of records of the sale and re-sale of free men who had committed no crime, their physical coercion, and uncompensated work in "mines, lumber camps, quarries, farms, and factories," supplies a harrowing tale of the lurid re-investment in the practices of "slavery by another name."[45] Blackmon's documentation also highlights the ruse that would help perpetuate the vulnerability of blacks to the justice system: "the capture and imprisonment of thousands of random indigent citizens, almost always under the thinnest chimera of probable cause or judicial process."[46] Confirming the extensive institutional legacy of blackness and criminality, Michelle Alexander argues that the United States criminal justice system incarcerates people of color disproportionately, stigmatizes them through felony labeling, deprives them of certain civil rights upon release, and, in effect, creates a caste system that continues to reproduce racial hierarchies and legitimize discrimination in education, jobs, and housing in the twenty-first century iteration of the New Jim Crow.[47]

As a result of this chronic discriminatory pattern, Ta-Nehisi Coates argues, "white supremacy is not merely the work of hotheaded demagogues, or a matter of false consciousness, but a force so fundamental to America that it is difficult to imagine the country without it."[48] White supremacy is, in short, the shaping force of the reader's repertoire, and congressional legislation has played a substantive part in sustaining white supremacy in the United States. In the year following the ratification of the US Constitution, the Congress of 1790 declared "that all free white persons," who met specific residency requirements, "shall be entitled to the rights of citizenship."[49] Although congressional leaders debated the requisite period of residency, the eligibility of Catholics and Jews, or foreign persons' rights to land ownership and inheritance, for example, the congruency of race and citizenship was already so ingrained that the criterion of whiteness was never questioned. In fact, Matthew Frye Jacobson observes, "the nation's first legislators saw the law as too inclusive rather than too exclusive, and nowhere did they pause to question the limitations of naturalized citizenship to 'white persons.'"[50] Across the legislative spectrum of the early colonies the racial designation "white" was enjoined to the practical work of citizens who could affirm civility against the barbarous "savages," propound Christian virtues, and help suppress slave rebellions or prosecute the Indian wars. The result was the creation of a public ideology of belonging and fitness to share in the republican virtue of self-government. Thus, Jacobson writes, "the word 'white' did attain wide usage in New World political discourse, and it was written into an immense body of statutory law" to grant vast amounts of social and legal privilege and never to curtail them, the exception being marital proscriptions to ensure the purity of the white race.[51] South Carolina law declared that state's restriction of the franchise to "a free white male," and in similar fashion in 1777, Georgia limited the right to vote to "all male white inhabitants."[52] By the time of the 1790

Naturalization Act, therefore, the legal enshrinement of white citizenship expressed widely held views about white male supremacy and competency in the work of self-government, cultural ownership, and national identity.[53]

For a country increasingly populated by immigrants, after aggressive indigenous displacement and removal, the project of immigrant gatekeeping tells the story of concerted white maintenance. Over the following century, debates about what it meant to be an American accelerated, in response to waves of immigration during the 1800s, and mounting restrictionism led Congress to take action, notably in the period between 1890 and the 1920s. The Dillingham Commission was established by Congress in 1907 to study and produce a report on this decades-long influx of immigrants relative to the degree of their assimilation, loyalty to their new country, and their degenerative impact on the American economy and culture. The forty-one volume Dillingham Commission report, published in 1911, drew a firm distinction between old immigrants, from northwestern Europe (England, France, Germany), and new immigrants, from southeastern Europe (Italians, Armenians, Poles). The report concluded that new immigrants were less likely to assimilate to American culture, values, and habits and recommended a literacy test that was adopted for exclusionary purposes in the 1917 Immigration Act. Desmond King remarks that the Commission's explicit focus on new European immigrants "reinforced the political marginality of African Americans: conducting the debate in terms exclusively of white immigrants emphasized a vision of the Unites States' identity as a white one."[54] Despite centuries of residency in America, African Americans were discounted when the "criteria of assimilability" were favorably identified with "Anglo-Saxon Americanism, which was white."[55] Importantly, the report, by relying on the work of anthropologist Franz Boas, gave unintended credence to the proponents of eugenics who wanted immigration policy to be based on their radical theories of racial management.[56] They got their wish in the Johnson–Reed Immigration Act of 1924, whose reliance on eugenic theories was cited as a model for the horrific experimental work in 1930s Germany.[57] The exclusion of "the descendants of slave immigrants" from the 1929 national origins legislation reconfirmed a sustained and closely held American identity as white.[58]

Although class, wealth, and education allowed for differentiation among whites, over time ethnic whiteness gave way to a racial whiteness that, in turn, was consolidated and mobilized against black social advancement.[59] In the antebellum era, arriving Irish immigrants lived and worked alongside free blacks, and "it was speculated," writes Noel Ignatiev, "that if racial amalgamation was ever to take place it would begin between these two groups."[60] The strategy of associating new immigrants with blacks would lead to a disassociation *from* blacks once the opportunities for white entry and acceptance presented itself. Already evident in the failed aftermath of Bacon's Rebellion of 1676, which united "slaves, indentured servants, and poor whites in a revolutionary effort to overthrow the planter elite," Alexander argues persuasively that a "racial bribe" was also instrumental in the defeat of Reconstruction and the rise of Jim Crow; the promise to whites of all classes of distance from the taint of black slavery and its persistent legacy was an effective political lure.[61] Union support for the dignity of work enabled European ethnic white assimilation while aggressive anti-black exclusion was enforced, in some instances, by white youth gangs.[62] This production of a white racial supremacy, the result of a deliberate blending and moderating of diverse European ethnics into American whiteness, holds powerful cultural sway in its reward system that continues to bar black legitimacy in maintaining the exclusivity of racial rank. Where debates around assimilation became central to the Dillingham Commission inquiry, highlighting the anxieties about outsiders and the degeneration of the texture of the American polity, strategies to facilitate shared whiteness were already serving as a cultural glue that mitigated any perceived erosion of American identity. Using the descriptive title *Working Towards Whiteness*, David R. Roediger posits the successful culmination of decades-long efforts of white ethnic inclusion at the end of World War II.[63]

The congressional and public debates about immigration have focused on an idea of a white nation whose existence is defensively predicated on posing the perennial question: "Who is an American?" Deeply interwoven in the institutional fabric of the nation, whiteness is not incidental or occasional, but structural; systemic whiteness is the intentional product of the racial disparities inherent in and generated by the nation's institutions. Not simply the idiosyncratic or unique identity of a single individual, but the product of fundamental social structures, whiteness establishes a group mandate, bears the imprimatur of institutional authority, and is gifted the social levers of power and privilege. In the United States, whiteness is the feature of the social system shaped and regulated by its institutions and affiliates. The nation's informing political framework of racial dictatorship suggests that systemic whiteness is always engaged in projects of power and self-normalization – that is, inventing self-serving norms that are the product of *mis*interpreting history.

My attempt to define the structures and practices of systematic whiteness as a product of history bears comparison to Bourdieu's habitus, or other similar constructionist theories of culture that, nevertheless, neglect race. According to Bourdieu, as subjects we inhabit homogenous environments whose social dynamics are informed by and reproduce seemingly commonsense ideas formed over time, or what he describes as "history turned into nature."[64] We are immanent bearers of an entire social and institutional history whose unguarded, improvisational acts reflect and reveal that social education. Bourdieu's theory relies on the "unconscious" dimension of the institutional acculturation and education of agents acquired through repetition over time: "The 'unconscious' is never anything other than the forgetting of history," a normalization that induces repeated, unreflective action.[65] Again he writes: "It is because subjects do not, strictly speaking, know what they are doing that what they do has more meaning than they know. The habitus mediates an individual agent's cultural practices, without either explicit reason or signifying intent, to be none the less 'sensible' and 'reasonable.'"[66] As such, a reader is engaged in an everyday cultural practice whose racial habitus is the subject of exploration.

Indeed, reading and acting within the constraints of systemic whiteness have powerful effects so routinized over the years that one assumes a recognizable, familiar, natural order of things that resonates as just and "reasonable" within a chosen environment such as academia. But to not challenge this version of the "unconscious" behavior is to let "reasonable" – because they have always been justified – defenders of white supremacist positions off the hook without any demand for accountability to themselves and society. I would emphasize, further, that in my reading, this idea of the "unconscious" is more akin to taking things for granted, or, when confronted, denying the already politicized status quo rather than an assertion that one can never have access to the knowledge and awareness about the operations of systematic whiteness – otherwise what would be the practical value of reflective education, the consciousness-raising of social protest, or engaged work for policy change? The passivity of the reader, to build on de Certeau's critique, whose reading activity is subjected to *racial* determinations or strategies, and not merely class, must be resisted by way of a series of tactical maneuvers that will allow for agency in the act of reading.[67]

White Reading as Distortion

One of the conventional difficulties arising from discussing reading resides in the seeming impossibility of grappling with the individual experiences of any number of persons, but the notion of systemic or structural whiteness allows for a collective account of readers reading. A mechanism is required by which a sufficiently compelling and real commonality among vast numbers of readers can be attested. Systemic whiteness embedded in the nation's origins, practices, institutions, and routines of daily life is such an analytical mechanism. In his use of the phrase "white culture," John Hartigan supports the quest for an inclusive, analytical approach to understanding cultural formation, arguing that the breadth implied by the word "culture" "establishes a register apart from individual identity."[68] As critics have observed, varieties exist within the broad racial category of whiteness because of education, wealth, class, and geographic region, of which we must be mindful.[69] And while the inclusive approach might appear "homogenizing," whiteness in the immigrant society of United States is the historic product of the homogenizing tendencies of cultural assimilation.[70] Thus, the question remains: What are the consequences for reading that follow from whiteness' shared, inclusive, and systemic effects? Whiteness, as "a set of institutional routines and 'white cultural practices'" consistently provides and ensures privileged material access across an array of social experiences like access to home financing, the funding of freeway projects, placements of dumps, and political campaign priorities. As a result, Hartigan argues, "whites benefit from being white whether or not, as individuals, they hold supremacist notions, harbor racist sentiments, or are made anxious by the physical presence of people of color." In a manner consistent with Bourdieu's theory of the "unconscious" function of the habitus, I would argue, Hartigan reiterates "the material relations and social structures that reproduce white privilege and racism in this country, quite apart from what individuals feel, think, and perceive."[71] Hartigan's primary concern with whites' access to material privileges leads him to identify a principle pertinent to the extra-individual analysis that a concept like systematic whiteness employs where readers, engaged in an explicitly social activity, might not even be conscious in the moment of their dependence on protocols and provisions of whiteness that pervade their everyday lives. Germane to systemic whiteness, therefore, are material, social, and epistemological privileges constantly available for those who qualify.

The individual becomes so enmeshed within structural whiteness that one might not always be aware of the operational forces and processes that are designed to produce white supremacist outcomes, yet the racial logic – one might say *illogic* – of systemic whiteness constantly plagues the individual. According to Charles W. Mills in *The Racial Contract*, understanding epistemology in a racial context requires acknowledging divergent realities, one actual and the other race-dependent, that is, built on retrofitting empirical, objective reality to its own particular purpose.[72] This reality-bending construct is the fantasy of whiteness projected onto the world to impose a self-serving order and vision of power that must distort truth, as in the baseless Enlightenment declarations of the natural superiority of whites that justified colonial exploitation and black enslavement. Traditional social agreements about what "counts as moral and factual knowledge of the world" are disrupted by a racial contract, as Mills describes it, committed to the peculiar demands of a racial order that relies on misinformation to distort lived reality and substitute an idealized alternative that selectively celebrates and validates everything white.[73] This "invented delusional world, a racial fantasyland, a 'consensual hallucination'" required by the racial contract has consequential material effects.[74]

The conscious and deliberate strategies employed for centuries to ensure normative white dominance have remained the untold story of Western political thought. "So here, it could be said," Mills writes of what is, in effect, a white epistemology, "one has an agreement to *mis*interpret the world. One has to learn to see the world wrongly, but with the assurance that this set of mistaken perceptions will be validated by white epistemic authority, whether religious or secular."[75] Systemic whiteness, which is the institutional validation of whiteness as officially sanctioned, not only entails histories and legacies of power, discrimination, and injustice, but is also invested in the kind of epistemological distortion that affects how we process information and read: "One could say then, as a general rule, that *white misunderstanding, misrepresentation, evasion, and self-deception on matters related to race* are among the most pervasive mental phenomena of the past few hundred years."[76] Central to the project of *Black Shakespeare* is the calling out of a white epistemology that *mis*interprets Shakespeare's investment in blackness and race along with the other reorienting adjustments that we are constantly compelled to make in order to render whiteness reasonable, true, and right. This study takes seriously Mills's thesis concerning the way a white epistemology bends and misrepresents race-specific reality to serve its particular purposes and extends the argument to a theory of reading. The book maintains as a central proposition that the epistemology of systemic whiteness reimagines and distorts a text through the operational principles of elision, erasure, and avoidance. History, too, is distorted, and its role in white epistemological formation is constantly under pressure of *mis*interpretation and forgetting, a looking away that vitiates race's thick, symptomatic formation. Whiteness's need to deliberately *mis*read reality is consequential for Shakespeare especially, considering the function of his work as a bulwark of White humanism and as a space for the free rein and implantation – with all of the term's colonizing implications – of the White imaginary.

Notes

1 James Baldwin, *Nobody Knows My Name* (1961) (New York: Vintage, 1993), 116.

2 Roland Barthes, "The Death of the Author," in *The Rustle of Language*, translated by Richard Howard (New York: Hill & Wang, 1986), 55, 49.

3 Ibid., 54.

4 Edith Snook, "Recent Studies in Early Modern Reading," *English Literary Renaissance* 43.2 (2013): 343–378 (370):" The field is, unsurprisingly, dominated by historicist approaches and includes the work of both literary scholars and historians who examine representations of reading in literature and investigate the archive of reading's records."

5 Jean E. Howard, "The New Historicism in Renaissance Studies," *English Literary Renaissance* 16.1 (1986): 13–43 (20). Howard provides a substantial account of the key inaugural texts that represent this turn to history (13.n1). The debate is crystallized in several texts, including Stephen Greenblatt, *Renaissance Self-Fashioning: From More to Shakespeare* (Chicago: University of Chicago Press, 1980); Jonathan Dollimore, *Radical Tragedy: Religion, Ideology, and Power in the Drama of Shakespeare and His Contemporaries* (Chicago: University of Chicago Press, 1984); Jonathan Dollimore and Alan Sinfield, eds., *Political Shakespeare: New Essays in Cultural Materialism* (Ithaca: Cornell University Press, 1985); and the later response by Robin Headlam Wells, *Shakespeare's Humanism* (Cambridge: Cambridge University Press, 2005).

6 Zeus Leonardo, "Through the Multicultural Glass: Althusser, Ideology, and Race Relations in Post-Civil Rights America," *Policy Futures in Education* 3.4 (2005): 400–412 (405). Similar concerns about the racial complicities of liberal humanism have been argued by Mills in *Black Rights/White Wrongs*.

7 Howard, "The New Historicism in Renaissance Studies," 21.

8 Evelyn B. Tribble, *Margins and Marginality: The Printed Page in Early Modern England* (Charlottesville: University Press of Virginia, 1993), 3.

9 Robert Darnton, "What is the History of Books?" *Daedalus* 3.3 (1982): 65–83 (67). See also Darnton's "First Steps Toward a History of Reading," *Australian Journal of French Studies* 23.1 (1986): 5–30.

10 On the genealogy of book and reading histories, see Jennifer Richards and Fred Schurink, "The Textuality and Materiality of Reading in Early Modern England," *Huntington Library Quarterly* 73.3 (2010): 345–361; William

H. Sherman, *Used Books: Marking Readers in Renaissance England* (Philadelphia: University of Pennsylvania Press, 2008); for a review of scholarship of early modern reading, see Snook, "Recent Studies in Early Modern Reading." Calling for a more expansive approach that is gender aware, see Heidi Brayman Hackel, "'Boasting of silence': Women Readers in a Patriarchal State," in Kevin Sharpe and Steven N. Zwicker, eds., *Reading, Society and Politics in Early Modern England* (Cambridge: Cambridge University Press, 2003).

11 Emma Smith, *Shakespeare's First Folio: Four Centuries of an Iconic Book* (Oxford: Oxford University Press, 2016), 121–182.

12 Stephen Orgel, *The Reader in the Book: A Study of Spaces and Traces* (Oxford: Oxford University Press, 2015), 2. In addition to Sherman's *Used Books* and Smith's *Shakespeare's First Folio*, see Jennifer Andersen and Elizabeth Sauer, eds., *Books and Readers in Early Modern England: Material Studies* (Philadelphia: University of Pennsylvania Press, 2002); Heidi Brayman Hackel, *Reading Material in Early Modern England: Print, Gender and Literacy* (Cambridge: Cambridge University Press, 2005); Jason Scott-Warren, "Reading Graffiti in the Early Modern Book," *Huntington Library Quarterly* 73.3 (2010): 363–381.

13 Richards and Schurink, "The Textuality and Materiality of Reading," 346; see also Wolfgang Iser, *The Implied Reader: Patterns of Communication in Prose Fiction from Bunyan to Beckett* (Baltimore: Johns Hopkins University Press, 1974); Hans Robert Jauss, *Toward an Aesthetic of Reception*, translated by Timothy Bahti (Minneapolis: University of Minnesota Press, 1982.)

14 Iser, *The Implied Reader*, 292.

15 Leonardo, "Through the Multicultural Glass," 405.

16 See Britton, "Recent Studies in English Renaissance Literature."

17 Deidre Shauna Lynch and Evelyne Ender, "Introduction: A Time for Reading," *PMLA*, Special Topic: Cultures of Reading, 133.5 (2018): 1073–1083 (1078).

18 Rita Felski, *The Limits of Critique* (Chicago: University of Chicago Press, 2015), 2. Felski does not take a position against interpretation, or, as she prefers, the term "critique" that encompasses similar practices; she writes in favor of more options than the limitations of a single method and critical style (8–10). For an engagement of this debate around the notion of "reparative reading," see Eve Kosofsky Sedgwick, "Paranoid Reading and Reparative Reading or, You're So Paranoid, You Probably Think This Essay is about You," in *Touching Feeling: Affect, Pedagogy, Performativity* (Durham: Duke University Press, 2003).

19 Sharon Best and Stephen Marcus, "Surface Reading: An Introduction," *Representations* 108.1 (2009): 1–21 (9).

20 Ibid., 1.

21 Ibid., 3. Elizabeth Weed debates Best and Marcus's reading of Althusser's use of the term "symptomatic reading" in "'The Way We Read Now,'" *History of the Present* 2.1 (2012): 95–106, esp. 101.

22 Best and Marcus, "Surface Reading," 13.

23 Fredric Jameson, *The Political Unconscious: Narrative as a Socially Symbolic Act* (Ithaca: Cornell University Press, 1981), 61.
24 Best and Marcus, "Surface Reading," 2.
25 Ibid., 15–16.
26 Lisa Freeman, "Why We Argue about the Way We Read: An Introduction," *The Eighteenth Century* 54.1 (2013): 121–124 (122).
27 Ibid., 123.
28 Weed, "The Way We Read Now," 95.
29 Crystal Bartolovich, "Humanities of Scale: Marxism, Surface Reading – and Milton," *PMLA* 127.1 (2012): 115–121 (116).
30 Jeffrey L. Williams, "The New Modesty in Literary Criticism," *Chronicle of Higher Education*, January 5, 2015, www.chronicle.com/article/The-New-Modesty-in-Literary/150993.
31 Freeman, "Why We Argue," 122.
32 Best and Marcus, "Surface Reading," 1.
33 Margreta de Grazia and Peter Stallybrass, "The Materiality of the Shakespearean Text," *Shakespeare Quarterly* 44.3 (1993): 255–283 (256, 257).
34 Weheliye, *Habeas Viscus*, 5.
35 Omi and Winant, *Racial Formation*, 55.
36 Roman Jacobson, "Linguistics and Poetics," in *Style in Language*, ed. Thomas A. Sebeok (Cambridge, MA: Technology Press of Massachusetts Institute of Technology, 1960). Jacobson's mapping of six aspects of language highlights the set toward the contextual (which has a "denotative" and "cognitive" function) as "the leading task of numerous messages" (353).
37 Wolfgang Iser, *The Act of Reading: A Theory of Aesthetic Response* (Baltimore: Johns Hopkins University Press, 1978), 68–95. While Iser theorizes a dialectic between the text's and reader's repertoires, my reading does not follow this formulation.
38 On systemic racism, see Joe R. Feagin, *Racist America: Roots, Current Realities, and Reparations*, 4th ed. (New York: Routledge, 2019), 1–34.
39 Omi and Winant, *Racial Formation,* 65. For their examination of racial dictatorship and European conquest, see 61–69; and for their definition of a "racial project," see 55–56.
40 Excellent discussions of the institutional history that produces what I describe as systemic whiteness are provided by Jacobson, *Whiteness of a Different Color* and Lipsitz, *The Possessive Investment in Whiteness.*
41 Omi and Winant, *Racial Formation,* 66.
42 Ibram X. Kendi. *Stamped from the Beginning: The Definitive History of Racist Ideas in America* (New York: Nation Books, 2017), 2.
43 Edmund S. Morgan, *American Slavery, American Freedom: The Ordeal of Colonial Virginia* (New York: Norton, 2003), 3–6.
44 Kendi, *Stamped from the Beginning,* 3.
45 Douglas A. Blackmon, *Slavery by Another Name: The Re-Enslavement of Black Americans from the Civil War to World War II* (New York: Anchor Books, 2009), 6.

46 Ibid., 7.
47 Michelle Alexander, *The New Jim Crow: Mass Incarceration in the Age of Colorblindness* (New York: The New Press, 2012). For a statistics-based approach to race and rates of incarceration, see Khalil Gibran Muhammad, *The Condemnation of Blackness: Race, Crime, and the Making of Modern Urban America* (Cambridge, MA: Harvard University Press, 2011).
48 Ta-Nehisi Coates, "The Case for Reparations," *The Atlantic*, June 2014, www.theatlantic.com/magazine/archive/2014/06/the-case-for-reparations/361631/.
49 Quoted in Jacobson, *Whiteness of a Different Color*, 22. On the importance of the legal definition of citizenship as codified in race, see also Paul Spickard, *Almost All Aliens: Immigration, Race, and Colonialism in American History and Identity* (New York: Routledge, 2007), 79–128, esp. 89–91.
50 Jacobson, *Whiteness of a Different Color*, 22. Jacobson's excellent study provides a detailed account of whiteness, immigration, and citizenship; see esp. 13–38.
51 Ibid., 25.
52 Ibid.
53 Painter, *The History of White People*, acknowledges that the insertion of "free" indicates that some whites in servitude were not included in the 1790 Congressional Act, but the 1800 census addressed the classification issue, and as "politics freed all white people and ideology whitened the face of freedom, 'free white males' seemed a useless redundancy" (106).
54 Desmond King, *Making Americans: Immigration, Race, and the Origins of the Diverse Democracy* (Cambridge, MA: Harvard University Press, 2000), 80.
55 Ibid., 81.
56 Boas has stressed the assimilability of new immigrants to the American environment, but his use of cranial measurements for his study allowed for the displacement of his cultural emphasis with a eugenic one. See King, *Making Americans*, 50–81.
57 Ibid., 167; for a recent study of the 1924 Act and its devastating social afterlife, see Jia Lynn Yang, *One Mighty and Irresistible Tide: The Epic Struggle Over American Immigration, 1924–1965* (New York: Norton, 2020).
58 Quoted in King, *Making Americans*, 224.
59 McDermott and Samson, "White Racial and Ethnic Identity," esp. 246.
60 Noel Ignatiev, *How the Irish Became White* (New York: Routledge, 1995), 2; see also 40–59. Nativist reaction qualified Irish Catholic Famine migrants as black to highlight the cultural xenophobia that viewed non-Protestant affiliation with suspicion. Ignatiev reminds us that while the oppressive Penal Laws of the eighteenth century forced Irish emigration, it was only with the Famine Migration of the nineteenth century that the bulk of arriving Irish could be described as Catholic (38–39). On the racial assimilation of the Irish and other European immigrants, see also Allen, *The Invention of the White Race: vol. 1: Racial Oppression and Social Control*, 2nd ed. (New York: Verso, 2012), esp. 177–199; Eric L. Goldstein, *The Price of Whiteness: Jews, Race, and American Identity* (Princeton: Princeton University Press, 2008).

61 Alexander, *The New Jim Crow,* 24, 25. The notion of the "racial bribe" was powerfully articulated by W. E. B. DuBois as "the public and psychological wage," the cost of white racial affiliation. See his *Black Reconstruction in America,* edited by Henry Louis Gates Jr. (Oxford: Oxford University Press, 2007), 573.

62 McDermott and Samson, "White Racial and Ethnic Identity," 251.

63 David R. Roediger, *Working Towards Whiteness: How America's Immigrants Became White* (New York: Basic Books, 2006), 136–137.

64 Pierre Bourdieu, *Outline of a Theory of Practice,* trans. Richard Nice (Cambridge: Cambridge University Press, 1977), 78; on the "habitus" and "homogeneity," see, 80–83. For a useful discussion of the habitus, see John Fiske, "Cultural Studies and the Culture of Everyday Life," in *Cultural Studies,* ed. Lawrence Grossberg et al. (New York: Routledge, 1992), esp. 156, 161–64.

65 Bourdieu, *Outline of a Theory of Practice,* 78–79.

66 Ibid., 79.

67 De Certeau, *The Practice of Everyday Life,* 174–176.

68 John Hartigan Jr., "Establishing the Fact of Whiteness," *American Anthropologist* 99.3 (1997): 495–505 (496, 497).

69 Paul R. Croll, "Modeling Determinants of White Racial Identity: Results from a New National Survey," *Social Forces* 86.2 (2007): 613–642, esp. 634–635.

70 Hartigan, "Establishing the Fact of Whiteness," 502.

71 Ibid., 496.

72 Charles W. Mills, *The Racial Contract* (Ithaca: Cornell University Press, 1997), 9–19.

73 Ibid., 17.

74 Ibid., 18.

75 Ibid.

76 Ibid., 19.

CHAPTER 2

Racial Blind Spots
Misreading Bodies, Misreading Texts

Antiliteracy Laws: Reading as a Racialized Event

The concept of the racialized reader rests on the predicate of an epistemological formation that shapes and influences how the reader decodes and digests racial matters. However, the reader's white racial formation, examined in the preceding chapter, is not circumscribed by post-Enlightenment theoretical and historical developments. Shakespeare provides us with evidence that illustrates the process of racialized reading, notably in a period earlier than many critics might have expected the self-awareness of whiteness to be an operative feature of identity, let alone reading and interpretation. In later periods, by contrast, reading in the Anglo-American tradition was an explicit and well-documented racialized activity and experience. If reason defined what it meant to be human, then Enlightenment thinkers consistently denigrated black persons as inferior to whites, going so far as to equate skin color with impoverished reasoning and mental accomplishments like reading. Immanuel Kant, elaborating on the thought of David Hume, writes: "So fundamental is the difference between these two races of man, and it appears to be as great in regard to mental capacities as in color."[1] Black illiteracy during this period was not reflective of a lack of native talent or natural ability, but the product of a systematic enforcement of brute ignorance. Consider the Negro Act of 1740 in South Carolina, which was added to the existing slave codes as the first of the antiliteracy laws in the American colonies. Passed in the wake of the Stono Rebellion of 1739, it was intended to suppress further incitement to resistance by limiting the access of enslaved blacks to literacy. The new legislation threatened that having "Slaves taught to write or suffering them to be employed in writing may be attended with great inconveniences."[2] Literacy in this instance appeared to target the edict passed by the Spanish king intending to undermine the British by luring enslaved blacks to Spanish Florida with the promise of freedom. The law's purpose was to prevent those slaves who could read and write from spreading subversive information contained in the edict and any similar documents. Black literacy, along with black freedom, was thus politicized as a threat to the British ruling authorities. With the adoption of similar antiliteracy laws in Georgia in 1755 and Virginia in 1819, the proven alignment of race and illiteracy as instrumental to state control in the new republic was firmly decided. The Nat Turner rebellion of 1831 led to the addition of the death penalty to Virginia's codes which, Birgit Brander Rasmussen observes, "became a model for antiliteracy legislation throughout the slave-holding South."[3]

The expansion of the Savannah antiliteracy statute in 1818, for example, to include "any person of color, slave or free," is of tremendous consequence.[4] The phrase, "any person of color, slave or free," points to the overriding of regulated legal status in favor of a color code that was subject to the onlooker's determination. The legislation not only broadened the scope of the repression of blacks, enslaved or free, it also instituted and sought to preserve the white class as a reading authority, vested with the power of the state. Racial demarcation based on a *reading* of skin color, and not legal status, had become the norm. Notably, the premise of the Savannah antiliteracy statute is based on the constitution and authorization of a white reader of black bodies whose ability to see and make distinctions among somatic forms and colors is assumed to be reliable. The ironies are significant, since the injunction against black literacy and social agency was predicated on the exclusive privilege of white reading of black bodies. White reading of skin color determined black persons' inferior social status absent any legal constraint and deprived them of skills that proved their humanity in the age of reason. Reading, specifically whites reading not just books or written legislation (since some blacks had proven their reading and writing abilities and destroyed the fabricated barrier of their unreason), but whites reading black bodies and demonstrating a racist literacy served as a powerful incentive to control, then as well as now.[5] This turn in the history of antiliteracy laws whereby seeing blackness justified the imposition of restrictions on literacy resonates with the hypervisibility of blackness linked to similar denials in housing, jobs, and equal treatment in the justice system. Seeing corporal blackness has become an American norm.

This prescription of whites reading authoritatively and reliably as granted in the antiliteracy codes is, however, not as settled a matter as the legislation might suggest; indeed, far from it. This chapter examines an alternative historical account, therefore, about the incompetencies and biases of white reading at pivotal moments in Shakespeare and beyond. That the history of reading in America concerns the legally forced, artificially configured authority of a privileged, free, white class, however, should give us considerable pause. Such reading expertise should be closely scrutinized for its historical indebtedness to the harsh, life-threatening politics of exclusion and enforced, structural inequality, evident in the antiliteracy ordinances. Importantly, however, instead of producing an authoritative, expert white reader, the history of systemic whiteness is one of racial illiteracy, the ignorance and destructive consequences of which are evident everywhere in modern society. Moreover, the Savannah code exposed a seemingly inescapable alignment that blurs differences between reading bodies and reading texts: a phenomenon of *race* construed as the seeing and reading of somatic signs in a social context, one that is also peculiarly suited to the audience experience of seeing black bodies in the early modern English theater. The creation and enforcement of antiliteracy laws made the concept and political fact of white reading visible, and this chapter attempts to unfold an early modern literary and performance example in that history.

Shakespeare, Racial Blind Spots, and the Crisis in Sight

Sight, construed as a stable guarantor of knowledge, has deep roots in the Western cultural tradition. Long considered the most reliable sense, sight achieved prominence through the seeming documentary robustness of the visual data recorded and relayed to the viewer. The presumed facticity of sight connected the observer to the external world in ways that inspired cognitive confidence and produced epistemological conviction; the assimilation of visual data constituted knowledge. Plato in the *Timaeus* declares that, "sight in my opinion is the source of the greatest benefit to us," and David Summers explains that Plato's exaltation of sight as providing "the clearest knowledge of the natural world" is coupled with "the sustaining principles of order and harmony."[6] In his *Metaphysics*, Aristotle establishes the firm connection between sight and knowledge in the text's famous opening and, guided by his fundamental belief in the relation between sensation and thought, extols sight as the sense that allows the mind to make fine discriminations and distinctions: sight "most of all the senses, makes us know and brings to light many differences between things."[7] Together, these two major classical statements by Plato and Aristotle have shaped the tradition surrounding sight, emphasizing access to the natural world as the basis of human knowledge.[8] The derivation of "idea" from the Greek *idein*, meaning "to see," sustains this intersection of sight and insight, vision and contemplation, viewing and reflection; or, as Chris Jenks writes, the "lexical etymology reminds us that the way we think about the way that we think in Western culture is guided by a visual paradigm."[9] To speak about sight is to opine about knowledge; the two are deeply interconnected. And to speak about the experience of seeing in the theater (from the Greek *theatron*, meaning the "seeing place") is to engage in a profoundly epistemological exercise.

The early modern period, however, experienced what might be described as a crisis in sight, which also meant it confronted a predicament about the reliability of knowledge. Stuart Clark's thesis in *Vanities of the Eye* is that for the early modern period, "several important developments unique to the cultural history of Europe over roughly two and a half centuries worked to undermine this inherited confidence and disrupted the relationship between human beings and what they observed."[10] Among these developments were the Protestant Reformation and the visual complications inherent in the distrust of icons and idolatry; the revival of Greek skepticism, rooted in doubt that challenged the validity of sensory evidence, especially data deriving from the eyes; and the fascination with demonology that prompted disturbing questions about vision and the real. In a chapter titled, "Ocular Proof in the Age of Reform," Huston Diehl, arriving at a similar conclusion about the impact of Protestant reform, notes the "epistemological crisis created by the reformers when they deny the magical efficacy of images and relics and yet assert the power of visible signs."[11] "In one context after another," Clark contends, "vision came to be characterized by uncertainty and unreliability, such that access to visual reality could no longer be normally guaranteed. It was as though European intellectuals lost their optical nerve."[12] Early modern society's increasing doubt about the certainty of sight created an exquisite opportunity for Shakespeare to enter the mix by exploring a new and consequential set of questions pertaining to seeing blackness and the evolving intellectual and cultural phenomenon of unreliable sight, meaning knowledge, in *Othello* (1604).

Sight and the questions surrounding its accuracy form the basis of the playwright's investigation into the audience as reliable observer of blackness and race, outlining, in effect, a project that animates the central issues of this book concerning systemic whiteness and readerly perception. What, in general, manifested as a broad, unfolding set of cultural and epistemological queries, became for Shakespeare an opportunity to pose specific questions about the unreliability of sight as a function of racial bias, what I argue is a form of debilitating white illiteracy. For an early modern play that locates a black man at the center of the dramatic action, we should probably not be surprised by the frequent references to sight, the textual evidence proving that despite specious contemporary denials about the relevance of blackness and race in the early modern period, Shakespeare foregrounds the cultural awareness of blackness and the attendant social reaction as a salient cultural phenomenon. In *Othello*, sight is interlaced in every aspect of the language and action – famously, even jealousy, a potentially destructive emotion, is construed as "the green-eyed monster" (3.3.169).[13] In the play's ocularcentric universe, Othello is a sight to behold, his spectacular difference identified repeatedly, as in Emilia's color-sensitive wish for her mistress, "I would you had never seen him" (4.3.16). Shakespeare serves notice that questions about the stability of sight and knowledge relative to blackness are critical to what might pass as otherwise unqualified and untested truths. Othello's demand for "ocular proof" (3.3.362), for example, devolves into a crisis of epistemology and belief. Proof ascertained by firsthand or eyewitness experience, it turns out, is not as foolproof as it might at first appear, and the play's tragic unfolding rests on this counterintuitive recognition exemplified in the cognitive confusion caused by a visible, peripatetic handkerchief that fails, in the end, to deliver the truth or knowledge Othello imagines, thereby urging the audience to reflect candidly and carefully on what we think we know – especially about blackness.

Seeing blackness is never simply a neutral sensory experience but *a fortiori* an ideologically encoded act complete with moral judgment and differential demarcation. Vision or perception, therefore, in contrast to the mere mechanics of sight, conveys the defining collective institutional ideas and practices that inform the structural homogeneity essential for the position from which a community's white power elite can declare other subjects black. Vision encapsulates the Venetian habitus in which an intersection of social and cultural factors gives shape to a way of life and thought.[14] In *Othello* this habitus is racialized so that the play represents the alienating effects of the Venetian system in which, to adapt Bourdieu's language, the black man is effectively pitted against the "cognitive and motivating structures" whose task it is to "reproduce the regularities immanent in" the self-identified white society.[15] The play powerfully dramatizes how vision compromises sight, insofar as the culturally engrained ideas infuse the collected data of the eyes to create epistemological distortions. What we see is overpowered by what we have been conditioned to know.

Clark's punning reference to "optical nerve" allows for a transition to recent theoretical considerations of a scotoma (from the Greek meaning "darkness") or blind spot, a physiological condition whose explanatory power is conceptually relevant to the questions of epistemological uncertainty regarding blackness that Shakespeare raises in *Othello*. Within human biology, a natural blind spot in the eye is the result of the lack of photoreceptors on the retinal disc at the point where the optic nerve, along with blood vessels, leaves the eye.[16] Humans do not typically notice blind spots, however, because the brain compensates by filling in those areas with learned information garnered from routine, habit, and cultural experience.[17] Thus, the analytical and metaphoric value of the blind spot is to call attention to our lack of awareness of something that is, however, truly there – a structural blindness that in cultural terms is caused by a systemic whiteness that is undiscerning of blackness, creating a modern day crisis in knowledge and racial literacy.

Given academic currency in the work of Emily Pronin and her colleagues, the idea of the blind spot is used to suggest bias, identifying the tendency to ascribe more objectivity to oneself than to others, called the bias blind spot: "individuals are likely to conclude that they are somehow less subject to biases than the people they observe and interact with in their everyday lives."[18] The relevance to seeing and reading white subjects in white-dominant societies is meaningful for explaining their sense of superiority, and for my purposes, defining and assigning value in literary studies. As a result, this bias blind spot misreads others through an overvaluation of one's own assumed objectivity. Judith E. Glaser notes that "through the incredible amount of neuroscience research taking place around the world right now, we are able to understand more about the way our minds create biases, blind spots, and filters that prevent us from seeing reality as it is."[19] Extending these neuroscientific and psychological insights into the realm of ethics, Max H. Bazerman and Ann E. Tenbrunsel write about the human limitations intuited in blind spot theory: "we are 'boundedly aware': our perceptions and decision making are constrained in ways we don't realize. In addition to falling prey to bounded awareness, recent research finds we are also subject to bounded ethicality, or systematic constraints on our morality that favor our own self-interest at the expense of the interest of others."[20]

In applying blind spot theory to critical race analysis, I argue that bounded awareness results from limitations induced by white racial formation. If sight is a function of cultural perception, as various critics have proposed – what we see is filtered through the lens of social conditioning and experiential formation – then that cultural and ideological data actually create epistemological blind spots that can blur or distort awareness and knowledge of race. Unlike the permanence of the retinal scotoma, the notion of the racial blind spot is proposed as a critical tool leading to remediation, not to describe an unchangeable condition, as I believe the opening scenes of *Othello* dramatize. Like Bazerman and Tenbrunsel, whose aim is to raise awareness of "the gap between who you want to be and the person you are," this book alerts readers to the human restrictions of systematic whiteness and the possibility of committing to an antiracist program of change.[21] Critiquing whiteness, despite its history of denial, dismissal, and recalcitrance poses several challenges, the most important of which, for critical race studies, is whether to simply stop at condemnation or, once again, create opportunities for productive inclusion toward a transformative politics of literacy, scholarship, and pedagogy. I am proposing the hard, important work of the latter.

The Racial Theater of the Audience's Mind

Othello is an immigrant, and his ambivalent status as a Venetian outsider mirrors the mounting social tensions arising from the substantial influx of foreigners in late sixteenth-century English society. Longstanding English xenophobia manifested in popular anti-alien feeling, while governmental oversight of homeland security competed with the pragmatic recognition of foreigners' utility to the Crown. "This apparent xenophobia often had its origins in economic jealousy," writes Laura Hunt Yungblut, "but whatever its basis, the perception of strangers as different and of their presence as deleterious echoed through centuries of English history."[22] Alert to the ever-present threat against the English Protestant state, the government understood, nevertheless, the contribution of aliens, "mostly urban artisans with a wide variety of technological skills, a potentially great boon for a country that was technologically backward compared to its Continental neighbors."[23] The hired general of the Venetian republic, Othello brings considerable skill in the technologies of war and, as a Christian convert, was welcomed in the home of Brabantio, a member of the ruling senate. His marriage to the senator's daughter unravels what was always a fragile social contract; Othello's marriage contract, alternately, grants him institutional validation. Brabantio's descriptors for Othello – "foul," "sooty," "thing" (1.2.62, 70, 71) – indicate the racist xenophobia that lurks beneath the social surface and informs his ultimate anxieties about the marriage: "For if such actions may have passage free, / Bondslaves and pagans shall our statesmen be" (1.2.98–99). Setting aside the "economic jealousy" commonly ascribed to the social unrest involving foreigners, *Othello* speaks directly, and in a recognizably modern voice, to the disturbances caused by the politics of a black presence.

It would be a mistake to read *Othello*, Shakespeare's most famous race play, with a sole focus on the fate of the Moor. Instead, the play offers rich possibilities for understanding Shakespeare's evocation and exploration of the white audience-as-reader. Ruben Espinosa and David Ruiter extend the important and always timely reminder: "In early modern dramatic representation of foreigners, the presence of immigrants often reveals more about the host society than it does about the immigrant him/herself."[24] What is the most valuable thing we learn about the host society? At stake in Brabantio's outrage is the threat of cultural miscegenation and reversal of political fortune with the feared ascendancy of slaves and pagans. Importantly, the senator's outburst reveals most tellingly the current republican racial praxis and what the state stands to lose: Venice has always known itself as white and prosecuted its rule with hierarchical rigor against interloping black strangers like Othello; this is a racial power structure that Brabantio intends to defend. In the context of this book, Venetian border protection speaks metaphorically to the larger questions of the history and politics of reading, race, and gatekeeping in the Shakespeare literary complex that expose a tenuous relationship to scholars and scholarship of color. Today, when immigration has, in some quarters, sadly become a byword for racist exclusion in a destructive cultural politics of division, skin color is made, once again, the cheap currency and target of surveillance. In *Othello*, by contrast, Shakespeare probes the audience's mental engagement with blackness that results in the construction of an early modern white identity.

Othello famously opens with the absent Moor, a Shakespearean dramaturgic decision that figures centrally in the carefully calibrated unfolding of the action that indicates a deliberate artistic agenda.[25] The repetition of "Moor" becomes a brilliant device through which physical absence is supplanted by rhetorical and ideological presence, the result of the verbal dilation or filling out of the word's increasingly magnified racial meanings.[26] The reaction of an irate father to the news of his daughter's elopement shatters the city's nocturnal calm, the verbal indictment of the unnamed "Moor" husband echoing in the night. Shakespeare's earliest London audience is obliged to try filling in the gaps concerning the unidentified man being discussed whose dehumanizing namelessness erases individual character and qualities. The term "Moor," however, offers three broad, important clues suggesting a markedly different cultural outsider: it references geographical origins, someone from the North African kingdom of Mauritania, meaning "land of the Moors"; a Muslim, member of the Islamic faith; and, importantly, racial blackness, because of the non-English, non-Christian, African associations.[27] With the repeated enunciation of "Moor," the audience formulates mental material that supplements information withheld by the dramatist. The language, moreover, reinforces the color and physical traits of a Moor who is famously described as a "black ram," "the thick-lips," and "the devil" (1.1.89, 67, 92), all phrases that mimic the optics of seeing by etching a black stand-in onto the audience's mental inner eye.

A theatrical corpus of works prior to *Othello* had already established a series of racial stereotypes closely identified with blacks, who were thought to be excessively jealous, deceitful, wicked, prone to violent acts, and overly sexual.[28] These works reflected and, in turn, reinforced existing attitudes about Moors, the cumulative evidence from early modern drama having the effect of turning blackness into a genre. Like a literary genre, a racial genre has recognizable, repeatable, familiar content, form, and effects; it works by creating a contract of social expectations with the audience that, in this instance, supplements the anxiety of ignorance by filling in the informational gaps with preconceived ideas gleaned from prior cultural and theatrical knowledge. The audience's expectations are reflected by Iago, Brabantio, and Roderigo who claim, in the interracial couple's elopement, theft, sexual abduction, prurience, and corrupt manipulation by the Moor, all of which are consistent with the generic black type. Confirmation of the audience's expectations amounts not only to congruence and complicity in thinking, that is, a racial ideology and belief. It also suggests that the audience members have acquired a perverse racist literacy that makes them seemingly apt readers: they believe they know who Moors are and what Moors are likely to do. With much left unstated – we also never learn the newlywed wife's name in the first scene – the audience has become increasingly sure about one thing: sexual crimes have been committed by a black man who is now firmly etched in the audience's mind as an outlaw and threat to cultural stability in the person of his white wife.

This opening scene is characterized by Shakespeare's exploration of the cognitive impact of racial stereotypes on an early modern audience. Using the figure of *energeia*, Shakespeare unlocks for analysis the mental operations of a white epistemology at work. As a distinctive feature of the larger category of description (*ekphrasis*) as developed in classical and early modern rhetoric, *enargeia* achieves amplification through the accumulation of striking narrative details that brings a scene vividly before the mind's eye.[29] Arguably the signature figure of the play, *enargeia* returns throughout, as in Othello's detailed account of his life story before the senate or Iago's dream narrative meant to verbally stage the scene of Cassio and Desdemona's purported infidelity. One of the most widely used classical rhetorics in the Renaissance provides a definition of *enargeia* that echoes Shakespeare's famous phrase ("ocular proof"): "It is Ocular Demonstration when an event is so described in words that the business seems to be enacted and the subject to pass before our eyes."[30] Other writers elucidate several points embedded in this compact statement. Quintilian calls attention to the forensic value of vivid description (*evidentia* in Latin) in persuading a judge, insisting that the goal is not simply to narrate but to display the facts "in their living truth to the eyes of the mind."[31] Henry Peacham explains the effect in *The Garden of Eloquence*: the listener's mind is, "therby so drawen to an earnest and stedfast contemplation of the thing described, that he rather thinketh he seeth it then heareth it."[32] The conjunction of rhetoric, sight, and audience finds its clearest statement in Erasmus' evocation of *enargeia*'s performative effect in painting a powerful verbal picture "so that at length it draws the hearer or reader outside himself as in the theatre."[33] With Brabantio presenting himself at an upper window, Iago has an audience whom he "draws . . . outside [itself]" and convinces of Othello's guilt in stealing the senator's daughter. Iago's deliberate ploy is to present the evidence of proof to Brabantio in such a graphic way that the father's mind is shocked by the explicit images that lay bare the acts of seeming sexual transgression. The passages are well known, a historical consequence of the effectiveness of the rhetorical impact of *enargeia* at work, so two brief examples will suffice: "Even now, now, very now, an old black ram / Is tupping your white ewe" (1.1.88–89); and "your daughter and the Moor are now making the beast with two backs" (1.1.115–16). Here, Iago's repetition of the deictic "now" punctuates the verbal illusion of a live event that, Heinrich Plett argues, is one of the effects of using *enargeia*: "the event described seems to be happening *hic et nunc* before the inner eye of the recipient."[34]

Erasmus's performative formulation, that the picture created through words "draws the hearer or reader outside himself as in the theatre," shifts the lexicon around *enargeia* sufficiently for us to grasp the metatheatrical construction of the opening scene, in which the audience in the theater functions as a prime interlocutor engaged. In the world of the play Brabantio might not be in a theater, but Shakespeare's audience is, making the cognitive demands implied in *enargeia* – the fictive making of a black man – more urgent. Brabantio is merely a test case for initiating the key theoretical examination that Shakespeare undertakes in unfolding the audience's racial imaginary. Othello's absence, in conjunction with the racially charged information brought forward, puts the audience in the position of having to use its mind to invent a black man, the fictive product of an assortment of acquired cultural knowledge and details. The audience sees blackness by recalling narratives recounted, dramas performed, and tales read in written texts, the remembered assemblage of images creating a strong mental picture. Elizabeth Spiller argues that in the sixteenth century, "written texts and paper images" were essential technologies that facilitated English encounters with foreigners.[35] The names Sir John Mandeville, Johannes Boemus, Sebastian Munster, Peter Heylyn, and Richard Hakluyt figure significantly in this tradition of cross-cultural print encounter.[36] Starting in the mid-1550s, the introduction of Africans in English society, as a result of capture, led to an appreciable growth of the black presence by the turn of the century, described by Imtiaz Habib as a largely shadow community "disliked but valued, politically debarred but quietly retained, legally non-existent but historically permanent."[37] But for the audience attending a performance of *Othello*, the encounters in reading and in the social environment of London notwithstanding, the stage tradition of presenting Moors played a significant educational role for those who had seen Muly in Peele's *Battle of Alcazar* (1588), Aaron in Shakespeare's own *Titus Andronicus* (1592), or Eleazer in Dekker's *Lust's Dominion* (1599).

Though the non-literary and social data might mitigate the portraits of Moors in some instances, the theatrical evidence was unrelenting in its dogmatic denigration of blackness.[38] "Moor," substituting for the absent Othello, is not just a blank, empty category label. The audience reacts to the deliberately unnamed and unseen Moor by testing, and most likely confirming, its portable knowledge about blackness against Iago and Roderigo's accusations while simultaneously *filling in the blanks* about the absent, as yet unknown black man (what I call the "Othello blind spot") with a mind conditioned by cultural information gathered from the available non-literary texts, real-life encounters, and accumulated knowledge from past theatrical performances. The theater, to follow Erasmus's thinking, is the ultimate instantiation of *enargeia*, for as the "seeing place," its images of blacks, past and present, come alive in full, animated degradation to be impressed on the audience's mind's eye. *Enargeia*, requiring mental imagery as convincing evidence, participates in and draws rhetorical power from the literacy of sight endowed since antiquity with the promise of certainty, in this instance, about the audience's assured knowledge of blackness obtained from an abundance of cultural sources.

Shakespeare and the Interpellated White Reader

Othello's entry in the play's second scene constitutes a dramatic tour de force in the service of a Shakespearean race and pedagogic theory. Citing the biblical narrative of Christ in the garden of Gethsemane on the night of Jesus' arrest, Shakespeare repositions Othello in terms that suspend the racial expectations that have driven audience investment to this point in the play. A nighttime scene with a confident Othello refusing to withdraw and hide; arriving officers armed with weapons intending to make an arrest; the Judas-like friend Iago who has already betrayed Othello; a brawl between the two rival factions involving drawn swords and threatened physical harm: these provide the recognizable context for a biblically literate early modern audience.[39] Additional details include, for example, lit torches carried by the arresting officers corresponding to the "lanterns and torches " (John 18:3) that are notable for an open-air Globe performance in daylight, which would have rendered them otherwise redundant. In Othello's command, "Keep up your bright swords, for the dew will rust them" (1.2.59), Shakespeare rewrites Jesus' order to Peter who attacks the high priest's servant: "Put up thy sword into the sheath" (John 18:11). The "Moor" the audience had imagined is reconstituted through the filter of biblical allusion as a black man who is a dramatic parallel to Jesus.

A reflective audience is asked to rethink its investment in the idea of an immoral, black Muslim and to see Othello instead through the interpretive lens of the central figure in English religion, Jesus. The earlier image of the violent social intruder and sexual predator is countered by Shakespeare's evocation of a man, like Jesus, calm and morally exemplary, who is the racial target of political jealousy. Shakespeare deviates from the predominant "social construction of visual reality," that is, the prevailing stereotypes of blackness, to produce an intellectual and "visual disturbance."[40] In reframing Othello as his phenomenological opposite, Shakespeare mounts an assault on racist assumptions, the sharp contrast between Muslim and Christian forcing the English playgoers' self-awareness of deeply held religious and racial bias. That such racial and religious misrecognition was the source of cognitive dissonance can be seen in Thomas

Middleton's *The Triumphs of Truth* (1613), a civic pageant in which Moors arriving in London excite the anxious crowds until the English learn that the Africans are Christian converts.[41] Shakespeare's conscious revision leads to important audience effects by undercutting everything playgoers thought they knew: it ruptures black stereotypes, shocks the mental system, fractures confidence in prevailing structures of racial knowledge, and initiates a series of interrogations and re-adjustments to racial bias that is the basis for self-questioning.

The fracturing of confidence in racial knowledge and the questioning of preconceived racial ideas are superseded by a third, most revelatory effect: the hailing or calling out of the audience's whiteness. In his seminal essay, "Ideology and Ideological State Apparatuses (Notes Toward an Investigation)," Louis Althusser argues that ideology, the dominant belief system, constitutes and defines subjects as produced by that system. The notion of ideology is inconceivable without the subject since the subject is an embodiment of ideology, the materialization, as it were, of a controlling set of beliefs.[42] Thus, ideology, he concludes, is a calling out or interpellation of the subject: "I shall then suggest that ideology 'acts' or 'functions' in such a way that it 'recruits' subjects among the individuals (it recruits them all), or 'transforms' the individuals into subjects (it transforms them all) by that very precise operation which I have called *interpellation* or hailing and which can be imagined along the lines of the most commonplace everyday police (or other) hailing: 'Hey, you there!'"[43] In contrast to Frantz Fanon's famous representation of the cultural hailing of blackness embodied in networks of power and discrimination – "'Look, a Negro!'" – Shakespeare turns his critical gaze to situating whiteness.[44]

While interpellation has been widely understood through the explanatory metaphor of the state authority hailing the subject ("Hey, you there!"), I would emphasize here Althusser's other metaphor of recruitment that best conveys the audience's ideological transformation by race at the opening of *Othello* – consonant with Erasmus's *drawing out* of the audience. The Shakespearean device of absence mimics and represents (in the theatrical sense) the ideological recruitment of the audience into the practice of vilifying blackness that only reveals the audience's whiteness. The compulsion to fill the knowledge gaps, to reproduce the beliefs, rituals, and practice of making blackness, is the theatrical equivalent that explains the allure and surrender to recruitment. By employing the notion of "filling in" throughout, I am alluding to and underscore the epistemological effects of the blind spot when the human brain compensates by filling in the absent or obscured material with previously learned information garnered from cultural experience and ideological habit.[45] The racial blind spot represents a true ignorance of racial otherness, that is, nevertheless, supplanted by a plethora of prefabricated racial biases. The audience's investigatory labor relies on previous configurations of blackness so familiar that they comprise a recognizable, generic norm, an "obviousness that we cannot *fail to recognize.*"[46]

The audience experience I am trying to theorize can be explored further by way of Norman Bryson's essay "The Gaze in the Expanded Field," in which he writes: "For human beings collectively to orchestrate their visual experience together it is required that each submit his or her retinal experience to the socially agreed description(s) of an intelligible world."[47] The cultural and historical conditioning that influenced how audiences saw, conceptualized, and thought about blackness in the early modern period is the product of "socially agreed description(s)" that confirm vision as "socialized."[48] Bryson invites us to see that the cultural or ideological conditioning that colors vision is, in an important sense, the source of blindness:

> Between the subject and the world is inserted the entire sum of discourses which make up visuality, that cultural construct, and make visuality different from vision, the notion of unmediated visual experience. Between retina and world is inserted a *screen* of signs, a screen consisting of all the multiple discourses on vision built into the social arena.[49]

The notion of vision as unimpeded retinal access to the world is revised to explain how sight is always compromised by "multiple discourses" – like the multiple white-derived anthropological, theatrical, print, and demographic constructions of blackness – and that a "*screen* of signs" blocks the view and "*casts a shadow.*"[50] In the case of race, prejudicial and broadly shared stereotypes of white invention, or the products of systemic whiteness, distort vision in ways that misrecognize blackness and make us poor readers of humanity. This is the problematic of white racial illiteracy that Shakespeare brilliantly dramatizes in the opening pair of scenes in *Othello.* The shadow cast by the multiple discourses that racialize blackness mimics the obstruction of vision that occurs in the ocular blind spot to explicate the full impact of racial conditioning and stereotype on the audience: a critical and intellectual blindness that produces supremely unreliable readers.

We must not fail to grasp that the full effect of the Shakespearean interpellation is the recruitment of the white subject, both the enlistment for a cause as well as the expansion of a racial group: "In the act of acknowledging that it is indeed he who is addressed, the individual thus recognizes his subjecthood."[51] The play's deliberate evocation of a racial belief system makes the audience complicit in a more comprehensive understanding of a complex ideology, that ideology being the audience's investment in whiteness, the position from which stereotypes about blackness can replicate and cause whiteness to propagate and flourish. From the literal recruitment of Brabantio by Roderigo and Iago into the racial scheme mounted against the Moor, whiteness has been the ideological predicate of the action among a group of white men to subvert an interracial marriage, itself an institution symbolizing social union and the promised legacy of self-replication through which ideological recruitment and recognition are traditionally maintained.[52] The many moral indictments of the Moor's licentiousness are more than a recycling of black stereotypes that undercut the sober regulation of marriage: "you'll have your daughter covered with a Barbary horse, you'll have your nephews neigh to you" (1.1.111–12). The conjunction of the Moor and animal sexuality situates him at the limits of the human, functioning as a racialized discourse within a long history of African abjection that works to centralize the human, that is the white human, as the subjective position from which such articulations of beastly otherness emanate.[53] Like any orientalism, black animalism is not only about the invented other but also represents a program to raise up the West, that is, Europe and whiteness, in a geo-political rhetoric of power.[54]

Gary Taylor's argument that the descriptor "white" served a generic, utilitarian purpose, for Africans and Amerindians to name Europeans in the global nexus of early modern overseas trade and colonizer expedition, relies on the undifferentiated pallor of fair skin.[55] Relative to the theater more specifically, he maintains that Middleton's *Triumphs of Truth* lays down a historical marker: "The earliest, unmistakably generic, unmistakably positive use of *white* in an extant dramatic text occurred in a pageant performed in the streets of London on October 29, 1613 – four months after the premiere of Shakespeare's last securely datable play."[56] It does not appear that Middleton's Moor king describing Londoners as "white people"[57] (412) who stare in astonishment at the pageant of Africans spectacularly conveyed by ship to the city, is qualitatively different from the protestations to preserve Desdemona's "whiter skin of hers than snow" (5.2.4), in Othello's words, from the sexually symbolic and culturally meaningful encroachments of the black invader. White skin seems to enjoy city-wide, institutional value. Taylor's conclusion appears to be a miscalculation that conceives somatic fairness narrowly rather than as part of a white racial complex, excludes Shakespeare's work from consideration, and, most importantly, ignores the positionality of whiteness that enables the performance and positing of identity. Employing a method like the one made famous by Theodore Allen, for whom "white" people did not exist in America until the post-Bacon Rebellion era of 1676 – they were English before then – Taylor's isolation of the word "white" obviates its operational capacity that literary analysis can make clear.[58] In employing the Moor, Shakespeare capitalizes on the global significance of such a figure and stages in the English theater the impact of transnational encounter on the emergent construction of white political identity.

Here, therefore, is the compelling feature of this Shakespearean *Othello* moment: the recruitment of whiteness, rendering it a visible, active component of defining the audience as a racialized subject, making whiteness something "we cannot *fail to recognize*." Shakespeare's dramaturgic conception achieves a conclusion that is comparably modern: "The ideology of race and its concomitant discourses interpellate *every* human individual into the racial formation. He/she is signified and brought into the racial universe, which gives him/her a racial label, White or otherwise."[59] In addition, Shakespeare's careful unfolding of the audience's mental operations amounts to an anatomy of reading, revealing a cognitive engagement of interconnected literacies – visual, biblical, rhetorical, print, narrative, demographic, and cultural – afforded by the theater and noting their complex, combinatory effects. The cognitive process of reading is presented within a theatrical modality that foregrounds whiteness as more than physiological content; it is a form of knowledge that shapes the reader's improvisational habits, behavioral orientation, and intellectual stance. Here, I am particularly interested in the ramifications of this recognition of whiteness with the understanding that the audience's work described thus far constitutes fundamentally, and importantly for literary studies, acts of reading – of the dramatic action and the social genres of blackness. Thus, I propose the notion of the interpellated reader, one who is constantly recruited by the density of the text and whose white positionality is hailed and made conscious for the purpose of calling attention to modern critics and scholars, readers whose comparable position as white is often muted in the theory and analysis of early modern studies.

This muting of the subject's whiteness forms a critical feature of any assessment of the current "*state* of the field" of early modern studies, meaning more than the status of scholarship and professional affairs, and highlighting here the realm or state of power that whiteness represents.[60] It comes as no surprise that the avoidance of race in early modern studies is contingent on this primary refusal and failure to recognize the "obviousness" of readerly whiteness. Accounting for scholars as readers in the predominantly white field of Shakespeare studies, therefore, poses challenges: white persons tend not to regard their own whiteness because they do not generally experience being raced and, therefore, imagine an existence outside of race. "'White,'" write Thomas K. Nakayama and Robert L. Krizek, "affects the everyday fabric of our lives but resists, sometimes violently, any extensive characterization that would allow for the mapping of its contours."[61] Seeing race in Shakespeare is, therefore, a difficult, alienating experience and commitment for readers "positioned as white." Nevertheless, understanding the historical formation and impact of systematic whiteness explains why whiteness that "affects the everyday fabric of our lives" must be regarded as the critical component in the social activity of reading. And while whiteness traffics in denial and strenuously avoids its own examination, the broad historical contours of white racial formation can, in fact, be delineated to explain how systemic whiteness has informed early modern and contemporary readers' racial repertoire.

Initiating the outline of such a history with Shakespeare, the opening scenes of *Othello* amount to a critique that provides substance and legibility to a white reading subject realized in the dynamic, interactive experience of the theater audience as an exemplum for our ongoing contemplation. Writing at the height of critical interest in the English history play, Peter Womack describes the early modern theater's creation of an imagined national community anchored in the audience's common heritage: "the theatre was inviting its audience not merely to contemplate the 'imagined community' but to *be* it."[62] In *Othello*, Shakespeare recreates an entirely other conception of an imagined commonality of whiteness for the audience not simply to ponder, "but to *be*." Whiteness, Shakespeare suggests, comprises an emergent cultural bond configured in and through the figment of blackness in the cultural imagination, a bond whose import would in time (if not already in 1604) rival the mutuality of national identity and belonging. As such, whiteness has an articulable existence prior to the well-documented, later developments in the uniquely oppressive institution of black slavery in the Americas.

White Preference and Racial Blind Spots

Today, as part of a historical legacy exemplified in the antiliteracy laws, black bodies are routinely seen, read, and subjected to proscription in

American culture. However, Shakespeare's interrogation of seeing, reading, and interpretation has an important highlight: he is addressing, in the context of the early modern theater, the issue of cross-racial reading. Shakespeare investigates an audience from a majority white culture that, due to multiple factors, sees and thinks from within racial stereotypes that the playwright, in turn, makes visible and available for conscious reflection. Iago's contention that Othello is handicapped as a reader of the Venetian scene because of racial and cultural differences is instrumental in Othello's gradual mental transformation. About the women, Iago claims: "I know our country disposition well: / In Venice they do let God see the pranks / They dare not show their husbands" (3.3.204–206), to which Othello replies incredulously, "Dost thou say so?" (3.3.208). Unlike Iago, who challenges Othello's ability to read white culture, Shakespeare makes the dramatic departure to question the majority white culture's ability and willingness to read blackness. I would like to iterate the continuing relevance of that particular Shakespearean inquiry today, so I return to blind spot theory to foreground the element that has been implicit throughout but deserves, at this point, more overt statement: the impact of own-race bias and its consequences for cross-racial reading. In addition to theoretical frameworks that have informed my analysis – identities structured in whiteness, the social orientation toward a set of learned collective practices, and the incipience of racial blind spots resulting from that ideological conditioning – I bring these considerations into the immediate present with the aid of recent empirical research in social psychology.[63]

In their recent study *Blindspot: Hidden Biases of Good People*, social psychologists Mahzarin Banaji and Anthony Greenwald examine hidden racial bias and its social effects. Developing their thesis within the framework of blind spot theory, they reiterate that in American society subjects are unaware of and blind to their own racial biases – what I have described as the crisis of sight, extended into the modern era where racial bias and ignorance of others have been exposed as significant factors in the American divide. The issues examined earlier in the context of early modern texts and culture – the panoptic order of whiteness, the imperative of cultural homogeneity, and unacknowledged racial bias – are found to operate in modern society but are subjected by these researchers to the evaluative scrutiny of experimental science. Rather than use explicit testing measures, such as direct response to questions, which carries a greater risk of subject interference, Banaji and Greenwald used another method, the Implicit Association Test (IAT), and developed the first Race IAT to "measure one of our society's most significant and emotion-laden types of attitudes – the attitude toward a racial group."[64] The researchers focused especially on black and white racial groups. Years of testing, now confirmed by other researchers, have produced the following findings.[65] First, they conclude "that automatic White preference is pervasive in American society" with 75 percent of those tested showing that preference: "This is a surprisingly high figure."[66] This preference holds true even when subjects subscribe consciously to different, non-biased outlooks.[67] Second, "the automatic White preference expressed on the Race IAT is now established as signaling discriminatory behavior."[68] Research by Brian Cutler and Margaret Bull Kovera into the reliability of eyewitness accounts elaborates the issue of cross-racial reading. Specifically, tests reveal that, "With respect to false identifications, White participants exhibited a larger own-race bias than did Black participants; the size of the own-race bias was comparable for White and Black participants with respect to correct identifications."[69] That is, while both black and white participants are equally adept in reading accurately within their own race, white participants show a higher incidence of error in reading blackness than do black participants in their ability to read cross-racially. These findings speak to unconsciously held attitudes that are especially challenging among white subjects, but their material and social costs in all areas of African Americans' lives, from housing discrimination, job discrimination, healthcare, police violence, to the criminal justice system, are all too real.[70]

As contemporary readers, especially within the discipline of English studies, we are not exempted from the conclusions that suggest, as Shakespeare has before us, that our ability to see and read blackness might be severely impaired by unconscious biases or blind spots that have been socially and culturally conditioned. That is, researchers and scholars are vulnerable to white racial illiteracy. Again, the use of the terminology of "unconscious" bias foregrounds a learned, reflexive behavior that has been subsumed within normalcy and does not imply that such behavior is either beyond conscious recognition and remedial action or without utility for social, educational, and labor policy. In fact, the impact of these discoveries in the experimental sciences has an immediate practical value for legal studies as well as Critical Race Theory, and should have an equally practical and imperative claim on literary studies regarding how we read, engage, and teach race.[71] While automatic white preference may result from conditioned behavior, Shakespeare's use of the play's second scene stands as an example of the importance of conscious intervention to disrupt oppressive racial orthodoxy and destabilize the sedimentation of reading and interpretive conventions. In the end, the inference to be drawn from the collectible data is that white bias significantly affects the casual, daily routines of seeing, thinking, and reflecting, so we must, like Shakespeare in *Othello*, explore how such bias influences acts of reading and interpretation within a profession whose scholars are, to use Morrison's memorable formulation, "positioned as white."

Textualizing Black Skin

Seeing blackness, as this most recent research indicates, helps us understand that race, in addition to naming historically inflected social relations of power, often begins from and is invested in the reading and interpretation of physiological signs of color informed by a reading subject's own-race bias. This own-race bias challenges, continuing into the contemporary era, the reliability of sight to produce effective, trustworthy knowledge, transforming the emergent early modern crisis of sight into an array of misinformed judgments and policy decisions affecting the lives of blacks and people of color across subsequent, recent history. This problematic of seeing blackness returns us to the emergence of the Western construct of the "Black Man" and the Savannah antiliteracy legislation that mandated two significant practices and outcomes regarding literacy: the free white subject who is legally authorized and sanctioned as a reader of black bodies; and the assumed reliability of that white subject's interpretive determinations and skills. A third, and final, lesson relative to the reading of black bodies can be intuited. This law imagines that seeing bodies represents a unique exercise akin to reading, involving the identification and decoding the somatic signs of blackness. We must differentiate here between reading blackness and race in literary studies and the textualization of black skin in real life and history.

Singled out historically as spectacularly visible, somatic blackness functions like a textual sign that is interpreted within a semantic field defined by particular cultural indices whose history I have outlined above. Blackness is not the singular corporal marker in the diversity of human existence, but it has acquired that narrowly construed, prominent status in American and post-Enlightenment social and political history. Black bodies have been rendered socially mobile codes that are constantly subjected to interpretive strategies within regimes of white reading. Importantly, therefore, whites see blackness and read race – that is, they observe and report on blackness' cultural significance acquired through the dynamic unfolding of history. Blackness and its learned visual response are critical to "the cognitive and motivating structures making up" the cultural and epistemological landscape of Anglo-American history. So, here is a curious thing: If blackness is conceived historically as generating a strong visual and cultural impression, why, in early modern criticism, is there such a discrepancy between the admittedly reductive but socially prevalent habit and practice of reading black bodies, a practice that is textually discursive in orientation, and the capacity or willingness to see, read, or admit to seeing blackness in literary works? Or, to use the formulation, why, when certain scholars see blackness, do they not read race? The resistance to reading early modern race is besieged with profound ethical, sociological, and epistemological problems so that the outcome too often results in misread bodies and texts.

Let us consider further that the Savannah antiliteracy law presupposes that black bodies should be treated like texts to be studied, read, and interpreted wherein blackness as a preemptive sign is made to minimize the totality of a black humanity. The great irony is that at the moment in 1818 when whites were being granted the extraordinary power to read, interpret, and determine the social fate of black bodies-as-texts, blacks were summarily being denied the fundamental legal access to textual literacy. Importantly, black bodies assigned the status of texts are subject to the fate of texts: inert and meaningless until the signs are made active and given meaning by the white reader, a meaning that does not reflect any truth about black persons but is, instead, the self-serving, projected fantasy of an already biased, defective white epistemology. The perversity of reducing a black body to a text in this historical instance seeks to enshrine black dependency, raising the question: Where is black agency? In this disturbing instance of American reading, the discrepancies in power and privilege are fully legible, but also map the crucial distinctions between textual illiteracy and racial literacy: between the politically enforced textual illiteracy of blacks as an integral strategy of white supremacy and the need for a wider educational program of racial literacy to combat centuries of persistent ignorance about the goals of a just, antiracist society. While white reading remains hobbled by unreliability and distortion, as the dramatic, theoretical, historical, and psychological evidence has shown, the particular effects not only on reading texts, but also the catastrophic impact on reading black bodies as endangered social subjects in contemporary America must be an issue of collective import that will be explored further.

Notes

1 In Emmanuel Chukwudi Eze, ed., *Race and the Enlightenment: A Reader* (Oxford: Blackwell, 1997), 55.

2 Birgit Brander Rasmussen, "'Attended with Great Inconveniences': Slave Illiteracy and the 1740 South Carolina Negro Act," *PMLA* 125.1 (2010), 201–203 (201).

3 Ibid., 202.

4 Ibid.

5 Recall the famous cases of Frederick Douglass and Phillis Wheatley, who were eager for and understood the life-altering significance of literacy and "who connected knowledge with power," in the words of DuBois, *Black Reconstruction in America*, 525.

6 Plato, *Timaeus*, 47a–b, in *The Collected Dialogues of Plato*, ed. Edith Hamilton and Huntington Cairns (Princeton: Princeton University Press, 1961).
See also the *Republic*, *The Collected Dialogues of Plato*, 507b–511d; David Summers, *The Judgment of Sense: Renaissance Naturalism and the Rise of Aesthetics* (Cambridge: Cambridge University Press, 1990), 32.

7 Aristotle, *Metaphysics*, 980a, in *Introduction to Aristotle*, ed. Richard McKeon, trans. W. D. Ross (New York: Random House, 1947).

8 See also "The Noblest of the Senses: Vision from Plato to Descartes," in Martin Jay, *Downcast Eyes: The Denigration of Vision in Twentieth-Century French Thought* (Berkeley: University of California Press, 1994), 21–82. Despite some disagreement from important figures like Lucien Febvre and Robert Mandrou, who rearrange the hierarchy of senses in the late medieval and early modern periods, Jay argues that their contention rests on marginal evidence (34–35).

9 Chris Jenks, "The Centrality of the Eye in Western Culture: An Introduction," in *Visual Culture*, ed. Chris Jenks (New York: Routledge, 1995), 1.

10 Stuart Clark, *Vanities of the Eye: Vision in Early Modern European Culture* (Oxford: Oxford University Press, 2007), 2.

11 Huston Diehl, *Staging Reform, Reforming the Stage: Protestantism and Popular Theater in Early Modern England* (Ithaca, NY: Cornell University Press, 1997), 134.

12 Clark, *Vanities of the Eye*, 2.

13 All quotations from the play are taken from *Othello*, ed. Norman Sanders (Cambridge: Cambridge University Press, 2003), cited in the text by act, scene, and line. On sight in the play, see Susan E. Schreiner, "Appearances and Reality in Luther, Montaigne, and Shakespeare," *Journal of Religion* 28.3 (2003): 345–80, esp. 371–75; Steven Baker, "Sight and a Sight in *Othello*," *Iowa State Journal of Research* 61:3 (1987): 301–309, esp. 302.

14 Bourdieu, *Outline of a Theory of Practice*, 80–83.

15 Ibid., 78.

16 Arthur F. Kinney, *Shakespeare and Cognition: Aristotle's Legacy and Shakespeare's Drama* (New York: Routledge, 2006), 19. On the distinction between the natural blind spot and artificial scotomas, see V. S. Ramachandran, "Filling in Gaps in Perception: Part II. Scotomas and Phantom Limbs," *Current Directions in Psychological Science* 2.2 (1993): 56–65; esp. 56–57.

17 Geraint Rees and Rimona Weil, "How Does the Brain Fill-in the Visual World?" *ACNR* 9.4 (2009): 12–15. They write: "Our awareness of the visual environment comes to us from the pattern of light on the retina. But this pattern is an incomplete record of the visual scene, because many pieces of the scene fall on the blind spot or are obscured by retinal vessels" (12). This idea of filling in has been studied and interpreted in various ways, too detailed to address here. See Dror Zur and Shimon Ullman, "Filling-in of Retinal Scotomas," *Vision Research* 43 (2003): 971–982.

18 Emily Pronin, Daniel Y. Lin, and Lee Ross, "The Bias Blind Spot: Perceptions of Bias in Self Versus Others," *Personality and Social Psychology Bulletin* 28 (2002); 369–381 (369–70). See also Emily Pronin et al., "You Don't Know Me, But I Know You: The Illusion of Asymmetric Insight," *Journal of Personal and Social Psychology* 81.4 (2001): 639–656; Emily Pronin, Thomas Gilovich, and Lee Ross, "Objectivity in the Eye of the Beholder: Divergent Perceptions of Bias in Self Versus Others," *Psychological Review* 111.3 (2004): 781–799.

19 Judith E. Glaser, *Conversational Intelligence: How Great Leaders Build Trust and Get Extraordinary Results* (New York: Bibliomotion, 2014), xviii.

20 Max H. Bazerman and Ann E Tenbrunsel, *Blind Spots: Why We Fail to Do What's Right and What to Do about It* (Princeton: Princeton University Press, 2011), 8.

21 Ibid., 1. See Ibram X. Kendi, *How to be an Antiracist* (New York: One World, 2019).

22 Laura Hunt Yungblut, *Strangers Settled Here Among Us: Politics, Perceptions, & the Presence of Aliens in Elizabethan England* (New York: Routledge, 1996), 9.

23 Ibid., 3.

24 Espinosa and Ruiter, *Shakespeare and Immigration*, 5.

25 Thomas G. Pavel, *The Poetics of Plot: The Case of English Renaissance Drama* (Minneapolis: University of Minnesota Press, 1985). Pavel's structuralist approach employs a grammar of "moves" that accounts for the dynamics of plot progression. I have attempted to map and explicate a broader complex that includes the audience's psychological, affective, and political entanglement in plot.

26 In addition to forms like "his Moorship's ancient" (1.1.33), the word "Moor" appears several times in the opening scene at lines 40, 58, 115, 125, 146, 163, and 176.

27 Jack D'Amico, *The Moor in English Renaissance Drama* (Tampa: University of South Florida Press, 1991), 1–4.

28 Foundational scholarship in early modern race studies by Barthelemy and Tokson addresses the negative portrayals of blackness in the drama. Heylyn's description of blacks operates as a template for several dramatic personae. Africans, he claims, are "much given to lying, treacherous, very full of talk, excessively venerous, and extream jealous," all of which attach to Othello at some point (Quoted in Tokson, *The Popular Image of the Black Man*, 17–18). While the term "Moor" was also sufficiently broad to cover a range of persons, it consistently identified persons of non-English and non-European origins

who were likely dark-skinned; see D'Amico, *The Moor in English Renaissance Drama,* 59–60, 224n.8.

29 On the history of and distinction between the terms, see Graham Zanker, "Enargeia in the Ancient Criticism of Poetry," *Rheinisches Museum für Philologie* 124 (1981): 297–311.

30 *Ad Herennium*, trans. Harry Caplan, Loeb Classical Library (Cambridge, MA: Harvard University Press, 1981), 4.55.68.

31 Quintilian, *Institutio Oratoria*, 4 vols., trans. H. E. Butler, Loeb Classical Library (Cambridge, MA: Harvard University Press, 1986), 8.3.62.

32 Henry Peacham, *The Garden of Eloquence* (London: H. Jackson, 1593), 134.

33 Desiderius Erasmus, *On Copia of Words and Ideas*, trans. Donald B. King and H. David Hix (Milwaukee: Marquette University Press, 1963), 47; see also Joel B. Altman, '"Preposterous Conclusions": Eros, *Enargeia*, and Composition in *Othello*," in his *The Improbability of 'Othello': Rhetorical Anthropology and Shakespearean Selfhood* (Chicago: University of Chicago Press, 2010), where he examines *enargeia* in relation to the theater, but for very different purposes from the ones argued here.

34 Heinrich F. Platt, *Enargeia in Classical Antiquity and the Early Modern Age: The Aesthetics of Evidence* (Leiden: Brill, 2012), 9.

35 Spiller, *Reading and the History of Race,* 16.

36 On the non-literary sources of images of blackness, see Tokson, *The Popular Image of the Black Man,* 1–19.

37 Habib, *Black Lives in the English Archives,* 118.

38 In the visual arts, a range of perspectives covering the African as slave, ambassador, and duke is documented in Spicer, *Revealing the African Presence.*

39 Accounts of Jesus' arrest can be found in Matthew 26 and John 18.

40 Norman Bryson, "The Gaze in the Expanded Field," in *Vision and Visuality*, ed. Hal Foster (Seattle: Bay Press, 1988), 91.

41 Thomas Middleton, *Thomas Middleton: The Collected Works*, ed. Gary Taylor and John Lavagnino (Oxford: Oxford University Press, 2010).

42 Louis Althusser, *Lenin and Philosophy and Other Essays*, trans. Ben Brewster (New York: Monthly Review Press, 2001). Althusser writes, "I say: the category of the subject is constitutive of all ideology, but at the same time and immediately I add that *the category of the subject is only constitutive of all ideology insofar as all ideology has the function (which defines it) of 'constituting' concrete individuals as subjects.* In the interaction of this double constitution exists the functioning of all ideology, ideology being nothing but its functioning in the material forms of existence of that functioning" (116).

43 Ibid., 118.

44 Frantz Fanon, *Black Skins, White Masks*, trans. Charles Lam Markmann (1952; New York: Grove Press, 1967), 109.

45 See Rees and Weil, "How Does the Brain Fill-in the Visual World?".

46 Althusser, *Lenin and Philosophy,* 116.

47 Bryson, "The Gaze in the Expanded Field," 91.

48 Ibid., 91.

49 Ibid., 91–2.
50 Ibid., 92.
51 Cindy Nguyen, "Interpellation," The Chicago School of Media Theory. https://lucian.uchicago.edu/blogs/mediatheory/keywords/interpellation/.
52 Following Althusser's argument, I count marriage among "the rituals of ideological recognition, which guarantee for us that we are indeed concrete, individual, distinguishable and (naturally) irreplaceable subjects" (*Lenin and Philosophy*, 117).
53 Francesca Royster, "'Working Like a Dog': African Labor and Racing the Human–Animal Divide in Early Modern England," in *Writing Race Across the Atlantic World: Medieval to Modern*, ed. Philip Beidler and Gary Taylor (New York: Palgrave, 2005); Kim F. Hall, "'Troubling Doubles': Apes, Africans, and Blackface in *Mr. Moore's Revels*," in MacDonald, *Race, Ethnicity, and Power in the Renaissance*; Derrick Higginbotham, "Women/Animals/Slaves: Race and Sexuality in Wycherley's *The Country Wife*," in Smith,. Jones, and Grier, *Early Modern Black Diaspora Studies*; Erica Fudge, Ruth Gilbert, and Susan Wiseman, eds., *At the Borders of the Human: Beasts, Bodies and Natural Philosophy in the Early Modern Period* (New York: Palgrave 2002).
54 Edward W. Said, *Orientalism* (New York: Vintage Books, 1979).
55 Gary Taylor, *Buying Whiteness: Race, Culture and Identity from Columbus to Hip-Hop* (New York: Palgrave, 2005), 97–119.
56 Ibid., 125.
57 Thomas Middleton, *Thomas Middleton: The Collected Works*, ed. Gary Taylor and John Lavagnino (Oxford: Oxford University Press, 2010), 412.
58 Allen, *Invention, vol. i*, 2nd ed., "Introduction to the Second Edition" by Jeffrey B. Perry, x–xii.
59 Leonardo, "Through the Multicultural Glass," 407.
60 Chakravarty has recently employed this pun to differentiate between "a state not only as a condition, but as an entity, a polity" ("The Renaissance of Race," 17).
61 Thomas K. Nakayama and Robert L. Krizek, "Whiteness: A Strategic Rhetoric," *Quarterly Journal of Speech* 81 (1995): 291–309 (291).
62 Peter Womack, "Imagining Communities: Theatres and the English Nation in the Sixteenth Century," in *Culture and History, 1350–1600: Essays on English Communities, Identities and Writing*, edited by David Aers (Detroit: Wayne State University Press, 1992), 138.
63 On the value of complementing theoretical work with empirical data, see Croll, "Modeling Determinants of White Racial Identity," 614.
64 Mahzarin R. Banaji and Anthony G. Greenwald, *Blindspot: Hidden Biases of Good People* (New York: Delacorte Press, 2013), 41.
65 Christian A. Meissner and John C. Brigham, "Thirty Years of Investigating the Own-Race Bias in Memory for Faces: A Meta-Analytic Review," *Psychology, Public Policy, and Law* 7.1 (2001): 3–35. A meta-analysis synthesizes the available data in a particular research area to provide "greater statistical

power"; see Brian Cutler, ed., *Expert Testimony on the Psychology of Eyewitness Identification* (Oxford: Oxford University Press, 2009), 15; and Kurt Hugenberg and Galen V. Bodenhausen, "Facing Prejudice: Implicit Prejudice and the Perception of Facial Threat," *Psychological Science* 14.6 (2003): 640–643.

66 Banaji and Greenwald, *Blindspot*, 47.

67 This is the effect of cognitive dissonance; see Banaji and Greenwald, *Blindspot*, 54–61.

68 Ibid., 47. Unlike Banaji and Greenwald, some recent research has opted to examine white identity in itself without an external focus on racial prejudice. See Ashley Jardina, *White Identity Politics* (Cambridge: Cambridge University Press, 2019); Eric Knowles and Kaiping Peng, "White Selves: Conceptualizing and Measuring a Dominant-Group Identity," *Journal of Personality and Social Psychology* 89.2 (2005): 233–241; and Mark M. Leach, John T. Behrens, and N. Kenneth LaFleur, "White Racial Identity and White Racial Consciousness: Similarities, Differences, and Recommendations," *Journal of Multicultural Counseling and Development* 30 (2002): 66–80. Croll, whose work subscribes to this approach, has determined, however, that even when it had been argued in the 1990s "that whites, by and large, were unaware of their own racial identity," up to 74 percent of whites in his more recent study "said their racial identity was either very important or somewhat important" ("Modeling Determinants of White Racial Identity," 614).

69 Brian Cutler and Margaret Bull Kovera, *Evaluating Eyewitness Identification* (Oxford: Oxford University Press, 2010), 39.

70 Banaji and Greenwald, *Blindspot*, 189–209; see also Bazerman and Tenbrunsel, *Blind Spots*, 43–8.

71 Marianne Novy expresses a brief interest in experiments covering weapons and the propensity for racial misrecognition, but she turns her attention to whether works "can be free from being read as exemplifying racist ideology." *Shakespeare and Outsiders* (Oxford: Oxford University Press, 2013), 103.

CHAPTER 3

Antonio's "Fair Flesh" and the Property of Whiteness

Pound of Flesh: The Historical Aftershocks

Writing from Liverpool, England in 1861, at a distance from the outbreak of the Civil War, J. W. C. Pennington introduces his readers to the American story of Jourden H. Banks, an escaped slave from Alabama.[1] The Missouri Compromise, first established in 1820 to delimit free states from slave states, resulted in the passage of the Fugitive Slave Law of 1850 intending to lay claim on the bodies of persons seeking their freedom and compel their return to the condition of slavery. Formerly an escaped slave from Maryland, Pennington is a suitable candidate to narrate Banks's story: he earned his education, becoming the first black student admitted to Yale, entered the ministry, and fought for the abolitionist cause. In his autobiographical narrative, *The Fugitive Blacksmith* (1849), Pennington is motivated to recall his time in slavery, even after many years have elapsed, because he fears the central evil, the very "being of slavery, its soul and body," is in danger of being misconstrued: the "chattel principle, the property principle, the bill of sale principle."[2] The slave's physical abuse, humiliation, and exploitation, though cruel and inhumane, do not alter the fundamental violation of his personhood enshrined in the "chattel principle" that renders him a living contradiction: a propertied person, a human thing, and a sovereign-less self. The prospect of the fugitive slave brought greater attention to the assertion of rights in property as slave-owners insisted on recovering their possession deemed "immoveable by the operation of law," as William Goodell remarks in *The American Slave Code* (1853).[3] Even the apologists' argument, in the light of abolitionist attacks, that it was the enslaved person's labor and not the slave himself that was the subject of property, obviated the central concern: the slave's labor could not be separated from the subjection of the slave's body, hence the forcible demands for bodily repossession.[4] The intense assertion of property rights triggered by the fugitive slave, and validated in the attendant laws, made clear the enslaved person's existential peril.

Captured in Illinois and held in Smithland jail, Jourden Banks is cautious about revealing his origins, knowing that any disclosure about his background might prove disastrous: "our only hope was in strict secrecy in regard to our owners, not to tell their real names or place of abode. We might just as well turn and go back home ourselves, and better, because it would save the masters expense and would be likely save us severer punishment."[5] Robert, a fellow inmate suffering from consumption, broke this cardinal rule among escapees, and shared all with the doctor who intended to purchase and liberate Robert from his owners. Informed of Robert's whereabouts, his inflexible owner arrived only to reject the doctor's offer, saying that he did not care for Robert's life, preferring to take him home dead as an example to the other slaves. Having witnessed the degree of the white slaveholder's obdurate cruelty, Banks recounts: "Here is a man offered more than the poor skeleton of his slave is worth, but the malicious gratification of getting him home dead or alive was so sweet that he would not receive the price of his pound of flesh."[6] The flight, pursuit, seizure, and repossession of the fugitive slave like Robert has the effect of reaffirming the slave's status as property since, as Stephen Best observes regarding nineteenth-century jurisprudence, "the correct disposal of 'things,' within property disputes often entails the added determination of the nature of things themselves."[7] The striking irruption of a quantifying Shakespearean allusion ("pound of flesh") in this context ties the well-known expression to a property discourse. At the same time, the insertion of the Shakespearean reference in the middle of this scene of corporal subjection reflects Pennington's intent to reframe the narrative to speak to an inclusive global audience using Shakespeare as a cultural broker in the abolitionist cause.

Pennington's reference to *The Merchant of Venice* is, however, revealing for reasons related to the articulations of race in the intersection of the two texts. The fame of Shakespeare's *Merchant* as one of the author's most performed and controversial plays is, perhaps, only superseded by the idiomatic currency of the instantly recognizable phrase, "a pound of flesh" (4.1.322).[8] Missing from the English stage since Shrovetide 1605 after two royal performances, *Merchant* reappeared in its original version in Charles Macklin's 1741 production, at about the time when the phrase "pound of flesh" began assuming extra-textual vitality.[9] The reference is, of course, to the loan negotiated between Shylock and Antonio, whereby the latter's body, specifically a pound of his flesh, is declared forfeit in the event of non-repayment. In the dramatic spectacle of the courtroom scene, Shylock insists on legal restitution, leading to the phrase's commonly accepted meaning: a harsh, though legal demand, displaying unremitting cruelty. For his immediate audience and many critics, Shylock's exercise of his legal rights is a thinly disguised murder attempt executed through conscripted state power.[10] This attempted assault by an "alien" (4.1.345) on the life of a Venetian citizen would appear to rehearse onstage the real, social anxieties evinced in circulated stories about Jews and the ritual murder of Christians.[11] As a result, much of the play's criticism has centered on questions of anti-Semitism, the culture of distrust and bias in England extending from the Jews' expulsion in 1290 by Edward I, and Shylock's Jewishness, difference, and threat to persons in the established social order.[12]

By contrast, Pennington's account locates the "pound of flesh" squarely within a racial narrative about blackness, corporeality, property, and subjection inflicted by the inhumane conditions of slavery. Notably, Pennington's narrative situates the white slaveholder in the role of Shylock making corporeal demands, while the black body of the distressed slave represents the site of the "pound of flesh." In Pennington's account, readers accept, almost without notice, the seemingly inevitable pairing of blackness and tortured flesh as if this is Shakespeare's formula rather than the intellectually corrosive legacy of slavery. That is, Pennington's narrative betrays an epistemological and textual distortion developed within the institution of black slavery as a dominant fact of American cultural formation. To be clear, this focus on a pound of *black* flesh is not Shakespeare's. In the case of the play's iconic forfeit, Shakespeare points in a very different direction toward Antonio's body, raising the stakes on examining the racial substance of his white flesh. As a result, Shakespeare's dramatic narrative in *Merchant* interweaves biblical, financial, and property discourses in elaborating an intense racial conflict between the two main protagonists, Shylock and Antonio, centered on the blunt political aggression of whiteness in the Venetian system. In the heat of their internecine racial contest, Shakespeare asks us to reflect on the impact of race on reading, and Pennington's account, because it presents a misreading of Shakespeare's "pound of flesh," is strategically positioned to introduce Shakespeare's own dramatized accusations of misreading by a self-appointed white authority. Antonio's race-averse enforcement of textual and social meaning should alert us as modern critics of Shakespeare to the hermeneutic limitations imposed by the conjunction of whiteness and misreading.

Antonio's "Fair Flesh"

While Shylock's exorbitant demand for his forfeit appears to epitomize his rancor, a closer analysis of the play's signature bodily referent foregrounds the materiality of Antonio's flesh, along with the interrelated matters of circumcision, castration, emasculation, and male erotics, as some critics have argued.[13] Teasing out the discursive intricacies of flesh, Paul Hammond points out the meaning of "purse" as slang for genitals, in Antonio's earnest offer of himself to Bassanio in what appears to be an asymmetrical homoerotic exchange: "My purse, my person, my extremest means / Lie all unlocked to your occasions" (1.3.137–38).[14] What interests me here is Hammond's claim about the reader's relationship to language: mapping the homoerotic content of early modern texts involves detecting the "affective spaces formed by the play of language, often by linguistic hesitations and ambiguities."[15] That is, the work of reading or making textual bodies more legible in a culture ambiguously saturated with male friendship requires being vigilant to strategies and moments of linguistic hesitation that cultivate silence and invisibility in order to make them articulate.[16] The representations of eroticized bodies, like racialized bodies, might not always seem to avail themselves to interpretive scrutiny and hermeneutic transparency; more pertinently, readers are not always attuned to their presence, not always prepared to recognize their discursive and material realities.

Shakespeare gives considerable attention to physical appearance, the "pound of flesh" being one of the most pivotal but underappreciated instances of corporal legibility. Examples range from demeanor and clothing worn to more complex indices of identity and identification. To be allowed on the trip to Belmont, Gratiano promises reformed deportment as "one well studied in a sad ostent" (2.2.167) or physical demeanor. The male disguises worn by the major female figures – Portia, Nerissa, and Jessica – consistently highlight body awareness in a manner similar to the "varnished faces" (2.592), or painted masks, worn by the men out on the town for a night of Venetian revelry. Shylock's "Jewish gaberdine" (1.3.104), by contrast, is not a disguise or superficial token and makes him a highly visible immigrant target. Skin color does not go unnoticed as in the contemptuous report of the "Negro's belly" (3.5.36), Portia's servant whom the audience does not even see. According to Portia, the letter bearing the news of Antonio's failed ventures and default on the debt owed to Shylock "steals the colour from Bassanio's cheek" (3.2.243). Shakespeare carefully insists on corporal visibility that only serves to amplify the audience's potential awareness of physical appearance as a sign of racial embodiment.

I propose that the "pound of flesh," located at the play's racial nexus, be read in terms of whiteness and for the value attached to this emerging early modern racial identity. I would like, therefore, to shift the corporal focus toward Shakespeare's representation of Venice's dominant white culture. On his entry in the play, Morocco makes what turns out to be a heartfelt but useless plea to Portia: "Mislike me not for my complexion" (2.1.1), echoing the anti-black language and rhetoric in Venice that she has already activated in denigrating his "complexion of the devil" (1.2.107). Even from the distant shores of the African littoral, given the maritime networks of commerce and trade that required cultural and communication links, Venice's reputation for white preference is well known. Structurally, therefore, Shakespeare ensures that Morocco's opening words of the scene follow immediately the first onstage meeting between Antonio and Shylock, calling our attention to the prevailing racial ethos. In the event of an oversight, the audience now has no reason to be ignorant of the white bias at work in a confrontation usually regarded as uniquely driven by religious division and, more importantly, the subsequent striking of the flesh-bond agreement. The actual language used by Shylock in stipulating the conditions of the bond is pertinent and revealing; though quoted routinely, the linguistic specificity of the negotiated terms is largely overlooked by commentators on the play. "Go with me to a notary, seal me there / Your single bond," he tells the merchant. Should Antonio default on the loan, "let the forfeit," Shylock states, "Be nominated for an equal pound / Of your fair flesh, to be cut off and taken / In what part of your body pleaseth me" (1.3.137–138, 141–144). The violence of the demand has been decried, and the initially undetermined site of cutting has yielded expansive readings, but Shylock's explicit naming of Antonio's "fair flesh," that is, his whiteness, has remained under the scholarly radar, seemingly the locus of a critical blind spot. Antonio has become the invisible white man.

It is true that fairness, meaning whiteness, has been recognized for some time as a philological site of racial identification, but as Kim F. Hall argues, "the language of fairness was associated specifically with women."[17] Consistent with this claim, Morocco praises "fair Portia" (2.7.43), and Lorenzo remarks Jessica's "fair hand" (2.4.12). Fairness signified both beauty and whiteness, explaining, in part, the critical inclination toward a gendered focus on women. Early modern women writers, Hall notes, "provide ample evidence of the racialized nature of the language of fairness and beauty as well as of the importance of the language of fairness in constructions of female subjectivity."[18] Bearing "the symbolic weight of the culture," women also became the repositories of meaning for an emerging white national identity in the era of overseas expansion.[19] Regarding Antonio as "fair" requires a gender shift, according to the orthodox approach, while foregrounding the following separate but overlapping meanings: white, beautiful, and just.[20] In the maritime republic of Venice, Antonio, the "royal merchant" (3.2.138), is esteemed as the leading figure among the mercantile male elite where fairness, also referencing beauty, is the implied aesthetic that rationalizes whiteness's desirable and exceptional status. In this city teeming with foreigners drawn by its commercial fortunes, whiteness is the coveted, dominant norm. Also, in this multicultural Mediterranean crossroads, riven by ethnic and religious conflict, fairness, here meaning a just accounting, is posited as the antidote to the city's daily racial discord. Antonio's racialized fairness is the proxy for embodied justice imagined as undercutting the violence under the guise of benign superiority. In Shakespeare's version of Venice, we find the representation of a dominant white culture sustained by the politics of white supremacy. However, for its representative merchant leader, who does not fit the gender-typical prescriptions of female beauty or achieve white racial visibility in the critical tradition, Antonio has become the invisible white man.

The implications are important for readers and scholars of Shakespeare. Whiteness, as a racial identity within society, has proven difficult to nail down because of its invisibility.[21] Richard Dyer states this truism in race studies whose significance continues to resonate profoundly: "The invisibility of whiteness as a racial position in white (which is to say dominant) discourse is of a piece with its ubiquity."[22] As a "pervasive nonpresence," whiteness jettisons all strands of racial particularity, assumes normative, colorless transparency (there is nothing to see here), and disappears behind the protective cover of socially marked others.[23] In an exercise of political will, invisible whiteness distances itself from others through differentiation, even stigmatization, disavows racial continuity with nonwhite persons, and disappears into normative superiority. In short, invisible whiteness withdraws in full retreat and disengages from the scene and substance of race: "As long as race is something applied to non-white peoples, as long as white people are not racially seen and named, they/we function as a norm. Other people are raced, we are just people."[24] But whiteness as invisible bears important ethical implications related to inattention all the way through to denial. Devised as a non-color because it consists of all colors, whiteness can evade responsibility for attending to race, since blackness bears the burden of high visibility, racial attribution, and cultural embodiment of the thing itself. That is, this silent, invisible racial majority can suspend direct, responsible involvement, rely on the privileges of being merely human, and redirect all things racial elsewhere. Not all instances of racial inattention are meant to be deliberately harmful; by definition, inattention can be motivated by factors ranging from distraction to apathy. Still, ignorance does not alter the inescapable racial conditions whose histories we embody, sometimes all too literally, and indifference is never the refuge of responsible cultural citizenship.

In Defense of Jacob's Racial Legacy

Antecedents of the flesh-bond story can be found in sources like the *Mahabharata*, which features a king's gift of his own flesh, equivalent to a dove's weight, in order to save it from a predatory hawk.[25] In the late medieval period, the more recognizable "tale of a wicked merchant who made a bond with the trusting debtor by which the latter must lose a part of his body" appeared in multiple versions.[26] The thirteenth-century *Gesta Romanorum* records a merchant's demand from his creditor: "make it to me a charter of thine own blood, on condition that if thou keep not thy day of judgement, it shal be lawful for me to draw away all of thy body from the bone, with a sharp sword."[27] By the sixteenth century, Alexander Silvayn's *The Orator*, translated in 1596, about the time of Shakespeare's composition of *Merchant*, tells the story of a Jewish creditor being owed nine hundred crowns by a Christian merchant in Turkey; the debt defaulted, the Jewish lender comes before a judge to claim his payment from the merchant, variously expressed as "a pound of the flesh of his bodie," "a pound of his flesh," and "paide with mans flesh."[28] It is the general consensus, however, that the immediate source of Shakespeare's play is Ser Giovanni Fiorentino's *Il Pecorone*, a collection of tales published in Milan in 1558. Shakespeare might have read the text in manuscript translation if not the original Italian, since the English version did not appear until 1632. In Ser Giovanni's version, a Bassanio-like figure named Giannetto causes his godfather to go into debt to underwrite his triple attempt to win a lady of Belmonte who has a deceptive bargain: she will endow any man with all her goods if he manages to sleep with her successfully over the course of one night; she drugs each man, rendering him incapable of performance and ensuring that Giannetto forfeits all his wealth. Because roughly two-thirds of the Italian narrative treats the young man's requests, his amorous misadventures, and the fallout leading to the financial ruin of his godfather, the Jew's entry is much delayed. The dramatic axis shifts entirely in Shakespeare, where the narrative compression of the early parts of the Italian tale catapults the racial conflict between Antonio and Shylock into prominence right from the beginning. In Shakespeare's dramatization, therefore, race, set against a culture of commerce, is pronounced in unique ways that allow for contemplating the significance of Antonio's whiteness.

Leading up to the flesh-bond arrangement in the play's third scene is an exchange in which Shylock cites a biblical account of the story of Jacob and Laban and the patriarch's strategic interest in sheep.[29] This first meeting between Antonio and Shylock is marked for importance because of what can be discerned from Shakespeare's creative imagination at work. His source, *Il Pecorone*, usually translated as "The Simpleton," offers better interpretive direction if we allow the closer approximation, "The Big Sheep," as a foregrounding clue to what is fundamentally Shylock's argument about nation and race by way of the biblical intertext.[30] From his opening statement, Antonio condemns the concept of interest, distancing himself from Shylock by citing his own practice: "I never lend nor borrow / By taking nor giving of excess" (1.3.53–54). The audience has already heard Shylock reflect, in an aside, on Antonio's public railings against the Jewish moneylender's earnings that the merchant disdainfully "calls interest" (1.3.43). In his defense, therefore, Shylock turns to the story of Jacob, who decides to cease working for his uncle Laban and create his own family legacy. The reference is to the events in Genesis 30, where Jacob proposes an agreement of separation: rather than be paid wages, he asks to divide Laban's livestock based on color. He will search out and have the black and spotted animals, "little or great spots among the goats, and black among the sheep," while Laban will retain the unmarked, white flock.[31] In the margins, the Geneva Bible notes "that which shall hereafter be spotted" as the accurate expression for "wages," clarifying that Jacob did not seek monetary compensation or wages, but the means to create a legacy specifically realized in the chromatic rhetoric of the narrative.[32]

Laban had not always played fairly or honestly. He had violated a marriage agreement with Jacob by substituting his daughter Leah on the wedding night unknown to his son-in-law, thereby forcing the younger man into an additional seven years of indentured labor for marriage to the intended daughter, Rachel.[33] Once again, devising a plan to break the deal, Laban directs his sons to round up and spirit away the black and spotted animals.[34] Jacob's ingenuity and countermeasures fire Shylock's imagination, as seen in the descriptive details. During mating season for "the woolly breeders," Shylock recounts, the "skilful shepherd pilled me certain wands" at the moment of copulation, setting them "up before the fulsome ewes, / Who then conceiving, did in eaning time / Fall parti-coloured lambs, and those were Jacob's" (1.3.75, 76, 78–80). Jacob finds a way to create a whole new stock of black and spotted sheep based on the theory of maternal imprinting, regarding the effect of sight on somatic and genetic transmission, an idea still circulating in the early modern period.[35] The "pilled," or peeled, branches created a streaking black and white image that impressed itself on the fetus at conception and resulted in the generation of dappled lambs. Thus, following the biblical conclusion that Jacob "increased exceedingly" as a result of this particular foray in animal husbandry, Shylock declares: "This was a way to thrive, and he was blest; / And thrift is blessing if men steal it not" (1.3.81–82).[36]

Critics have variously described Shylock's narrative selection as "odd" or a "slightly baroque biblical story."[37] Still, it remains true that "Jacob's stratagem, if it is not evident to some modern critics, would have been explained by any biblical commentary in the Renaissance."[38] Antonio does not question the biblical story or the commonly acknowledged pseudo-scientific, psychological theory of maternal imprinting that modern readers find opaque. Instead, Antonio challenges Shylock's legitimacy as a reader and textual interpreter while exposing his ignorance of the text's racial significance.[39] "The devil can cite Scripture for his purpose" (1.3.90), Antonio scoffs, presupposing that Shylock's sole intent is a defense of "interest," using the metaphor of natural propagation to contest the received claim from Aristotle about the sterility of money and the unnaturalness of interest.[40] Admittedly, a rationalization of his economic practices in Venice is part of Shylock's layered argument, comparing, in Marc Shell's well-known formulation, the sexual generation of "ewes" with the monetary generation of "use" or usury.[41] But he is invested in much more. When Antonio questions whether Jacob took interest, Shylock replies, "No, not take interest, not as you would say / Directly interest" (1.3.68–69), suggesting that he uses the Jacob story to make indirect claims that might lie outside Antonio's narrow range of financial comprehension.

To begin, Jacob's entry into Laban's employ marked the genesis of his uncle's financial prosperity, so his announced departure is met with skepticism combined with deception intended to ensure the retention of his skills for additional economic benefit. An early modern audience would be familiar with a comparable, ambivalent English and European attitude toward Jews, who were reviled in many quarters, but deemed dependable sources of liquid assets in a changing cash economy, reliable targets for aggressive taxation and fines, and useful for their knowledge of trading networks in expanding international markets. "The great economic utility of Shylock – and of the Jew in the period," Stephen Greenblatt reiterates, "is his possession of liquid assets, assets which he is committed, for his very existence, to employ actively."[42] Sir Thomas Sherley's proposal to James I to "profit" from relocating Jews to England or Ireland highlights their business acumen as well as the potential revenues to be earned from the "great customs" and severe fines to be levied for the privilege of trading in English ports.[43] Nicolas de Nicolay marvels at the superior market knowledge, trading skills, and language facility of Jews in Constantinople and the cities of Greece, but concludes that, "this detestable nation of the Jews, are men of all malice, fraud, and subtle dealing, exercising execrable usuries amongst the Christians."[44] In citing Jacob's story, Shylock makes the historical, biblical text resonate with his contemporary social identity as a needed but despised member of a community who embodies the pressures, compromises, and contradictions of the transitional economy of late sixteenth-century England, where the parliamentary debates concerning the 1571 Usury Bill finally conceded moneylending with interest as a practical measure.[45] Insofar as sexual and monetary generation intersect in Shylock's economic narrative, the result will be a nonwhite or discursively black economics based on the narrative's color dynamics. Jacob's tactical choice of spotted and black sheep was initially designed to minimize any perceived threat to Laban's domestic economy and preference for white livestock; then, to escape further exploitation, Jacob's black progeny became instrumental to his freedom, increase in estate, and the down payment on the future patriarch's legacy.

Politically, therefore, Shylock's Jacobean construction of blackness is coterminous with ingenuity, resilience, and tactical surety that resists cooptation and disputes the valorization of whiteness as transcendent. His black economics must not be confused with increasingly outmoded (because of market pressure) yet resilient early modern views about usury. Rather, his notion of blackness is recuperative and equates to the rhetorical and tactical measures aimed at ensuring his own prosperity and survival in a hostile, white early modern environment. Shylock's proposition is all the more striking in the context of the discursive disparagement of early modern Jews as black.[46] Sebastian Munster's disputation between a Christian and a Jew, for example, presents blackness as the Jew's distinguishing and defining feature: "I knew you to be a Jew: For you Jews have a peculiar colour of face, different from the form and figure of other men; . . . for you are black and uncomely, and not white as other men."[47] The play's community of Venetian Jews is imbricated in racialized blackness and includes Shylock's countryman Chus (3.2.284). The name symbolizes the offspring of Noah's son Ham who disobeyed the interdiction against copulation in the ark, wanting the first born after the flood to be the inheritor of the world by primogeniture, and was punished by having his son born black, the archetype of the black Jew and prototype for black humanity, as recounted by George Best in *A True Discovery* (1578).[48] Antonio's hurled invective, "devil," expresses religious contempt and somatic scorn consistent with the commonly held view that blackness was the devil's color. Launcelot's taunting malapropism, "Certainly, the Jew is the very devil incarnation" (2.2.20–21), makes the notion of Shylock's black flesh all too literal and performatively real for the audience (Latin *incarnare*, "to make flesh"). As such, Shylock continually struggles against a dominant discourse that denies him ontological and social legitimacy because he is "not white as other men." Consciously adopting a recuperative legacy of blackness, Shylock renews its possibilities for artful political and legal resistance.

The articulation of an authorized history of blackness as redemptive and political is sharpened by Shylock's mobilization of a vocabulary of race. Race understood as genealogy, common ancestry, lineage, and stock is one of the medieval and early modern period's fundamental conceptions.[49] Shylock's account draws heavily on this formulation. Jacob's role as Jewish patriarch and ancestor to a lineage, whose history of displacement extended into the early modern European present, is emphasized for effect: "This Jacob from our holy father Abram was / (As his wise mother wrought in his behalf) / The third possessor, ay, he was the third" (1.3.64–66).[50] Other familial references like "mother" enhance the genealogical considerations, especially given the significance of the matrilineal principle in Judaism in determining racial status.[51] The core narrative of breeding sheep is predicated on the creation of a group sharing a color that defines a common descent. In narrowing the biblical animals down to sheep only, which commentators admit were typically white in ancient times, Shakespeare magnifies the production of a nonwhite race into whose legacy Shylock consciously inserts himself. Race as genealogy, with its implied reliance on biological processes, is joined to blackness in Shylock's presentation in ways that were new to early modern thinking. The neat fit of Jewish cultural traditions with early modern ideas of race as lineage and common ancestry is complicated by the introduction of blackness as having similar properties of shared group identity to suggest that a historical development, though not a radical break, was being made in paying attention to somatic forms of racial identity.

Shylock's Resistance to White Dominance

It is in the context of his assertion of racial awareness that we read Shylock's negotiation for a pound of Antonio's "fair flesh" with renewed somatic force. This deal, like its ancestral counterpart, hinges on flesh specifically coded in terms of color, but its displacement into the realm of contested social interaction makes Antonio's whiteness visible as the symbolic locus of racial aggression in a white-dominant city. Antonio's open hostility – chastisement about moneylending, name calling, kicking, and repeated spitting – is not mitigated by any signs of embarrassment. Rather, he pledges continued demeaning action, confidently asserting power over someone he regards as his cultural inferior. Shylock's wry inquiry, about whether he should simply respond to these verbal and physical humiliations with, "Fair sir" (1.3.118), is a subtle interpellation that exposes white violence as normative and self-justifying. Disgraced by the ever-evolving volley of slurs – "misbeliever, cut-throat dog" (1.3.103) – Shylock construes the collective degradations as "the shames that you have stained me with" (1.3.132). Stained, or blackened, in the social intercourse of Venice, Shylock is supremely sensitive to Antonio's merciless whiteness. Thus, Shylock is not merely launching a random assault on Antonio's body; he precisely targets Antonio's whiteness, the embodiment of profligate power, that has been deployed to inflict maximum harm and further alienate the alien Jew.

In the suspenseful moments of the flesh-bond negotiations, Bassanio is quickly alert to the racial meaning and intent. "I like not fair terms and a villain's mind" (1.3.172), he warns the insufficiently attentive Antonio, who is blinded by his immoderate hatred of Shylock along with his extravagant fondness for Bassanio. The expression "fair terms and a villain's mind" has proverbial antecedents ("Fair face, foul heart"), that explicitly contrast physical, facial features and internal qualities, "between outward attractiveness and inner corruption."[52] Preoccupied with his own amorous distractions, a spendthrift who takes advantage of his friend's emotional generosity, Bassanio is the unlikely candidate for unusual insight. Thus, the audience understands that what he observes amounts to what the average Venetian would recognize. Bassanio grasps the metonymic force of "fair" as deployed by Shylock, highlighting the moneylender's "fair" speech or rhetorical deftness in matching the bond's conditions or "fair terms" with the whiteness of the borrower to whose "fair flesh" these conditions apply. Additionally, the semantic flexibility of "fair" raises a central question: who is considered fair or white in Venice according to physical characteristics?[53] And, despite that seeming hermeneutic flexibility, is whiteness a more rigidly construed, complex cultural coding of certain forms of physical fairness marking it off as special, different, and superior? The social, ethnographic, and stage emphasis on the Jews' physical appearance – identifying hats and badges, red hair, and prosthetic nose – suggests that Jews were fair and otherwise indistinguishable from other white Europeans, or why would one need such an overdetermined imposition of external artificial signs?[54] Still, the historical record shows the persistence in representing Jews as dark-skinned or black in the medieval period and later centuries when "the 'blackness' of the Jew was not only a mark of a racial inferiority, but also an indicator of the diseased nature of the Jew."[55] The alleged physical disparities are designed to cultivate difference where very little or none exists, and the fair skin of Jews, like Jessica's and Shylock's, is questioned and subject to ideological darkening. The complete effect is not simply to denigrate Jews, but to allow whiteness to stand alone in oppressive racial splendor.

In the climactic courtroom scene, the play dramatizes a salient dimension of the politics of whiteness in a white normative society: its strategic invisibility. Portia, reading from the notarized agreement, turns the tables on the unsuspecting Shylock: "This bond doth give thee here no jot of blood. / The words expressly are 'a pound of flesh'" (4.1.302–303). The specific reference to "fair" flesh, detailed in Shylock's first mention of having the bond notarized, disappears here and from all the other "pound of flesh" formulations throughout. What might appear at first to be a lapse in continuity, or an error, is better understood as a function of visual rhetoric in the theater (and for readers). After Morocco's first onstage appearance, highlighted by a plea that names his blackness, the audience continues to see and register his skin color throughout the play without any *need* for further verbal reference. The same is true for Antonio's whiteness in the theater except for the different ideological expectations attendant on blackness and whiteness. Blackness persists as a visual fact, the product of cultural tendencies to admit its high visibility as evidenced by Portia even prior to Morocco's entry; it lives long in the imagination. Whiteness complicates this phenomenon of theatrical visuality because of white invisibility. Antonio's whiteness is constantly present, but our modern bias toward white invisibility obstructs our vision and distorts our ability to read Shakespeare's racial text effectively. Ironically, repetitions of the "pound of flesh" hide what is in plain sight for the modern audience. Each reference to Antonio's "pound of flesh" enacts whiteness' absent presence, challenging not just theater audiences but also early modern scholarship to read whiteness even when it appears textually missing.

Thus, when Walter Cohen in a landmark essay ponders whether Shylock is merely financially incompetent for demanding Antonio's flesh, the answer is now clear. "Shylock's desire for revenge," Cohen claims, "is both motivated by economics and possessed of a large degree of economic logic . . . . But when the grasping moneylender refuses to relent in return for any repayment – 'No not for Venice' – he goes beyond the bounds of rationality and against the practices of a ruthless modern businessman."[56] Overlooking the racial specificity of Shylock's demand, Cohen ignores the intensity and nature of the conflict Shakespeare has produced. Shylock is not an inept businessman; he is an astute immigrant, alert to the daily, brutal discipline of whiteness. In fact, Shylock calls attention to this seeming lack of economic "rationality," when he insists that the market value of a piece of Antonio's flesh (as opposed to the intact body sold as a slave) is less profitable than animal meat for consumption: "a pound of man's flesh, taken from a man, / Is not so estimable, profitable neither, / As flesh of muttons, beefs, or goats" (1.3.158–160). Consciously throwing out the laws of economic reason, Shylock's statement implies that he is motivated by another cause as a man bound to the logic of racial resistance. Living in a city identified with international commerce, Shylock, choosing to go against the grain of profitability, speaks to the urgency of superior and compelling racial concerns to which he must attend. In Shakespeare's Venice, Shylock's negotiated bond is a thoughtful, subtle, and strategic political act of resistance to the oppressive systemic whiteness that marginalizes and blackens him relentlessly through Antonio's cultural agency. Shylock is not merely launching a random assault on Antonio's body: he targets Antonio's whiteness, the embodiment of republican power, that has been deployed to inflict maximum harm and further alienate the alien Jew.

The Racial Contingency of Early Modern Investment Capital

The heated exchange precipitated by Antonio's loan request exposes social tensions that go way beyond the religious clash between Christian and Jew to reveal a conflict cast in terms of black and white racial animus. A closer examination of the loan instruments considered by the two men further explains how fully focused Shakespeare is on an evolving understanding of group racial dynamics, whiteness, property, and rights. The negotiation between Shylock and Antonio actually unfolds in two phases. The first concerns lending or borrowing with interest, widely recognized as usury. While the association of Jews with usury had become a theatrical and cultural commonplace, their expulsion from England in 1290 and later resettlement in small communities in London after 1540 suggest their role as convenient social scapegoats. While Europeans and Englishmen found creative loopholes and strategies that circumvented the religious constraints on usury that allowed them to enter the moneylending business, James Shapiro concludes, "Jews enabled the English to imagine a villainous moneylender whose fictional excesses overshadowed their own very real acts of exploitation."[57] Importantly, however, considerations of scapegoating or projecting actually argue that Jews or their Jewishness might not be the primary focus. One might look instead to the English subjects – the white English subjects – engaged in strategic acts of projection. Jews did not only signify Jewishness, but in the racialized context of the early modern period, and specifically in Shakespeare's play, they also raise profound questions about competing forms of whiteness for the single, compelling reason that Jews could pass as white. Whiteness for the English, compared to the enduring Jewish question, was the self-serving, new racial identity that required proof and protection.

Discredited in Aristotle, usury was roundly condemned by the Church up through Charlemagne, the fourth Lateran Council, and Aquinas, and while usury was not banned in civil law, the more religious the culture, the more likely was the opposition to this form of lending, which was regarded as extortion.[58] The most serious questions raised concerned its unnaturalness (barren metal breeding money) and the idleness encouraged in creditors; its legitimacy as a financial arrangement and the potential for exploitation; and its morality based on the transgression of biblical tenet.[59] Thomas Wilson's *Discourse upon Usury* (1572) lays out these objections and offers the summary judgment: "all lending in respect of time for any gain, be it never so little, is usury, and so wickedness before god and man, and a damnable deed in itself, because we are commanded to lend freely, and to look for nothing over and above that we lend."[60] Wilson's work, published in 1572, responds to the government's restoration of a statute in the previous year of a ten percent interest rate on loans originally enacted under Henry VIII in 1545 but abolished under Edward VI in 1552.[61] Earlier, in the twelfth century, a renaissance of trade had emerged alongside the renaissance of learning, resulting in new commercial forces being exerted on traditional religious beliefs.[62] By the sixteenth century, "the swift rise of a commercial civilization" introduced social change that prioritized the issue of "credit, money-lending and prices," ultimately centered on charging interest on loans.[63] A total church ban on interest-bearing loans would have decimated business enterprise, so "the argument continued to center on excessive interest charged by socially undesirable moneylenders and its potentially damaging economic effects."[64] The English parliament's action in 1571, therefore, reflected the economic pressures to reconcile the prohibitions with the existence of black market practices and the demands of an expanding economy, increasingly including the kinds of mercantile investments dramatized in the play.[65]

Antonio initially intends to borrow the sum of three thousand ducats with interest in violation of his own longstanding opposition to usury that has led to repeated vicious attacks against Shylock the moneylender. Antonio "lends out money gratis, and brings down / The rate of usuance here with us in Venice," Shylock complains, adding that Antonio "rails / Even there where merchants most do congregate / On me, my bargains, and my well-won thrift / Which he calls interest" (1.3.36–37, 40–43). Antonio engages in financial sabotage and declares his own moral superiority in never charging interest, even while pan-European anti-Semitism had prevented Jews from owning land and set severe limits on Jews' professional opportunities to secure a livelihood.[66] It is easy to claim moral superiority when the competition is hampered by restrictions and denied an equal playing field. In fact, allowing Jews to charge interest on loans was permitted because it benefited the increasing white, European demand for borrowed capital, similar to what we see fictionalized in the fair-fleshed Antonio's request.[67] Now that Antonio desires to help his friend Bassanio, given his current financial shortfall, he finds it convenient to turn to Shylock and the usurious practice he claimed to abhor. This racially skewed and unjust atmosphere within which Shylock is forced to operate explains his frustration at what turns out to be Antonio's self-serving, unjust condemnation.

Usury's negative associations can be traced back to the religious admonitions against charging interest to the poor that would worsen their already compromised state.[68] The effect of exorbitant interest is intentional economic ruin, for "usurers destroy and devour up, not only whole families," Thomas Wilson maintains, "but also whole countries, and bring all folk to beggary."[69] As Charles R. Geisst observes, "the history of usury in the Western tradition begins with the comments about it made in the Old Testament."[70] Had anyone "been asked why usury was wrong, he would probably have answered with a quotation from Scripture."[71] Religious voices weighed in on the subject, from Melanchton, Calvin, and Zwingli on the continent to Latimer, Crowley, and Jewel in England.[72] Importantly, therefore, the proscription against usury that arises in the exchange between Antonio and Shylock is based on the biblical injunction against violating racial and clan division encoded in the concept of brothers of the same covenant.[73] Deuteronomy 23:19–20 forbids charging interest on loans to fellow Hebrews, a principle carried over into Christian practice that rendered usury morally questionable.[74] The historical context concerns the Hebrews' economic development from an agrarian society, employing interest-free subsistence loans for harvest expenses, to the later period of monarchical trade, foreign agents, and private commerce around the ninth century BCE, when the "Deuteronomic Code seems to indicate the beginnings of investment practices."[75] The relaxation of the ban on interest-bearing loans to foreigners, who were likely traveling merchants, resulted from "incipient commercial motives" in a new age of commercial activity.[76] While some biblical historians, who are sensitive to the cultural implications, take great care to clarify what appears to be a "dual ethic" or "Deuteronomic double standard," it is precisely this cultural distinction between Hebrew brothers and foreign others that, when translated and transplanted in Europe, casts Christian and Jew as financial strangers.[77] "For hundreds of years during the medieval period," writes Klaus Issler, "not only did [the ethnic status or two-tiered view] hamper the commercial activity for merchants, traders, and shopkeepers – at times including the threat of excommunication – it also contributed to the unintended consequence of various waves of anti-Semitism throughout Europe."[78]

The encounter between Antonio and Shylock is steeped in biblical reference, befitting the early modern usury debate, with the explicit mention of the Jacob story that, as I have demonstrated, contains a racial argument. Moreover, since "Jews consider themselves descendants of Jacob, they are brothers and cannot charge each other interest, but they can charge interest to foreigners or non-Jews."[79] Antonio's expectation, spurred on by his hostility, reflects the religious foundation of this financial and racial divide: "If thou wilt lend this money, lend it not / As to thy friends," or brother Jews (1.3.124–125). The permission – not the requirement – to charge interest to a "stranger" ("unto a stranger thou mayest lend upon usury") led to the widespread financial arrangements, as seen in the play, where Jews were moneylenders in Europe, charging interest to a Christian clientele outside their tribe and racial group.[80] Naming Shylock "stranger cur" (1.3.110) alludes to the Deuteronomic precept and situates him squarely within the tradition of financial otherhood.[81]

Antonio's boast that he neither lends or borrows with interest (1.3.53–54) thus rests on his heretofore exclusive dealings with white Christians; Shylock's resort to Tubal to help shore up the full amount of the loan represents the free exchange among fellow Jews. The free circulation of money was contained within racially separate groups, and a changing economy, with the rising demand for investment capital, heightened and reinforced the awareness of those divisions as individuals made conscious decisions to cross clearly demarcated racial boundaries in search of capital outlays. Offering a systemic analysis, Shakespeare allows us to see that, beyond Antonio's intense, personal bigotry and racial hatred, the entire early modern commercial enterprise, often based on borrowed capital from "strangers" and others, is profoundly race-sensitive. It is important to remember, bearing this religious anthropology of debt and interest in mind, that the rise of capital in early modern Christian cultures, and the shift toward a mechanistic market, bears significantly on the heightened awareness of racial difference among participants engaged in the financial transactions of evolving markets. Financial operations, we learn, are contingent on racial awareness and labeling.

Crediting Whiteness

Shylock rejects Antonio's commitment to a conventional financial paradigm based on racial estrangement ("lend it not / As to thy friends") and offers instead a reformation of friendship by way of a second loan instrument: the debt bond. "Forget the shames that you have stained me with" (1.3.132), Shylock implores, offering to disregard the past and current interactions in which he is repeatedly harassed for his "stained," nonwhite, or black identity and status. The racial rapprochement will suspend the charging of interest; Shylock will "take no doit / Of usuance for [his] monies" (1.3.133–134) and thus opens a new phase of negotiation between the two men. A legally binding, sealed document, typically drawn up by a scrivener or notary, a bond secured a loan for a borrower, declared his indebtedness to a named creditor, and stated the terms and conditions of repayment.[82] What distinguishes Shylock's new proposal is that, contrary to usurious practice, the debt bond is, technically, interest-free.[83] Although the bond was conditional, with a penalty attached for failure to repay the borrowed amount at a specified date, the penal sum would be canceled if all obligations were met. The penal sum was, therefore, not considered a charge for the actual use of the money borrowed; that would constitute interest. Rather, the penal sum was instated as compensation to protect against the loss to the creditor of the amount loaned in instances of forfeiture.[84] Bolstering the common law practice that affirmed the debt bond as an interest-free instrument is the fundamental contractual fact: "the obligor could always save the penalty by prompt payment, and so the oblige was not as a result of the contract certain to gain it."[85] The Statute of Usury of 1487 and the act legalizing interest in 1545 both excluded the penal bond as an interest-bearing instrument: "it is clear that the legislature consistently followed the policy of the common law, which in its turn simply accepted the canonical view that penalties for non-repayment of debts were not usurious or objectionable."[86] As a second option proposed by Shylock, therefore, the debt bond is introduced to indicate an ostensible shift away from usury and its overt racial discontents toward something more financially hospitable, something more "kind" (1.3.135).

The widespread use of the bond was symptomatic of debt's integral place in early modern society.[87] After 1530, expanding commercial activity, the rise in consumer demand spiked by sharp population growth, the increased need for money undercut by a chronic coin shortage, a high incidence of failed repayments, and a jump in inflation helped create an environment in which the need for credit across all social ranks, including the Crown, became a fact of sixteenth and seventeenth-century English culture.[88] The effect was an interlocking network of creditors and debtors in which a borrower would often simultaneously be a lender, given the pressures of high consumer spending and the constraints of the short supply of money. Such concentrated levels of financial interaction were intensely personal, requiring considerable trust among the contracted parties, here bearing in mind the etymology of credit in *credo*: to believe or trust. From Keith Wrightson's cultural history of neighborliness and debt to Craig Muldrew's social networks of obligation, scholars have detailed the intersection of the affective, contractual, and economic bonds that defined early modern credit transactions.[89] The business of debt belonged to "an ethical tradition concerned with credit, honesty and reputation" to ensure loans, Muldrew argues, and these "ethics meant that wealth was gained through reputation, not accumulation, individualism, or inward piety."[90] The premium placed on personal creditworthiness in a period pre-dating formal means of risk assessment privileged the performative management of reputation for potential creditors.[91] The early modern market cannot be viewed solely through the lens of financial accounting or the impersonal, mathematical calculus in the exchange of goods. Instead, money's social meaning points to the affective, highly interpersonal dimension of the economy that depended on credit.[92]

Muldrew employs the notion of "the *culture* of credit, because more than anything credit was a public means of social communication and circulating judgement about the value of other members of communities."[93]

This description of the social environment within which debt bonds thrived is consistent with Shylock's proposed culture of "friends" and "kindness" (1.3.131, 135). Employing a discourse of kindness, Shylock invokes the Christian social principle of neighborliness, which extolls exemplary moral character befitting community standards, encourages reciprocal aid, and promotes harmony that boosts goodwill. Good neighborliness, most "crucially, was essentially a horizontal relationship, one that implied a degree of equality and mutuality between partners to the relationship, irrespective of distinctions of wealth or social standing."[94] The concept of friendship elevated these principles even further "to an altogether unusual degree of emotional compatibility and trust."[95] However, the arrival of newcomers in a neighborhood might reveal the limits of friendship's ideal: these new residents might not benefit from the reciprocal obligations of an otherwise dutifully cooperative community. During Elizabeth's reign, xenophobia destabilized the norms of neighborliness, and suspicion of foreigners diminished the standards of hospitality. England's reputation for deep distrust of outsiders tested the conventional ideals of sociability and friendship, as the heavy influx of religious and economic refugees into England in the sixteenth century escalated anti-alien sentiment.[96] Demographic expansion affecting in-migration to London made the city "an increasingly miscegenated space" that complicated the forced interactions with foreigners gathered from different parts of the realm.[97] Social adjustments to long-held principles prompted compromise between neighborliness and xenophobic insularity. Moreover, patronage and paternalism enforced systemic social verticality so that in "a culture so permeated by gross inequalities it was, of course, impossible for all social ties to be established on the basis of reciprocity for effective equals."[98] The challenge confronting Shylock in Shakespeare's representation is that of an alien, immigrant, and social newcomer, marginally attached to the elite social structure, who is additionally burdened with the "gross inequalities" of race.[99] He stands racially apart, isolated from the economic circle of trust. If friendship and kindness, informed by the equality of "a horizontal relationship," underwrite the ideal conditions of credit transactions, then Shylock's investment in the debt bond is destabilizing and threatens to disrupt the status quo.

The introduction of the debt bond prioritizes the social conditions and relationships that facilitate its use, and Shylock, very pointedly, reproduces the rhetoric of the affective functions of kindness, friendship, and love for his own purposes: "I would be friends with you, and have your love" (1.3.131), "This kindness will I show" (1.3.136), and "This is kind I offer" (1.3.135). Given the bond's popularity in a credit-conscious England, entrepreneurs, traders, members of the general public, Shakespeare's audience, and practitioners in all areas of the commercial theater would easily recognize the relational structures the debt bond implied and appreciate the political import of any alterations Shylock intends.[100] To sharpen our focus further, Shakespeare distills the principles of affective communities, mutuality, reciprocity, neighborliness, and trust, identified in modern scholarship, into the grammatically layered notion of "kind." Through this rhetorically powerful move, Shakespeare ensures that the full racial intent of the discussion cannot be overlooked. An examination of the early modern meanings of "kind" reveals the following definitions: a "species, breed," and a "group of people descended, or claiming descent, from a common ancestor; a family, a clan; an ethnic group, a tribe."[101] "Kind," therefore, overlaps with early modern definitions of "race" insofar as they both cover similar terrain designating genealogy, type, and kin. In the face of deeply ingrained racial custom in Venice, Shylock proposes an alternative view of racial kinship. The language of kindness, friendship, and love that Shylock employs signifies not just mutuality, but more strikingly similarity – of the same racial "kind" – that advances an entirely new argument about political and racial equity. At the same time, his language is deliberately twofold, rehearsing the reciprocity of community and trust only to reveal its insular racial character, admitting known insiders for preferential treatment. This culture of trust replicates the racial structures of exclusive, intra-group fidelities identified in ancient biblical loan practices.

Quite tellingly, Shylock's offer to be kind does not signal surrender to Christian custom or naïve incorporation of tradition. It is a strategic bid to seize the moment to attempt to reorganize, whether symbolically or temporarily, the seemingly permanent inequality of the current racial structure. Shylock posits a realignment of social positions and identities that adheres to the principle of similarity and not division, meaning that a recognition of his humanity and an opening up of the category of whiteness are required. Failure to grant that accommodation will result in a penalty directly proportional to the financial benefit: literally paid in the bond's legal tender of whiteness. At the center of this political and racial reimagining is the pound of white flesh that corresponds to what anthropologists describe as "primitive money": culturally specific items that have significant purchasing power far in excess of the minimal transactions of buying and selling. Such items, David Graeber argues, "are used to create, maintain, and otherwise reorganize relations between people," consistent with Shylock's venture in making visible whiteness' unchecked power.[102] Money, it is worth emphasizing, has more than simple commercial, exchange value. It has a "social currency" that foregrounds the nature of the interaction among participants engaged in specific transactions.[103] The debt bond epitomizes this principle: the highly contested racial relationship between the two men is mirrored in the bond's stated forfeiture of whiteness. Any possible resolution might also occur through restructuring the racial conditions embedded in the cultural relations signified by this financial instrument. Shylock's insistence on a cultural reset of "kindness" and "kind" represents a pointed critique of a color system that disqualifies his kind and denies him kindness.

Despite the celebrated myth of Venice as a republic where aliens have near equal rights under the law, Shakespeare's London, in the dramatic guise of Venice appropriated, destroys that myth to expose a city that is home to vicious racial hostilities, perpetrated along a color spectrum, that exist above and beyond the law. The multiple references to "kind" and its cognates infuse the bond exchange with a racial discourse that extends the earlier discussion concerning discriminatory whiteness in the Jacob and Laban narrative. Shylock, then, has been speaking consistently about race because it matters to his life and social wellbeing, while others suffer from a blind spot that prevents them from acknowledging or understanding racial injustice even as they engage in behaviors that weaponize whiteness. It is important to remember that the merchant Antonio is indebted to others, not just Shylock. Tubal recounts, "There came divers of Antonio's creditors in my company to Venice that swear he cannot choose but break" (3.1.89–90), and a little later we are told that the "creditors grow cruel" (3.2.315). But by focusing uniquely on Antonio's credit relationship with Shylock, Shakespeare carves out a space specifically to make visible the questions of race in the evolving early modern English culture and economy. Similarly, amid the broad scholarship on credit detailing the intricacies of loan negotiations and accounting within village and urban communities, examining advice handbooks instructing merchants on how to maximize profit through the cultivation of an ideal public profile of trust, or documenting the sharp increase in the numbers of debt cases before the Queen's Bench between 1560 and 1740, Shakespeare's play remits an expansive social account that, by its very existence, raises questions about the role of racial blind spots in contemporary scholarly practice.[104] Shakespeare pushes the boundaries of our received scholarship on credit, neighborliness, and obligation to explore its racial content and dynamic.

Whiteness as Property

Understanding the central function of the play's debt bond requires additional analysis of its status and the severity of the penalty itself. At first glance, the pound of flesh in lieu of non-performance appears opportunistically cruel, but as recent critics have observed, corporal discipline is consistent with the early modern practice of physical imprisonment for insolvent debtors.[105] For an unpaid obligation, the creditor could move directly to attach any available goods or land without filing suit. Failing that, immediate imprisonment of the debtor was possible. Importantly, "*money* could not be seized from a debtor, and in the absence of goods imprisonment was a creditor's last resort."[106] A gruesome precedent in Roman law granted the creditor the choice of cutting and dividing the insolvent debtor's body into prorated parts or leaving him alive to be sold into slavery along with his family.[107] Early modern creditors' pursuit of distraint or property seizure gave proof of creditors' seemingly willful intent to inflict harm on a debtor, as recounted by Samuel Cottesford in a sermon: "I care not so much for my money, as that I may have the will of the villaine. . . . I will have his skin, I will make Dice of his bones."[108] Despite the debt bond's popularity in avoiding the moral stain of usury, the "borrower who made use of a sealed bond gave his creditor a formidable collection mechanism" that implicated his person.[109] The marked increase in debt litigation belied the harmonious construct of a culture of trust even as it protected and enforced the stability of a credit system open to the legal abuse of overextended debtors. By the beginning of the seventeenth century, most legal "attachments were made against a defendant's person rather than goods," and until the debt was settled, many languished in prison indefinitely.[110] These conditions are directly applicable to Antonio who, should he be delinquent in payment, will be subject to the aggressive corporal seizure of debt bondage.

Framed historically, Shylock's stipulation of a pound of flesh is consistent with the early modern corporal obsession that reinforced the economic and social stability of the state's financial instruments. Several playwrights, including Middleton and Dekker, fell afoul of the credit system and ended up in prison, and credit's corporal fixation was a familiar reference point for the commercial theatrical establishment.[111] Since debt was in practice a bodily affair, Shakespeare exploits this ubiquitous corporal compulsion to examine its often obscured racial and material potential. To begin, the debt bond is an equitable instrument and has its origin in property law. The legal restitution permitted to unpaid creditors – seizure of goods and thereafter the person – forged a functional equivalence among all the elements to suggest the status of the body as property. In her recent study on debt, property, and personhood, Amanda Bailey states similarly: "In a juridical context in which flesh and money were regarded as comparable forms of property, to distinguish between them was to pose a false dichotomy." In her reading, the ethical dilemma presented by a credit system that used "human beings as collateral" is paramount.[112] The result is an intriguing argument in which the insolvent debtor, rendered "increasingly subjected to the domain of property" through the operations of debt bondage in sixteenth-century common law, becomes the genealogical forebear to chattel slavery and its legal reduction of persons to the status of property. Within their respective historical frameworks, both the debtor and the slave retained something of their humanity under the law, since object status was partial and not absolute. Bailey, thus, concludes that it was "not the slave's status as property but his 'liminal incorporation' into his host culture that connected him to the insolvent debtor."[113] Bailey's bold attempt to connect economic insolvency, human collateral, and property navigates the legal constraints and provisions in sixteenth-century common law, but it overlooks the glaring matter of race as color in the history of "priced persons" leading up to plantation slavery.[114]

Medieval and early modern common law identified goods and domestic animals as property in the process of settling disputes over the rights of contending parties. Horses, cows, plows, bedding, pots, jewelry, plate, and rugs filled out an overstuffed category of movable or transportable property. Land, the paradigm of property from a modern perspective, was not included under this rubric, being regarded as patrimonial, hereditary, and transferable as a gift.[115] Economic historians argue the impact of the market evolution where consumerism intensified the effect of fungibility that eventually incorporated land as salable, divisible property especially in urban areas. As a response to these changes, the sixteenth century saw developments in common law practice that expressed greater similarities in the way land and chattels were conceived. For Martha Howell, movables became a signature event in the early modern period insofar as they represent the ascendancy of salability and the abstraction of a thing to a price.[116] At the center of the evolving definition of property was a recurring concept related to ownership that endured into the sixteenth century and beyond: "medieval law did not conceive of property rights as absolute. One did not 'own' property; one 'had rights in' property."[117] This definition places the emphasis squarely on the idea of rights or legal interest one might have in a thing. It also calls attention to the agency of rights in the transformation of a thing into property, whether material or immaterial: "It is the real right attaching to the object (especially the real right of ownership) which turns the physical object into 'property' or a '*res*': the property objects in law are only the creation of the real rights attached to them."[118] Importantly, this definition of "rights in" property acknowledges the philosophical and practical distinction between rights exercised and the thing itself as separable entities. Someone may possess an object, a runaway animal or stolen utensil, but not have rights in the thing, a common occurrence that required legal resolution.[119] Understanding this separation, in theory and in practice, gives rise, in turn, to the dematerialization of the object that constitutes its status as property so that theories of property will come to include abstractions like intellectual property and money or, crucially, in the case of *Merchant*, whiteness.[120]

Because debt was classified as property, Shylock's defense of his bond and right to the pound of flesh is explicitly stated in the recognizable items of property law. In the courtroom scene, when he rejects exceptional sums of money for the bond's defeasance and is castigated for being unmerciful, Shylock asks rhetorically: "What judgement shall I dread, doing no wrong? / You have among you many a purchased slave, / Which, like your asses and your dogs and mules, / You use in abject and in slavish parts/ Because you bought them" (4.189–193). Citing the classic examples of domestic animals (asses, dogs, and mules), he builds his case by referencing movables, the emblematic category in early modern property law. Venetians' unimpeachable property rights in their animals as well as their slaves, Shylock insists, are akin to his own rights in the excised pound of flesh whose transportability makes apparent its literal status as movable property. The crucial comparison of slaves to domestic animals extends the argument to the human domain, making prominent the hybridization of human flesh as property that is embedded in the debt bond's claims and constraints on the body. But Shylock's rhetorical enterprise is directed specifically toward the assertion of his rights in the pound of white flesh and, by extension, his rights in the immaterial property of whiteness itself. In this regard, the unnamed slaves serve another vital function: the slaves Shylock references are white, or, at least in the multi-ethnic port of Venice, they embody various forms of whiteness. No textual markers indicate otherwise, in striking contrast to the racially overdetermined black servant girl in Portia's employ. The slaves' textual transparency, and subsequent racial invisibility, accords with the notable erasure of Antonio's whiteness. Venetian slavery, still active in the late sixteenth century, was multiethnic.[121] The prohibition against Christians enslaving other Christians, though often unheeded, led to slaves being captured and sold from diverse geographical backgrounds, especially the Ottoman-controlled regions of the Black Sea, Adriatic, and the Aegean as well as Sub-Saharan and North Africa. Slaves in Venice were not, to be sure, universally black despite evidence for this preference in some fashionable quarters. Rather, they bore multiple traces of mobility, imperial seizure and competition, religious conversion, altered social status, and fair skin. Fair-skinned slaves form the relevant correlate in the analogy to Shylock's ownership of Antonio's white flesh, along with his stubborn insistence that conveys both the forfeit's attributed value and property status.

This moment in the play represents a shift that encapsulates the extraordinary opportunity the debt bond affords. Since Jews were not allowed to own landed property, the debt bond creates a loophole whereby Shylock envisions an even more bold social restructuring that permits him to own whiteness as property and challenge the exclusionary principle on which property rights are predicated in Venice.[122] In the context of the Venetian racial foment that disqualifies Shylock's fair skin, owning whiteness through legally state-sanctioned financial mechanisms is an attempt to dismantle insidious hierarchies of color – here, the multiple forms of whiteness. In this, the play is consistent in its recognition that despite the prevalence of commerce, the significance of economic value does not compare to the city's racial politics and the valuation placed on the exclusive property rights in whiteness. Against John Wheeler's judgment in *A Treatise of Commerce* (1601) concerning the ubiquity of commercial practice and the merchandising mindset in England, Shakespeare offers his own cultural assessment in *Merchant* by calling attention to the emergent institution and power of whiteness as defining English phenomena as real and, perhaps, more consequential than the case for economic vitality.[123]

In response to Shylock's palpable threat of owning whiteness as property, a massive private and public campaign is launched to prevent such a turnabout. Antonio's friends, acquaintances, and the state (in the person of the Duke) rally to protect him in a manner that, when read through the play's racial lens, constitutes the community's collective political will to protect whiteness' integrity and power. Shylock's property-claim in whiteness results in a perceived crisis among the Venetians: one cannot separate or extract whiteness from the body without bloodshed or death just as, we have already seen, the attempt to separate the slave's labor from the slave's body results in the stalemate of corporal discipline and perpetual bondage. The dramatic turning point in the courtroom's contest centers on blood, an early modern marker for race. To the sudden joy of Antonio's supporters and Shylock's dismay, Portia unveils the infamous legal technicality that curbs Shylock's will and vitiates the contract: Shylock may have his pound of flesh, because it is explicitly stated in the bond, but he must not spill even "a jot of blood," which is notable for its "juridical absence" (4.1.302).[124] While the blood-trick appears in earlier sources, like Ser Giovanni's narrative, it takes on an entirely new meaning about protecting whiteness in Shakespeare's treatment. Blood (like "kind" discussed above), once more, reproduces the discourse of "race" in the early modern period in referring to group, lineage, and family.[125] Its recurrence in contexts of nobility, distinguishing those of noble blood from ordinary, less morally qualified human subjects, is culturally resonant for Shakespeare's audience and aligns with the historical construction of a new class of superior man in an age of commerce, the "royal merchant" (3.2.248), as Antonio is adoringly called.[126]

The pure-blood laws of Spain's inquisitorial courts served as an aggressive reaction to the threat of erosion of difference that religious conversion presented. Jewish conversion in significant numbers ignited fears of their infiltration into the Spanish mainstream, undetected and becoming physically indistinguishable from their hosts.[127] The parallels to *Merchant* suggest similar racial strategies at work. Blood, as Portia asserts, is not mentioned in the bond, and yet its absence becomes the centerpiece of the legal defense. The begrudging recognition of the physical similarity between Shylock and Antonio as fair-fleshed men is exposed when Portia asks upon entering the courtroom, "Which is the merchant here and which the Jew" (4.1.170)? The legal claim of racial similarity, inherent in Shylock's bond strategy, initiates a counter-discourse of blood purity – Antonio's blood as something not to be touched, wasted, or nakedly exposed through bleeding – to contain Shylock's racial advancement and maintain a boundary of difference. The phrase "flesh and blood," used in the familial context of Gobbo with his father (2.2.75–76), tries to sustain the uniqueness of white flesh through the idealization of blood and proves to be a cultural rallying point around which the white Venetians reinforce their identity as family.[128] For white Venetians, flesh and blood are bonded in a novel racial discourse of corporal property that resists any attempt to deconstruct this invented union. Shylock must undergo the injustice and indignity that separate "owners from their rights" to accommodate a countervailing predicate of union in order to shield Antonio and protect whiteness, buttressed with differential notions of superior blood, as a historically powerful, unique racial identity.

The Aggressive Property of Whiteness

I began this chapter citing an instance of racial misreading in *Merchant* as reported in J. W. C. Pennington's Civil War account of a white slave owner's rejection of a proffer for the recaptured fugitive slave named Robert: "Here is a man offered more than the poor skeleton of his slave is worth, but the malicious gratification of getting him home dead or alive was so sweet that he would not receive the price of his pound of flesh." The text remains ambiguous as to whether the Shakespearean phrase belongs to the slave owner, Banks, or is inserted by Pennington, the first African American admitted to Yale's all-white educational institution. What is clear is that a contextually driven adaptation is built on a textual misreading of the "pound of flesh" that equates blackness and embodied cruelty in an environment where such violence was the predictable norm. Pennington's narrative reads Shakespeare into the plantation history of human oppression and depravity, although Shakespeare's representation of contending forms of whiteness has been narrowed and transformed by this mid-nineteenth-century account into the racial agon of modernity. Shakespeare insists on exposing white violence in the person of Antonio, whose corrosively dehumanizing attitude triggers the revolt against his fair or white flesh and the culture of bias it represents.

The question remains: What is the relevance for modern readers and audiences of the interaction between Shylock and Antonio, and especially Antonio's particular brand of whiteness – aggressively assured and self-righteous; full of contempt and condescension; dominant, demanding, and exploitative for its own narrow interests? We come full circle to the scene of institutional escape for men like Pennington, Jourden H. Banks, and the mono-named Robert: flight, legal penalty, incarceration, and the recovery of property as presented in the historical fact of frightening, dangerous fugitive slave experience. Within this concatenated history, it is worth reemphasizing that Shakespeare's period was a time during which the debt bond, with its legal seizure of the body as forfeit, laid the conceptual foundation for understanding the forcibly asserted plantation rights in human property. Recognizing, therefore, the filiation of Antonio's brand of whiteness with the institution of black slavery is to observe a particular character of whiteness, an attitude, an ideal, and way of being that speaks not just to the tenuousness or outright rejection of the idea of *whiteness as property* but more to the notion of the *property of whiteness*, which is essential to the emerging early modern English identity Shakespeare examines.[129] In early modern usage, "property" also means an "attribute, characteristic, or quality" of a person or thing, the same attribute of willful superiority that, from Antonio to American scenes of white institutional control exerted over the slave's life and limb remains remarkably, frustratingly consistent.[130]

To regard transatlantic black slavery as the moment when this readily identifiable form of aggressive whiteness explicitly exerted its destructive power invites a return to Shakespeare's play and its evocation of the late sixteenth century as a time when the international contacts were being formed that facilitated the commerce and shipment of ocean survivors and newly constituted human chattel. Before the fully fledged plantation commerce in human bondage in the Americas, *Merchant* makes a notable contribution to our expanding historical awareness of whiteness' emergence as a distinct social factor recognizable and meaningful to Shakespeare in his day. At the beginning of the twentieth century, W. E. B. DuBois "insisted that the very existence of 'personal whiteness' was a problem American scholars needed to explain," since it was a phenomenon of recent vintage (since the nineteenth century) in the scope of world history.[131] Theodore W. Allen's "invention of the white race" is a late seventeenth-century ruling-class response to the threat posed by the consolidation of laboring classes.[132] *Merchant* can be situated, therefore, in this historical framing of whiteness as personal and political identity, rebutting Allen's temporal thesis and pushing DuBois's timeline back further into the sixteenth century. But the play's culture of white dominance, articulated in that famous theatrical property, the pound of "fair flesh," has been obscured by a second misreading of greater scope and magnitude involving the core critical complex of race, analytical method, and textual interpretation. The seeming unwillingness among scholars to address the textual evidence, admit its racial content, and grapple with Shakespeare's critique of whiteness has only reproduced, in this instance, one of whiteness's most strategically ontological and political maneuvers: invisibility that renders the text racially irrelevant.

Shakespeare's play as I have examined it pushes against that invisibility to call attention to whiteness as an aggressive identity and cultural force we cannot ignore. Invisibility is, moreover, code for the human actant's innocence through non-involvement ("I was never present; therefore, I am not accountable; I know nothing"), a hands-off stratagem that, when applied to reading, attempts to negate history and responsibility. It is imperative, therefore, that we recall the play's pivotal third scene where the flesh bargain is struck as the moment that dramatizes a third instance of misreading. Antonio's inability or refusal to admit the racial content of Shylock's unpacking of the biblical story of Jacob and Laban constitutes his direct attack on Shylock's capacity and legitimacy as a reader of a commonly held and canonical cultural text, the Bible. I intend, of course, the metadramatic analogy with contemporary scholar–readers and the canonical status accorded Shakespeare's work today. Antonio's disconcerting rejoinder, the "devil can cite Scripture for his purpose," simultaneously delegitimizes Shylock and installs himself as the decisive white reader – the contrast to the black "devil" Shylock – selectively rejecting and deploying race to suit his epistemological "purpose" in forcefully pairing whiteness and misreading. This jarring assertion of the right to determine legitimate reading practices prefigures contemporary debates in early modern studies about the role and value of reading race. Shakespeare authorizes racial analysis and critique, I argue, for, already in the late sixteenth century, he rehearses in Antonio the combined effects of racial positionality, whiteness' divisive effects, and the contested readings it produces. In a broad historical view, the play's contemporary value resides in its ability to ask us to ponder the significance of whiteness and misreading, particularly when, as demonstrated by Antonio, emotional and epistemological violence, dismissal, and an intransigent belief in a pre-ordained right to *read white* dominate the practice and experience of reading and interpreting texts.

Notes

1 J. W. C. Pennington, *A Narrative of Events of the Life of J. H. Banks, an Escaped Slave, from the Cotton State, Alabama, in America* (1861) (Gloucester: Dodo Press, 2009).
2 James W. C. Pennington, *The Fugitive Blacksmith* (Gloucester: Dodo Press, 2009), 4.
3 William Goodell, *The American Slave Code in Theory and Practice* (London: Forgotten Books, 2018), 10.
4 Stephen M. Best, *The Fugitive's Properties: Law and the Poetics of Possession* (Chicago: University of Chicago Press, 2004), 8–9.
5 Pennington, *Narrative*, 64.
6 Ibid. On the quantification endemic to the slave experience, see Daina Ramey Berry, *The Price for Their Pound of Flesh: The Value of the Enslaved, from Womb to Grave, in the Building of a Nation* (Boston: Beacon Press, 2017).
7 Best, *The Fugitive's Properties*, 29.

8 All quotations follow the New Cambridge edition of *The Merchant of Venice*, ed. M. M. Mahood (Cambridge: Cambridge University Press, 2003).

9 On the performance history of the play, see Charles Edelman, *The Merchant of Venice*, Shakespeare in Production (Cambridge: Cambridge University Press, 2002).

10 Critics have explained Shylock's seemingly extreme behavior in relation to biblical models: Michelle Ephraim, "Jephthah's Kin: The Sacrificing Father in *The Merchant of Venice*," *Journal for Early Modern Cultural Studies* 5.2 (2005): 71–93; David Nirenberg, "Shakespeare's Jewish Questions," *Renaissance Drama*, n.s., 38 (2010): 77–113.

11 Mary Janell Metzger, "'Now by My Hood, a Gentle and No Jew': *The Merchant of Venice* and the Discourse of Early Modern Identity," *PMLA* 113.1 (1998): 52–65; she reports that Foxe's *Actes and Monuments* represents Jews "as child murderers whose historical and bloody destruction confirm their rejection by God" (54). See also Edgar Rosenberg, "The Jew in Western Drama: An Essay," in *The Jew in English Drama: An Annotated Bibliography*, ed. Edward Davidson Coleman (New York: New York Public Library and Ktav Publishing House, 1970), 1–50, esp. 6–8.

12 One recalls Harold Bloom's blunt assessment in his *Shakespeare: The Invention of the Human* (New York: Riverhead Books, 1999): "One would have to be blind, deaf, and dumb not to recognize that Shakespeare's grand, equivocal comedy *The Merchant of Venice* is nevertheless a profoundly anti-Semitic work." He continues: "If I were a director, I would instruct my Shylock to act like a hallucinatory bogeyman, a walking nightmare flamboyant with a big false nose and a bright red wig" (171, 172). See also Herbert Bronstein, "Shakespeare, the Jews, and *The Merchant of Venice*," Shakespeare *Quarterly* 20.1 (1969): 3–10.

13 James Shapiro, *Shakespeare and the Jews* (New York: Columbia University Press, 1996), 113–130.

14 Paul Hammond, *Figuring Sex Between Men from Shakespeare to Rochester* (Oxford: Clarendon Press, 2002), 91.

15 Ibid., 90. Bruce R. Smith similarly notes the power of articulate silences in *Homosexual Desire in Shakespeare's England: A Cultural Poetics* (Chicago: Chicago University Press, 1994), 68.

16 On the widely accepted practice and ambiguity of male friendship, see Steve Patterson, "The Bankruptcy of Homoerotic Amity in Shakespeare's *Merchant of Venice*," *Shakespeare Quarterly* 50.1 (1999): 9–32; Alan Bray, "Homosexuality and the Signs of Male Friendship in Elizabethan England," *History Workshop* 29 (1990): 1–19.

17 Hall, *Things of Darkness*, 177.

18 Ibid.

19 Ibid., 9.

20 For these meanings, see "fair," adj.1.a, 11, 14.a and b. *OED Online*, Oxford University Press, March 2022, www.oed.com/view/Entry/67704.

21 Ann Louise Keating, "Interrogating 'Whiteness': (De)constructing 'Race,'" *College English* 57.8 (1995): 901–918, esp. 904–905; and Frankenberg, *White Woman, Race Matters*.

22 Richard Dyer, "The Matter of Whiteness," in *White Privilege: Essential Readings on the Other Side of Racism*, ed. Paula S. Rothenberg, 4th ed. (New York: Worth Publishers, 2012), 11.

23 Keating, "Interrogating 'Whiteness,'" 904.

24 Dyer, "The Matter of Whiteness," 10.

25 A review of the flesh-bond narrative, along with additional sources, is found in Geoffrey Bullough, ed., *Narrative and Dramatic Sources of Shakespeare*, vol. *i* (New York: Columbia University Press, 1977), esp. 446–54.

26 Ibid., 447.

27 Ibid.

28 Ibid., 483, 484, 485.

29 On the Jacob and Laban story in *Merchant*, see Marc Shell, *Money, Language and Thought: Literary and Philosophic Economies from the Medieval to the Modern Era* (Baltimore: Johns Hopkins University Press, 1982), 48–55; Lauren Garrett, "True Interest and the Affections: The Dangers of Lawful Lending in *The Merchant of Venice*," *Journal for Early Modern Cultural Studies* 14.1 (2014): 32–62, esp. 42; Heather Hirschfeld, "'We All Expect A Gentle Answer, Jew': *The Merchant of Venice* and the Psychotheology of Conversion," *ELH* 70.1 (2006): 61–81; Lars Engle, "'Thrift is Blessing': Exchange and Explanation in *The Merchant of Venice*," *Shakespeare Quarterly* 37 (1986): 20–37, esp. 31.

30 Mahood, introduction to *Othello*, 2.

31 Genesis 30:33. *The Geneva Bible*, 1560 edition (Madison: University of Wisconsin Press, 1969). As a point of clarification, the *Contemporary English Version* notes: "In ancient times sheep were usually white, and goats were usually black or dark brown; only a few sheep would have black spots, and only a few goats would have white spots." This explains the delineation among the outcome regarding spotted goats, spotted sheep, and the black lambs.

32 Genesis 33:32.

33 Genesis 29:15–30. Jacob wished to marry Rachel and agreed to work for seven years to gain her; on the wedding night, unknown to Jacob, Laban substitutes Leah in his bed to enlist him for another seven years' labor.

34 Genesis 31:7 speaks specifically about Laban's repeated deceptions concerning Jacob's wages; the removal of the black and spotted animals appears similarly problematic. Elizabeth A. Spiller notes that the removal "seems to be motivated not just by greed but by a desire to reassert a kind of 'purity' within the flocks that represents his life and family." "From Imagination to Miscegenation: Race and Romance in Shakespeare's *The Merchant of Venice*," *Renaissance Drama n.s.* 29 (1998): 137–164; 139.

35 Martin Japtok and Winfried Schleiner. "Genetics and 'Race' in *The Merchant of Venice*," *Literature and Medicine* 18.2 (1999): 155–172, esp. 157–62; M. Lindsay Kaplan, "Jessica's Mother: Medieval Constructions of Jewish

Race and Gender in *The Merchant of Venice*," *Shakespeare Quarterly* 58.1 (2007): 1–30, esp. 23–26.

36 Genesis 30:43.

37 Mary Jo Kietzman, "*The Merchant of Venice*: Shylock and Covenantal Interplay," *ELH* 84.2 (2017): 423–452 (434); Simon Critchley and Tom McCarthy, "Money and Morality in *The Merchant of Venice*," *Diacritics* 34.1 (2004): 2–17 (8).

38 Japtok and Schleiner, "Genetics and 'Race,'" 156.

39 Ephraim, "Jephthah's Kin," 74–76. She argues that the Reformist "struggle for scriptural mastery, emblematic of tensions between Protestants and Catholics during the Reformation, is played out directly against the Jew in *Merchant*" (74). On the matter of superior biblical exegesis by Jews, William Bedell, chaplain to the English ambassador in Venice, criticized the Venetian Catholic friars for their "strange wresting of the Holy Scripture," preferring the more disciplined "sermons of the Jews." Quoted in M. Lindsay Kaplan, ed., *The Merchant of Venice: Texts and Contexts* (Boston: Bedford/St. Martin's, 2002), 148–149.

40 Aristotle, *Politics*, trans. H. Rackham, Loeb Classical Library (Cambridge, MA: Harvard University Press, 1977), 1.3.23. On the hermeneutic disparities posed by the Laban passage, see Julia Reinhard Lupton, "Exegesis, Mimesis, and the Future of Humanism in *The Merchant of Venice*," *Religion and Literature* 32.2 (2000): 123–139. She writes: "It is not simply that Shylock's Jewish hermeneutics are rejected in favor of Christian techniques, but rather that the very possibility of imagining a specifically Jewish community of readers itself exists within the typological framework as an essential part of its historical vision" (125).

41 The well-known formulation is from Shell, *Money, Language and Thought*, 50.

42 Stephen J. Greenblatt, *Learning to Curse: Essays in Early Modern Culture* (New York: Routledge, 1990), 42.

43 In Kaplan, *The Merchant of Venice*, 224.

44 In Ibid., 227.

45 In Ibid., 200–206. Recent scholarship on usury's moral and economic efficacy includes Laurence Fontaine, *The Moral Economy: Poverty, Credit, and Trust in Early Modern Europe* (Cambridge: Cambridge University Press, 2014); Charles R. Geisst, *Beggar Thy Neighbor: A History of Usury and Debt* (Philadelphia: University of Pennsylvania Press, 2013); David Hawkes, *The Culture of Usury in Renaissance England* (New York: Palgrave Macmillan, 2010).

46 Shapiro, *Shakespeare and the Jews*, 170–172. Working from the evidence of medieval psalters, Kaplan argues "that the representations of Jews with dark complexions [are] not indiscriminate," but reveal "the developing idea of a distinct Jewish racial identity manifesting itself as physical difference." "Jessica's Mother," 5, 10. See also her more recent essay, M. Lindsay Kaplan, "The Jewish Body in Black and White in Medieval and Early Modern England," *Philological Quarterly* 92.1 (2013): 41–65.

47 Sebastian Munster, *The Messias of the Christians and the Jews Held Forth in a Discourse between a Christian and a Jew*, in *Race in Early Modern England: A Documentary Companion*, ed. Ania Loomba and Jonathan Burton (New York: Palgrave, 2007), 249.
48 In Kaplan, *The Merchant of Venice*, 177.
49 Margo Hendricks, "Surveying 'Race' in Shakespeare," in *Shakespeare and Race*, ed. Catherine M. S. Alexander and Stanley Wells (Cambridge: Cambridge University Press, 2000), esp. 15–18. Silvayn's *Orator*, one of *Merchant*'s possible sources, uses this racial typology negatively, to refer to the Jewish moneylender: "But it is no marvaile if this race be so obstinat and cruel against us." In Bullough, *Narrative and Dramatic Sources*, 486.
50 Spiller explains: "Understood by early modern readers as an account in which the moral fall of man was expressed in terms of his genealogical 'descent,' Genesis became a text into which early modern readers interjected their concerns about racial lineage and difference" ("From Imagination to Miscegenation," 140).
51 Shaye J. D. Cohen, "The Matrilineal Principle in Historical Perspective," *Judaism* 34.1 (1985): 5–13. Rebekah, Jacob's mother, and Rachel, her niece and his wife, play significant roles in this custom.
52 John Drakakis, ed., *The Merchant of Venice*, The Arden Shakespeare (London: Bloomsbury, 2010), 221.
53 Jacobson, *Whiteness of a Different Color*; Melanie Kaye/Kantrowitz, *The Colors of Jews: Racial Politics and Radical Diasporism* (Bloomington: Indiana University Press, 2007); John O. Calmore, "Jews and the Problem of Whiteness," *Race, Racism, and the Law*, August 26, 2011. http://racism.org/index.php/articles/race/66-defining-racial-groups/white-european-american/370-white01a2.
54 Thomas Coryate, for example, writes of the different colored hats and turbans Jews wear in Venice in *Coryats Crudites*, in Kaplan, *The Merchant of Venice*, 141.
55 Sander Gilman, "Are Jews White?" in *Theories of Race and Racism: A Reader*, ed. Les Black and John Solomon (New York, Routledge, 2009), 296.
56 Walter Cohen, "*The Merchant of Venice* and the Possibilities of Historical Criticism," *ELH* 49.4 (1982): 765–789 (769).
57 James Shapiro, *Shakespeare and the Jews*, 99. See also Geisst, *Beggar Thy Neighbor*, 32–33.
58 See Geisst, *Beggar Thy Neighbor*, 13–57.
59 Lloyd Edward Kermode, ed., *Three Renaissance Usury Plays* (Manchester: Manchester University Press, 2009), 1–11. In the ancient and medieval worlds, with the debate intensifying in the sixteenth century, usury was opposed in theory while allowed in practice. See Geisst, *Beggar Thy Neighbor*, 58–96.
60 In Kaplan, *The Merchant of Venice*, 196.
61 Kermode, *Three Renaissance Usury Plays*, 2.

62 See Geisst, *Beggar Thy Neighbor,* where he addresses the "revival of trade in Europe that brought traders into better contact with the Eastern Empire and the Muslim world" (31).

63 R. H. Tawney, *Religion and the Rise of Capitalism: A Historical Study* (Gloucester: Peter Smith, 1962), 150.

64 Geisst, *Beggar Thy Neighbor,* 34.

65 Donna M. Kish-Goodling, "*The Merchant of Venice* in Teaching Monetary Economics," *The Journal of Economic Education* 29.4 (1998): 330–339, esp. 337. Max Weber argues that the emergence of the powerful Florentine bankers in the fifteenth century forced the Church to capitulate to the financial realities shaping a new course for European history in *General Economic History,* trans. Frank H. Knight (New York: Greenberg, 1927), 269–270.

66 Brian Weinstein, "Shakespeare's Forgivable Portrayal of Shylock," *Jewish Bible Quarterly* 35.3 (2007): 187–191, esp. 188, where he notes the early modern restrictions placed on Jews. See also Geisst, *Beggar Thy Neighbor,* 52: "Jews were permitted to lend money to avoid an even greater evil – that of being forced by necessity to allow Christians to practice usury."

67 On Jews' role as "financial brokers" in the changing early modern English economy, see Shapiro, *Shakespeare and the Jews,* 98–99, and Norman Jones, *God and the Moneylenders: Usury and Law in Early Modern England* (Oxford: Basil Blackwell, 1989).

68 Exodus 22: "If thou lend money to my people, that is, to the poor with thee, thou shalt not be as an usurer unto him: ye shall not oppress him with usury" (Geneva Bible). See also Leviticus 25:35–37. These, along with Deuteronomy 23:19–20, are the three OT Torah passages on usury.

69 In Kaplan, *The Merchant of Venice,* 197.

70 Geisst, *Beggar Thy Neighbor,* 51.

71 Tawney, *Religion and the Rise of Capitalism,* 153.

72 Ibid., 81–82.

73 The crux of the usury debate concerns the emphasis on the poor in Exodus and Leviticus in contrast to the focus on brotherhood in Deuteronomy. See Klaus Issler, "Lending and Interest in the OT: Examining Three Interpretations to Explain the Deuteronomy 23:19–20 Distinction in Light of the Historical Usury Debate," *Journal of the Evangelical Theological Society* 59.4 (2016): 761–789.

74 Benjamin N. Nelson, *The Idea of Usury: From Tribal Brotherhood to Universal Otherhood* (Princeton: Princeton University Press, 1949), 3–28.

75 Bernard J. Meislin and Morris L. Cohen, "Backgrounds of the Biblical Law against Usury," *Comparative Studies in Society and History* 6.3 (1964): 250–267 (260).

76 Ibid., 264. The introduction of commerce has led Issler to see in the Deuteronomy passage an "economic contrast rather than an ethnic status contrast" ("Lending and Interest in the OT," 775; see also 774–779). The foreigners in question are not marked so much by their ethnic difference, but as traveling merchants, who borrow for financial increase and not out of need;

as such, they do not require the remission of interest. See also Jeffrey H. Tigay, *Deuteronomy, The JPS Torah Commentary* (Philadelphia: Jewish Publication Society, 1996), 218.

77 Meislin and Cohen, "Backgrounds of the Biblical Law," 264; for a military explanation, see Weber, *General Economic History*, 267–268.

78 Issler, "Lending and Interest in the OT," 782; for an account of the ethnic status interpretation, see 780–785.

79 Kish-Goodling, "*The Merchant of Venice* in Teaching Monetary Economics," 332.

80 Deuteronomy 20:20.

81 Nelson, *The Idea of Usury*, 86–89.

82 A. W. B. Simpson, "The Penal Bond with Conditional Defeasance," *The Law Quarterly Review* 82 (1966): 393–395.

83 This is also the position taken by Amanda Bailey, *Of Bondage: Debt, Property, and Personhood in Early Modern England* (Philadelphia: University of Pennsylvania Press, 2013). Garrett, however, insists on reading the penal sum as interest ("True Interest and the Affections," 34).

84 Simpson, "The Penal Bond," 412–13.

85 Ibid., 414.

86 Ibid.

87 Craig Muldrew, *The Economy of Obligation: The Culture of Credit and Social Relations in Early Modern England* (New York: St. Martin's Press, 1998), 95–119.

88 Ibid., 3–5; 15–36; David Landreth, *The Face of Mammon: The Matter of Money in English Renaissance Literature* (Oxford: Oxford University Press, 2012), esp. 14–15; Jean E. Howard, *Theater of a City: The Places of London Comedy, 1598–1642* (Philadelphia: University of Pennsylvania Press, 2007), 80–81.

89 Muldrew, *The Economy of Obligation*, 3; Keith Wrightson, *English Society, 1580–1680* (1982) (New Brunswick: Rutgers University Press, 2003), 59–65; Theodore B. Leinwand, *Theatre, Finance, and Society in Early Modern England*, rev. ed. (Cambridge: Cambridge University Press, 2003); Huey-ling Lee, "The Social Meaning of Money in Dekker's *The Shoemaker's Holiday* and Shakespeare's *The Merchant of Venice*," *Comparative Drama* 49.3 (2015): 335–366.

90 Muldrew, *The Economy of Obligation*, 2.

91 Aaron Kitch, "The Character of Credit and the Problem of Belief in Middleton's City Comedies," *Studies in English Literature, 1500–1900* 47.2 (2007): 403–426, esp. 407.

92 Muldrew, *The Economy of Obligation*, 5, 151–152.

93 Ibid., 2.

94 Wrightson, *English Society*, 59.

95 Ibid., 63.

96 Yungblut, *Strangers Settled Here Amongst Us*.

97 Howard, *Theatre of a City*, 11; see also her discussion of the tensions of a cosmopolitan city, 1–28. Foreigners, Howard reminds us, referred to persons from outside the city and not freemen, members of the guilds (8).

98 Wrightson, *English Society,* 65.
99 Ibid.
100 On credit, bonds, and the theater, see Bailey, *Of Bondage,* 4–5; Kitch, "The Character of Credit," 411–412; on commercial enterprise, see D. M. Palliser, *The Age of Elizabeth under the Later Tudors, 1547–1603* (New York: Longman, 1983), 267–268.
101 See "kind," n.7a, 10a. *OED Online*, Oxford University Press, March 2022, www.oed.com/view/Entry/103444.
102 David Graeber, *Debt: The First 5,000 Years* (New York: Melville House, 2011), 130.
103 Ibid., 130, 158.
104 Ceri Sullivan, *The Rhetoric of Credit: Merchants in Early Modern Writing* (Madison, NJ: Fairleigh Dickenson University Press, 2002); John Walter, *Crowds and Popular Politics in Early Modern England* (Manchester: Manchester University Press, 2006), 124–180; C. W. Brooks, *Pettyfoggers and Vipers in the Commonwealth: The Lower Branch of the Legal Profession in Early Modern England* (Cambridge: Cambridge University Press, 1986).
105 See Bailey, *Of Bondage,* 1–25, where she has written engagingly on this issue; see also Garrett, "True Interest and the Affections," 38, 47–48.
106 Alexandra Shepard, *Accounting for Oneself: Worth, Status, and the Social Order in Early Modern England* (Oxford: Oxford University Press, 2015), 44.
107 Nirenberg, "Shakespeare's Jewish Questions," 92–93.
108 Quoted in Garrett, "True Interest and the Affections," 47.
109 Bailey, *Of Bondage,* 1.
110 Muldrew, *The Economy of Obligation,* 275.
111 Robert Bearman, *Shakespeare's Money: How Much Did He Make and What Did this Mean?* (Oxford: Oxford University Press, 2016), 176–178. Shakespeare's father was also imprisoned for debts owed (10–22).
112 Bailey, *Of Bondage,* 52.
113 Ibid., 145.
114 Ibid.
115 For the medieval and early modern history of property, specifically land, I have relied on the thorough research of David J. Seipp, "The Concept of Property in the Early Common Law," *Law and History Review* 12.1 (1994): 29–91. Seipp actually identifies a gap in the terminology of property in relation to land during the Year Book period, that language returning in the sixteenth century after being articulated in the treatises of Glanvill and Bracton centuries before (31–37).
116 Martha C. Howell, "The Language of Property in Early Modern Europe," in *The Culture of Capital: Properties, Cities, and Knowledge in Early Modern England*, ed. Henry Turner (New York: Routledge, 2002).
117 Ibid., 20. See also Seipp: "One did not say, 'this is my property,' as we use the term now. Rather, one said, 'I have property in it,' or 'the property of it is to (or with) me.' Property was thus a characteristic or attribute (or 'property') of a cow or a jewel or a sum of money, not a shorthand referent to the thing itself" ("The Concept of Property," 33).

118 Andreas Rahmatian, *Lord Kames: Legal and Social Theorist* (Edinburgh: University of Edinburgh Press, 2015), 229.

119 Seipp, "The Concept of Property," 51–57.

120 On the concept of dematerialized property, see Rahmatian, *Lord Kames*, 228–230.

121 Though medieval legislation prevented the sale of slaves in Venice, the practice was widespread, and slaves formed part of Venetian society up through the early seventeenth century with children being a popular choice. A fashion for black slave children, in particular, had already reached its height in the fifteenth century. The unmarked character of Shylock's slaves, however, suggest that they are fair-fleshed. On the multi-ethnic scene of slavery in early modern Venice, see E. Nathalie Rothman, "Contested Subjecthood: Runaway Slaves in Early Modern Venice," *Quaderni storici* 47.140 (2012): 425–441, Stephen Ortega, "Across Religious and Ethnic Boundaries: Ottoman Networks and Spaces in Early Modern Venice," *Mediterranean Studies* 18 (2009): 66–89, and Hugh Thomas, *The Slave Trade: The Story of the Atlantic Slave Trade 1440–1870* (New York: Simon & Schuster, 1997).

122 On whiteness as property in the American context, see Cheryl I. Harris, "Whiteness as Property," *Harvard Law Review* 106.8 (1993): 1707–1791.

123 John Wheeler, *A Treatise of Commerce* (London: John Harrison, 1601). Wheeler writes, for example, "for there is nothing in the world so ordinarie, and natural unto men, as to contract, truck, merchandise, and trafficke one with another" (6).

124 The apt phrase, "juridical absence," is taken from Drakakis, *The Merchant of Venice*, 35.

125 Loomba, *Shakespeare, Race, and Colonialism*, 22–24.

126 For discussions of nobility, morality, and external beauty, see James I, *Basilikon doron* and Thommaso Buoni, *Problemes of Beauty and All Humane Affections*, both in Loomba and Burton, *Race in Early Modern England*, 152–153, 165. In the play, Bassanio, for example, echoes the conventional assertions of noble blood and its social value even when he is penniless: "I freely told you all the wealth I had / Ran in my veins" (3.2.253–254).

127 Janet Adelman, *Blood Relations* (Chicago: University of Chicago Press, 2008), 79–84.

128 On the recurrence of this phrase in Shakespeare, see Clayton Koelb, "The Bonds of Flesh and Blood: Having it Both Ways in *The Merchant of Venice*," *Cardozo Studies in Law and Literature* 5.1 (1993): 107–113.

129 On the double sense of "property, see Seipp, "The Concept of Property," 33.

130 See "property," n.1.b. *OED Online*, Oxford University Press, March 2022, www.oed.com/view/Entry/152674.

131 Stephen Middleton, David R. Roediger, and Donald M Shaffer, eds., *The Construction of Whiteness: An Interdisciplinary Analysis of Race Formation and the Meaning of a White Identity* (Jackson: University Press of Mississippi, 2016), 3.

132 Allen, *Invention, vol. i*, 2nd ed., esp. 1–24.

CHAPTER 4

Hamlet
Playing in the Dark

Desiring Hamlet?

January 6, 2021, instantly became a date that students will rehearse in future classrooms; on that day rioters and insurrectionists invaded the US Capitol, foot soldiers of a falsehood about a presidential election that has its roots in what has been journalistically dubbed the Big Lie. In the following months, the combination of conspiracy theories hardwired to white extremism made clearer America's long, complicated, but predictable, history of racial animus, division, and violence. Renewed partisan voter suppression tactics mounted in multiple state legislatures, fraudulently declaring widespread voter fraud, comprise a bundle of attempts to disenfranchise nonwhite voters and protect the power of a white electorate. The Big Lie is ostensibly a massive, sprawling deception about election fraud, but its legitimizing cause is entangled in the country's original and enduring lie (lower case) about the superior and prevailing interests of whites, the lie of longer historical vintage about which Eddie S. Glaude Jr. has written lucidly. In *Begin Again*, Glaude notes: "The lie is more properly several sets of lies with a single purpose. If what I have called the 'value gap' is the idea that in America white lives have always mattered more than the lives of others, then the lie is a broad and powerful architecture of false assumptions by which the value gap is maintained."[1] He continues, "Taken as a whole, then, the lie is the mechanism that allows, and has always allowed, America to avoid facing the truth about its unjust treatment of black people and how it deforms the soul of the country."[2] Such a cultural and political analysis is pertinent for literary studies, for it explains the distorting reading and writing experiences that many have endured in the Western diaspora.

Thus, in her 1991 essay, "On Seeing England for the First Time," Jamaica Kincaid describes the longing for a country she had not seen or known except in the Caribbean colonial classroom, where dates and events of British history had been committed to lasting memory. Tests bore the repeated instruction, "Draw a map of England," a seemingly innocuous, admittedly tedious, act that was, she recalls as an adult, "a process that would result in my erasure, not my physical erasure, but my erasure all the same."[3] She had been taught the lie that English lives, white lives, mattered more than her own. Like Kincaid, I always felt that I had to like *Hamlet*, the most canonical play by that most canonical English author, a text whose philosophical and metaphysical cogitation stirred critics and whose eponymous hero seemed, by all accounts, a depressive melancholic. To echo Kincaid: What was there to love for someone like me or "all the people who look like me?"[4] I began to suspect that the cultivated admiration for Hamlet, like Kincaid's longing for England, was born of a consequential cultural exercise in blindness and forgetting, a tacit agreement not to probe too inquisitively, not to demand too insistently, or look closely at what one had to concede or trade away in order to happily, naïvely love *Hamlet*. I cannot help but suspect that, his pensive, world-weary skepticism aside, Hamlet's whiteness resides at the core of what has remained an unexamined racial desire.

The chapter title provides a clue to my view of Hamlet's whiteness. I allude to Toni Morrison's *Playing in the Dark: Whiteness and the Literary Imagination*, discussed in the introduction, a work that addresses how blackness is manipulated, toyed with, and exploited in the white imagination of literary authors, a form of experimentation in race that amounts to unrestrained play and the furtherance of a stable idea of cultural whiteness. Driven by his assumptions about race, Hamlet, as a white prince and dilletante of the theater, dabbles in the newly emergent stage representations of Africans and is thrust headlong into rationalizing his ambivalent relationship to blackness as he ponders revenge to set Denmark right again. Hamlet largely operates in the world of the theater, even as he intends to make an impact on the court, but insofar as real-life black people live and endure as a function of a system that plays in the dark, black life will continue to be disposable, raising the proposition again: "that in America white lives have always mattered more than the lives of others." The next chapter builds, therefore, on the groundwork laid here to insist more explicitly on how modern readers and scholars navigate blackness and race through Shakespeare and travel beyond the confines of art, theater, and criticism to contemplate the lived experience of black life in the United States today. My belief that *Hamlet* and *Othello* are bound in an overt racial dialogue – that they constitute a hitherto unacknowledged pair of race plays – provokes a substantial rethinking of their traditional relationship and place in Shakespeare's canon.

Hamlet and Modernity

Hamlet is not typically associated with race.[5] Yet this canonical play has a role in creating and circulating the idea of the Violent, Murderous Black Man that was emergent in Shakespeare's time and which, importantly, remains dangerously functional today. To this end, my examination of *Hamlet* concentrates not only on the play's often noted concern with theater, but more specifically on the staging of blackness, the latter emphasis being generally invisible to the history of the play's criticism.[6] In this view, I argue against the weight of critical tradition that has been hampered by a learned incapacity to be alert to Shakespeare's constant iterations of blackness and its cultural significance as race. Instead, modern critical assessments of the play have coalesced around the idea of inwardness based, in part, on the unfolding dramatic action and the prince protagonist's famous delay in avenging his father's murder. Between the Ghost's sonorous command for revenge, "Remember me" (1.5.91), and Hamlet's return from England when he happens upon the gravedigger, the prince is often buried in what he himself fears is retardant reflection, questioning the veracity of the Ghost's revelation of fratricide, deciding his just course of action, or debating the ethics of suicide.[7] Shakespeare's technical distillation of Hamlet's pensive propensity has been hailed by Stephen Greenblatt as the distinctive achievement in the playwright's creative development circa 1600: "By the turn of the century Shakespeare was poised to make an epochal breakthrough. He had perfected the means to represent inwardness."[8] G. R. Hibbard, the editor of the Oxford edition, opens his introduction with these claims: "Up to the end of the First World War and for some time thereafter, *Hamlet* was generally regarded as the greatest of all Shakespeare's plays, the most exciting, absorbing, and profound drama ever written," concluding that "Hamlet himself is part of the consciousness of the modern world."[9]

The scholarly consensus on inwardness in *Hamlet* has a traceable history, and Margreta de Grazia's account locates the critical engagement with Hamlet's "intransitive inwardness" in the Enlightenment period.[10] Interest among critics in the material effects of Hamlet's dispossession of the kingship, through a disrupted succession and loss of entitlement to the land, has been surpassed by other concerns. In fact, de Grazia argues, "Hamlet's disengagement from the land-driven plot is the very precondition of the modernity ascribed to him after 1800."[11] Uprooting Hamlet from the politics of land and monarchical succession unmoors him sufficiently to enable dematerialized readings of psychological inwardness. However, the elevation of inwardness as a defining feature of modernity occurs against a historical backdrop of material import that rivals de Grazia's return to monarchical succession. This emphasis on inwardness in *Hamlet* during the period of Enlightenment defense of the transatlantic slave trade and subjugation of black bodies suggests two points of note. First, the focus on inwardness represents a withdrawal from the externality of social instruments of exploitation and violence as well as the politics of oppression and white supremacy. Second, and relatedly, where African enslavement enacted the politics of high visibility through various forms of coercion and bodily discipline, talk of inwardness not only shies away from corporal matters, but also specifically sidesteps the racialized body for the safe, unraced, interior spaces of consciousness.

I propose that Hamlet's combination of inwardness and delay is centered in his ruminations on blackness, thereby challenging and redefining the constitutive claims of the play's so-called "epochal breakthrough." Achille Mbembe submits that a "critique of modernity will remain incomplete if we fail to grasp that the coming of modernity coincided with the appearance of the *principle of race* and the latter's slow transformation into the privileged matrix for techniques of domination, yesterday as today."[12] If Hamlet's famed inwardness does, in fact, constitute a racial consciousness, then the play's entire relationship to modernity must be radically reconsidered. Herein lies the irony: we now know that modernity is inconceivable without a proper grasp of the collateral effects of black enslavement, so Hibbard's and others' positioning of *Hamlet* as exemplary of modernity would be enhanced by understanding the play's contribution to the damning racial narratives of bodily disposability. *Hamlet*, I maintain, is relevant to the emergence of this "*principle of race*," yesterday and today. Therefore, if we are to persist in this implanting of Hamlet as modern man, we might wish to consider a more complex view in which the play's accommodation within modernity does not conveniently neutralize its entanglement with violence against black subjects and bodies. And the widespread tendency of critics to identify with Hamlet, epitomized in Hazlitt's famous embrace of the Danish prince, "It is *we* who are Hamlet,"[13] would demand renewed interrogation: In what sense, exactly, do critics share in the racial consciousness and debate that Hamlet exemplifies? Within the project of Shakespeare studies and the canonization of

Hamlet, this is the pivotal question posed to contemporary scholars and critics.

Revenge and Racial Resemblance

Hamlet's first words in the play introduce a thematic that locates the drama squarely within the revenge tragedy tradition. To Claudius's proposition, "my cousin Hamlet, and my son," the skeptical prince responds in the now famous aside, "A little more than kin, and less than kind" (1.2.64–65), immediately raising questions about resemblance and familial affinity between the two men. Claudius's marriage has, after all, illegitimately overdetermined their kinship relations. The Tables of Kinship and Affinity of 1560 and 1563 declared marriage to a brother's surviving widow to be incestuous, resulting in an excess of familial bonds signified in the phrase "more than kin," as Hamlet is nephew and stepson to his uncle–father.[14] The sheer aural, visual, and linguistic contingency of "kin/kind" elicits an inescapable resemblance that is rooted in the early modern idea of "race" that precisely signified questions of genealogy, lineage, and parentage.[15] As is often the case, Shakespeare sets out a specific template or schema as guide, and in Hamlet's statement, often regarded as enigmatic or riddling among critics, makes a metatheatrical invocation of resemblance on which revenge tragedy turns. In order to fulfill his mandate, the revenger must, for all practical purposes, become like the original perpetrator in committing to deceit, manipulation, and murder.

To compound matters, the play's motivating fratricide is executed by the ostensibly white Claudius whom the punning prince calls a "Moore," a fluid early modern term for African and black person, here instantly identified with acts of betrayal, violence, blood lust, and murder.[16] Incredulous that his mother would so soon forget his father, memorialized and elevated as "this faire Mountain," Hamlet in the closet scene exalts the deceased "faire" or white king in contrast to the murderous black "Moore," Claudius.[17] While many modern editions erase the racial content of Hamlet's language by using the lowercase "moor" or ignore the matter altogether in the textual commentary, both the Second Quarto and First Folio are explicit in capitalizing "Moore." To be sure, "fair mountain" and "moor" (3.4.66–67) confer through geographic verticality a value system that locates the whiteness of the deceased king over the low-lying blackness of the "Moore." Similarly, the agronomic poverty suggested by the marshland "moor" contrasts whiteness' supreme cultural nourishment, inherent in King Hamlet, with

Gertrude's decision to "batten" (3.4.67) or gorge herself on the "Moore," the excess in appetite allowing for the hypersexuality attributed to all forms of intimate racial congress. For editors and scholars to obviate the racial import of "Moore" is, further, to misconstrue Hamlet's evocation of King Hamlet, hailed twice as Hyperion, the sun god referenced only to intensify Claudius's contrastive blackness (1.2.140; 3.4.56). In fact, Hamlet's plangent appeal to his mother as he juxtaposes the pictures of the brothers, her two husbands, "Have you eyes?" (3.4.65), imagines a racial visuality that physically materializes Claudius's blackness. Hamlet's naming the deceitful, murderous Claudius a "Moore" betrays a sinister and fairly rapid evolution in early modern racial thinking: in Hamlet's mind, violence is already racialized and attached specifically to a black identity and population.

As a consequence, the play's complex proposition of resemblance and identity, "more than kin, and less than kind," comes into powerful analytical focus. "Revenge tragedy," writes Ronald Broude, "is usually understood to center around a figure who conceives himself to have been seriously wronged, and who, overcoming obstacles both within and outside himself, contrives eventually to exact retribution, becoming in the process as depraved as those by whom he has been wronged."[18] Arguably, revenge tragedy carries a moral injunction against behavioral identification that is, nevertheless, impossible to avoid, resulting, as James J. Condon remarks, in "the protagonist's gradual and increasingly problematic resemblance to the villain whom he stalks," and foregrounding the ethical dilemma inherent in the genre itself.[19] Moreover, as Tanya Pollard observes, "the revenge invariably exceeds the original crime, creating new victims, and the revenger is always eventually punished for taking the law into his or her own hands."[20] Having insisted not only on Claudius's criminality, but also specifically on the intercalation of racial blackness and violence, Hamlet has implicated himself fully, if rather uneasily, in a disturbing and damaging ideation of the "Moore." For Hamlet, the revenge genre's principle of resemblance leading to excess has special meaning, as it points to the racial identification attendant on the avenging prince, a recognition that must now become an unavoidable priority among scholars. While blackness impinges on Hamlet's identity, given the structural inevitability of the revenger's behavioral and moral destiny, his open hostility to Claudius, grounded in the deeply racial constructs of the period, suggests that Hamlet's career will be fraught with attraction and repulsion, the push and pull of doubt, ambiguity, and delay.

Hamlet and the New Black Drama

The prince's particular investment in the racial concept of the "Moore" can be contextualized further within revenge tragedy as that genre intersects with a set of emerging theatrical traditions. Usually identified as originating with Thomas Kyd's *The Spanish Tragedy* (c.1586–87), to be followed by such works as Shakespeare's *Titus Andronicus* (1594), *Hamlet* (1600), John Marston's *Antonio's Revenge* (1602), and Thomas Middleton's *The Revenger's Tragedy* (1606), revenge tragedy achieved considerable theatrical popularity through satisfying an audience's visceral emotions. While the actual name *revenge tragedy* is a twentieth-century invention, first used by A. H. Thorndike in 1902 and developed in a landmark study by Fredson Bowers in 1940, critics have discerned consistent patterns across a number of dramatic works: a targeted criminal offense that must be privately avenged generates sensational plots featuring deception, gruesome deaths, ghosts, skulls, madness, and horror.[21] In this view, revenge drama appealed to the basic human instinct for justice and also spoke to the lingering frustrations of an older cultural order that had relied on familial blood feud or individual responsibility for self-protection. Once described among critics as a literary embarrassment, revenge tragedy has been reimagined in historical terms that argue the genre's relevance to the increasingly centralized European monarchies that outlawed private revenge as the prerogative of the state.[22] So, revenge tragedy, in insisting on private vengeance, dramatizes the ineffectiveness or plain failure of modern centralized systems of justice. The plays' European, often Catholic, settings, contrasted the political mayhem and disarray in foreign courts with the stability of the Protestant English Crown. Wendy Griswold argues, therefore, that revenge tragedy had a distinct ideological function where "stable government, English superiority, and Protestantism were mutually reinforcing."[23]

I propose approaching *Hamlet* to reexamine and expand these standard theories of revenge tragedy by revisiting the genre's trademark mix of incandescent, hate-fueled anger and excessive, bloody acts of vengeance in the context of the emerging "black drama" of the period. For Stevie Simkin, "explicitly staged violence is a vital constitutive feature of revenge tragedy. Furthermore, there is a general tendency in the invention and representation of such acts of violence to accentuate the grotesque, the macabre, and the horrific."[24] For example, Piero, the criminal protagonist of Marston's *Antonio's Revenge*, arrives onstage as a startling and emblematic figure of the genre's blood-soaked excesses: "*his arms bare, smeared in blood, a poniard in one hand bloody*" (*S.D.* at the opening of 1.1).[25] Violent criminals and avengers in the group of plays typically included in the genre are white, although that racial identification has not traditionally been explicitly featured in the genre's poetics. Despite the substantial scholarship on revenge tragedy, the question of white violence has generally remained unaddressed by scholars of this genre, partly because the villainous acts performed and avenged are construed as private interactions, the result of a contemptable yet individual aberration, the unfortunate, even unnatural, behavior of just one person.[26]

A fuller assessment would admit readers' systemic failure to see whiteness due to the epistemological conditioning toward white invisibility that is a function of the racial blind spot. By contrast, Hamlet's attribution of violence to a group or type of black person as a criminal agitator suggests the moral condemnation of an entire black population. As such, blackness supersedes specific acts of violence to become by itself, "the grotesque, the macabre, and the horrific," in the process eroding the difference between the doer and the deed. Understanding *Hamlet*'s complicity in the portrayal of black men situates the play in an entirely different literary and cultural aesthetic than has previously been recognized, and complicates Griswold's contention that revenge drama argues political and national superiority while ignoring her formulation's white racial premise. Promoting violence as the cultural bailiwick of black men proves exculpatory for white criminality, especially when individual, aberrant behavior is minimized against the greater whole of an altogether superior white Protestant state.

Hamlet owes much to and intersects with what I have described as the new "black drama" of a few years earlier. We are, of course, familiar with Shakespeare's now iconic *Othello*, but that work is part of a larger response to the racial impact of black persons on the consciousness of English citizens. The growing numbers of black Africans secured as personal servants and court musicians amplified their cultural reputation as display objects fulfilling white fantasies of material and symbolic self-aggrandizement.[27] Civic pageants, celebrating London's economic fortunes deriving from international commerce, often featured African figures paraded in London's streets, barely acknowledged as trading partners, but rather displayed as embodiments of commercial products destined for the English marketplace.[28] But it was in the commercial playhouses where the idea of black Africans as untrustworthy, violent, and dangerous flourished at the intersection of commerce, entertainment, and audience demand. *Hamlet*, I argue, offers a salient insight into this phenomenon of the white consumption of blackness, and the unique propensity of this aesthetic and commercial encounter to produce narrow racial perceptions that serve whiteness's self-interests.

When the "negro Muly Hamet" of George Peele's *The Battle of Alcazar* stepped onto the stage in 1589, audiences in the mimetic theater had their first real taste of the racialized, threatening black man: "Black in his look and bloody in his deeds, / And in his shirt, stained with a cloud of gore, / Presents himself with naked sword in hand."[29] The combination "Black in his look and bloody in his deeds" established a racial paradigm that would have an enduring stage legacy: the seamless integration of the literal and connotative meaning of a black man's skin and the evil that colors him within. Medieval drama had set the stage for Muly Hamet by making a firm connection between blackness and evil that, with the demise of the miracle and mystery plays in the sixteenth century, evolved into black stage characters that bore the moral and morphological burden of their medieval archetypes.[30] The souls of the damned, represented in miracle plays by actors painted or dressed in black clothing, or the fallen angels in mystery plays, blackened forever to denote their doomed plight, found new theatrical life in the perfidious black Moor of Peele's play and his stage successors. Shortly after *Alcazar*'s debut, Shakespeare's *Titus Andronicus* gave audiences a spectacular and deadly concoction of devilish ingenuity in "Aaron the Moor" (4.2.53), who announces his theatrical ancestry with vengeful relish: "If there be devils, would that I were a devil, / To live and burn in everlasting fire, / So I might have your company in hell / But to torment you with my bitter tongue" (5.1.147–150). He is explicitly referred to as "this incarnate devil" because of his wanton acts of cruelty and destruction (5.1.40). In the popular theater, the idea of black men construed as living, human devils elaborated color identification to declare racialized blackness as a sign of abject inhumanity unworthy of civil inclusion. Already, the English national Protestant mythology found its antitype in the diabolical black Moor. Such a figure was destined to serve as both a functional contrast for the English state and a cultural depository for all social and spiritual ills that, if not rhetorically and politically dislodged, would otherwise compromise the national identity.

Thus, whereas the medieval legacy was a fully articulated epistemology of blackness as diabolical and evil, the early modern dramatic evolution and achievement was to ground these moral categories in concrete human flesh and personalities, however consistently repugnant and homicidal these black subjects appear. In *Titus*, set in the imperial wars of ancient Rome against the barbarians, murder, rape, human dismemberment, and deceit number among Aaron's weapons in his resistance to his Roman captors: "Vengeance in my heart, death in my hand, / Blood and revenge are hammering in my head" (2.2.38–39). Arguably, Shakespeare provides Aaron with a political reason that explains his revolt against his imperial captors. His memorable defense of his threatened baby, who bears the "seal" of the father's blackness "stamped in his face," is encapsulated in the provocative racial query: "is black so base a hue?" (4.2.129, 74). At the same time, blackness as difference was being cultivated, in part, to distract from the violence of the white Andronici whose revenge plot animates the drama. Thus, the theater's delight in sensational representations of wanton blackness has racial and political purpose and can be intuited from Aaron's many repeated, self-conscious assertions of his villainy: "'Twill vex thy soul to hear what I shall speak: / For I must talk of murders, rapes, and massacres, / Acts of black night, abominable deeds" (5.1.62–64). The frisson of black danger experienced from the safe space of the playhouse audience had a far more enduring and damaging power in lodging denigrating notions of blackness, contrasted with positive affirmations of whiteness, in the early modern English mind. Black and white were groomed, from an English perspective, to inhabit different, seemingly incompatible but codependent worlds.

Lust's Dominion (1599) and *All's Lost by Lust* (1619) perpetuate the legacy of the ruthless black killer in Eleazar and Mulymumen, respectively, both dramas set against the Moors' 700-year occupation of Spain, ending in the Reconquista of 1492. Once again, the context provides a historical anchor for the ruthless black men that would threaten political anarchy for white, Christian Europe. In *Lust's Dominion*, Eleazar the Moor manipulates and murders his way to the Spanish throne with homicidal efficiency: he tricks the Queen Mother into killing Philip, her son, murders her, and finally stabs King Ferdinando.[31] In *All's Lost by Lust*, Mulymumen's amorous intentions are rejected by the Spanish general's daughter Jacinta, who disdains and fears his blackness: "base African, / Thine inside's blacker then thy sooty skin" (5.5.14–15).[32] Mulymumen's revenge is, therefore, motivated by lust and racial aggrievement: he blinds the general and later tricks him into becoming the "fatall butcher" who stabs his own daughter to death (5.5.181). Consistent with the plays' anti-Spanish bent, the Moors are deployed to suggest a politically vulnerable Spain susceptible to a horde of bloodthirsty black invaders – presumably unlike the superior, savvy English. Along with *Titus Andronicus*, these two plays underwent multiple revivals and adaptations that reinforced and legitimized the cold-blooded black killer as their most topical cultural legacy.[33]

Claudius's indebtedness to racialized black violence is only one important starting point for examining *Hamlet*'s hitherto unexplored role in this theatrical and cultural evolution of a disturbingly violent racial theatrical type. Among the pioneering early modern race scholars, Eldred Jones, Elliot Tokson, Anthony Gerard Barthelemy, and Jack D'Amico have documented the black drama and the negative stage representations of Africans and Moors in the period, but placing *Hamlet* within this theatrical history opens up dramatically new critical vistas for the play.[34] From the beginning, therefore, Hamlet's provocative phrase, "more than kin, less than kind," is charged with proleptic power and racial meaning, saying much about a racial destiny, the terms of which he defines. Imbued with dramatic irony, therefore, his riposte, "less than kind," anticipates his career as revenger complicated by his own racial conception of black persons as violently cruel – not kind. While proving Claudius's guilt, Hamlet will, in fact, test his own tolerance for identifying with violent forms of blackness that have a historical provenance in the cultural laboratory of the early modern English theater.

Black Pyrrhus

Hamlet is self-consciously metatheatrical, with its multiple verbal references to "show, act, play," as Maynard Mack pointed out in the 1950s.[35] Well over half a century later, Lyell Asher maintains that the several instances of the word "stage" constitute the most in any individual Shakespeare play, making *Hamlet* "among other things a play about playing, a show of shows."[36] As a "connoisseur of plays, playing, and playgoers,"[37] Hamlet is deeply aware of theater's purpose, conventions, and contemporary debates. Hamlet's reference to the spatial architecture of the theater alludes to the innovation in permanent structures dedicated for playing since 1576, citing the newly built Globe Theater that Shakespeare's company, the Chamberlain's Men, occupied in 1599 (2.2.283–286). It would seem that the idea of the theater's participation in something noteworthy or transformational is embedded in the play's language of spectacular performativity. In his conversations with Rosencrantz and Guildenstern, Hamlet is intrigued by news of the "late innovation" (2.2.308–309) in the city, the growing popularity of the boy actors pitted against the adult companies for market share of the audience, which has apparently precipitated the arrival of the traveling company of players in Elsinore. This so-called war of the theaters has become an editorial fixture (2.2.308–333).[38] Still, while much discussion has centered on the purported internecine theatrical rivalry in the city theaters, scholars have not paid sufficient attention to the rhetorical and dramatic effect of the subsequent theatrical fare, initiated by Hamlet himself, as Shakespeare's particular "innovation" to which we must attend: the play's disturbing conjunction of revenge, violence, and blackness.[39]

The developments unfolding in the distant city are important only insofar as they introduce and amplify the conceptual framework of competitive innovation that Shakespeare locates in Hamlet's interaction with the newly arrived acting troupe. The visit of the players is, therefore, the play's centerpiece. Twice, Hamlet explicitly states that a theatrical presentation will serve to extract the truth of Claudius's deeds, including his memorable objective, "The play's the thing / Wherein I'll catch the conscience of the king" (3.1.557–558) and his invitation to Horatio to observe closely during the "play tonight before the king" (3.2.65). Structurally, such statements foreground the traveling company's arrival and performance at Elsinore enough to justify a fresh reassessment of these scenes. In particular, when Hamlet references a black Pyrrhus during his exchange with the First Player, we recognize in his racial insistence an important act of theatrical citation: the Violent or Murderous Black Man of relatively recent theatrical vintage. Moreover, Hamlet's improvisational tendencies, already evident in his self-theatricalizing "antic disposition" (1.5.179), explain his choice of a black Pyrrhus as his most bold, innovative example of self-dramatization through verbal blackface and racial drag.

The history of critical commentary on the Player's Speech ranges from indifference to doubt concerning its artistic relevance. Writing in 1953, Andrew J. Green remarked that "recent criticism of Dover Wilson, Granville-Barker, Kittredge, Stoll, J. Q. Adams, and others is as oblivious to the dramatic purpose of the passage as is the older."[40] For Arthur Johnston, almost a decade later, the question remains as true then as it does today: "what function does the speech have in the play?"[41] The source of the Player's Speech is Aeneas's tale to Dido in Book 2 of Virgil's *Aeneid*, with a contemporaneous treatment in Christopher Marlowe's *Dido, Queen of Carthage* (2.1.213–264) published in 1594.[42] The Player's Speech captures the epic scene of the fall of Troy when Pyrrhus, seeking revenge for his dead father Achilles, goes on a murderous rampage that climaxes in the brutal slaughter of old Priam, king of Troy, leaving Hecuba, the old king's wife, in inconsolable grief. The First Player delivers, therefore, a fairly faithful rendition of antecedent texts (2.2.426–476). However, the section that often goes by the name of the Player's Speech is actually divided into two, with Hamlet speaking the first and, as it turns out, original part that marks

Shakespeare's innovation in this history of telling the famed story of Troy along with its narrative of imperial decline and rebirth. The tendency among critics to pass directly to the so-called Player's Speech and give much less attention to Hamlet's section results in passing over that pivotal, innovative portion that deals with his fantasies of blackness and race.

Eager to reconnect with the players whom he had encountered in one of his earlier theatrical forays, Hamlet cannot wait for the formal performance and asks for an immediate display of their acting craft: "Come, give us a taste of your quality, come, a passionate speech" (2.2.423–424). He suggests a speech that he had heard one of the players deliver once before: "'twas Aeneas' tale of Dido, and thereabout of it especially where he speaks of Priam's slaughter" (2.2.437–438). Hamlet begins:

> 'The rugged Pyrrhus, like th'Hyrcanian beast' –
> It is not so. It began with Pyrrhus –
> 'The rugged Pyrrhus, he whose sable arms,
> Black as his purpose, did the night resemble
> When he lay couchèd in the ominous horse,
> Hath now this dread and black complexion smeared
> With heraldry more dismal. Head to foot
> Now in total gules, horridly tricked
> With blood of fathers, mothers, daughters, sons,
> Baked and impasted with the parching streets,
> That lend a tyrannous and damnèd light
> To their vile murders. Roasted with wrath and fire,
> And thus o'er sized with coagulate gore,
> With eyes like carbuncles, the hellish Pyrrhus
> Old grandsire Priam seeks.'
>
> (2.2.441–455)

Hamlet's choice of theatrical speech focuses on Pyrrhus, the ferocious killing machine of classical literature whose deadly excesses are central to his story. Also named Neoptolemus by ancient writers, Pyrrhus, meaning fiery or red-haired, is bent on a bloody rampage to avenge the death of his father Achilles at the hands of the Trojans. Exiting the baleful wooden horse, he lay such waste to the entire city that he is covered with thick clots of blood that make him appear monstrously oversized "with coagulate gore" as he moves through the burning streets searching for Priam. The relevance of Hamlet's choice of subject, a son avenging his father's murder, is immediately clear for the audience who knows of the Ghost's call for revenge. Through his insistence on not only citing, but also reciting and enacting this legendary moment in literary historiography, Hamlet imagines himself as Pyrrhus abandoning delay in toppling Claudius in this Virgilian fantasy of gore.

Importantly, the descriptions of Pyrrhus from Homer, Virgil, Euripides through to Marlowe are consistent regarding this ultimate warrior: there is no mention of his blackness, whereas in Shakespeare's account, Pyrrhus is a black, grotesquely bloody avenger who far surpasses in brutality any ruthless black man early modern audiences had seen. Classical writers, in fact, emphasized both the physical appearance and the fierce Greek's fair, good looks. In *The Odyssey*, he is praised by Odysseus as the "most handsome man / I ever saw, next to great Memnon," and in contrast to the quaking warriors about to exit the Trojan horse, the narrator avers, "Not your handsome boy! / I never saw his face grow pale."[43] Notably, at the close of the bloody Trojan conflict, Homer insists on the corporeal detail: that Neoptolemus's beautiful body is left unscarred and "unhurt by all the skirmishes / endured in war."[44] In *Andromache*, Euripides tells the story of Neoptolemus's ambush and murder at the shrine at Delphi, during which his "whole fair form was rent with terrible wounds."[45] Even in Neoptolemus's death, writers highlight his fair beauty, his white appearance, which stands in sharp distinction to Hamlet's somatically black avenger, whom the lethargic prince seeks to appropriate for himself.

Much of the play's criticism has either avoided discussing this black Pyrrhus passage altogether or ignored Shakespeare's vivid details, thereby producing a whitewashed or race-neutral analysis. Even among those who discuss the Pyrrhus figure, the result is the same, as if a racial blind spot has effected textual erasure.[46] Shakespeare's rhetoric of heraldry is, of course, fitting for the warrior son of Achilles, but its overlapping meanings with racial blackness have elicited a narrow, scholarly preoccupation with the technical and specialized system of armorial wear at the expense of plainly visible corporal markers of race. Several terms in the passage denote heraldic designs and colors: *sable*, *trick'd*, *gules* are commonly glossed by editors, and de Grazia also adds to the list *carbuncles* and *gore*.[47] She concludes that the "armorial assignment – the result of enemy bloodshed rather than his own noble blood – transforms the avenger into a stalking escutcheon. As if in recognition of his cold-blooded savagery, he achieves a coat of arms intended as the insignia of chivalry."[48] But I would argue, in addition, that for Shakespeare, and for Hamlet, the traveling company consciously reinvents the classical story to produce a black-skinned Pyrrhus, "whose sable arms, / Black as his purpose, did the night resemble." Meaning black, generally, as well as the specific color in heraldry, the term "sable" describes the skin color of Pyrrhus and at the same time employs the heraldic system of colors as a proto-racial identity category.[49] That is, the heraldic color sable represents a code that systematizes lineal descent and defines familial belonging in the same way that early modern "race" signified lineage, genealogy, and bloodline.

The words, "whose sable arms, / Black as his purpose, did the night resemble," also belong to a discourse of racial ontology that fixated on the universal malignity of black skin. Like the language used by Jacinta in her rejection of Mulymumen in *All's Lost by Lust*, "base African, / Thine inside's blacker then thy sooty skin," the descriptors for Pyrrhus are consistent with a familiar unitarian ontology that understood the material body as a reliable and cogent sign of spiritual, mental, and moral darkness. The equation of skin and what lies within connects Pyrrhus's black "purpose" with its external manifestation in his "sable arms." Befitting the plot of the Trojan horse, the Greeks infiltrate the city of Troy at night, when, according to Shakespeare's version, Pyrrhus's black skin that "did the night resemble" functions as a quasi-cloaking device for this Trojan invader. Once launched on his path of vengeful excess, however, his body is physically altered by the sheer mass of clotted blood it accumulates, and the black and red combined are stark emblems of the life and career of the early modern black killer. Cutting a path through the streets of Troy, black Pyrrhus presents a freakish picture that elicits the most familiar racialized emotion: fear. He is a man whose textually explicit "black complexion" refers to his physical appearance, not internal humoral constitution,[50] and could logically inspire "dread" similar to Brabantio's expected reaction from his daughter to Othello: "a thing," he warns, "to fear, not delight" (1.2.90).

Upon hearing from Rosencrantz that he, along with Guildenstern, passed the players who were making their way toward the castle to "offer [Hamlet] service" (2.2.116), Hamlet immediately begins to rehearse some of the character types he might expect to find in their repertory: the Adventurous Knight, the Lover, the Humorous Man, the Clown, the Lady (2.2.299–303). Earlier in the same scene, the audience has just witnessed in Polonius another theatrical type, the Foolish Old Man (2.2.117–120). This foregrounding of theatrical types constitutes the helpful and requisite frame for Hamlet's selection of a scene for the players' impromptu performance, where he has chosen to highlight the Murderous or Violent Black Man as a relatively new, crowd pleasing, but devastating theatrical type. Shakespeare ensures that the audience pays attention to the unfolding of this theatrical type by carefully disrupting Hamlet's rhetorical delivery through "misquotation."[51] Deciding on the speech he wants to hear performed by the First Player, Hamlet launches into reciting from memory the speech he has heard only once before: "'The rugged Pyrrhus, like th'Hyrcanian beast' – / It is not so." He pauses, corrects himself, supposedly having altered the opening of the original through faulty memory, before restarting with the proper version: "The rugged Pyrrhus, he whose sable arms did the night resemble." Misquotation, pause, and correction are strategically introduced disruptors to mark Shakespeare's borrowing and unique departures from classical sources to write a new racial project.

In a companion passage from Virgil, the epic simile explains the explosive arrival of Pyrrhus at Troy's gates, like a snake erupting from winter's sod, in shining armor – a dazzling contrast to Shakespeare's black avenger:

> There at the very edge of the front gates
> springs Pyrrhus, son of Achilles, prancing in arms,
> aflash in his shimmering brazen sheath like a snake
> buried the whole winter long under frozen turf,
> swollen to bursting, fed full on poisonous weeds
> and now it springs to light.[52]

Hamlet's error in the opening lines echoes the epic simile, calling attention to the classical pedigree of the moment cited, but also signaling the deliberate Shakespearean alteration. Shakespeare gestures to the epic simile only to dismiss that classical architecture to allow Pyrrhus to appear instead in his own early modern guise and type. Hamlet does not refer to Virgil's snake but to the notoriously ferocious breed of tiger, native of the region south of the Caspian Sea, and replaces the "Hyrcanian beast" with "sable arms" as the descriptor for Pyrrhus.[53] The purpose of the linguistic substitutions is clear: the ancient beast has its early modern equivalent in the savage, sable-armed black man. Into that edited, vacant linguistic place of the "Hyrcanian beast" enters Shakespeare's Pyrrhus, a cultural figure whose blackness is alone sufficient to speak to the danger, ferocity, and beastliness of the Murderous or Violent Black Man type.

Hamlet's striking verbal hesitation structurally emulates Pyrrhus's pause, featured only in Shakespeare, sword held aloft as if frozen in time before its momentous dispatch of king Priam, punctuating the Trojan imperial collapse.

> for lo, his sword,
> Which was declining on the milky head
> Of reverend Priam seemed i'th'air to stick.
> So as a painted tyrant, Pyrrhus stood,

And like a neutral to his will and matter,
Did nothing.

(2.2.435–440)

Only some twenty lines later does Pyrrhus "make malicious sport / In mincing with his sword" Priam's limbs (2.2.471–472). Shakespeare highlights the primordial slaying of Priam that emblematizes the fall of Troy through this freeze-frame, a verbal ekphrasis, of the "painted tyrant" etching a black Pyrrhus indelibly on our consciousness as we attend the final deadly blow. Jonathan Bate affirms that Virgil's and Marlowe's accounts of Priam's slaughter are notably swift and efficient in contrast to the dramatic pause and slow unfolding, "the particular Shakespearean innovation that is without precedent in either" the *Aeneid* or *Dido*.[54] In Virgil, Pyrrhus drags the aged ruler from the altar, "twisting Priam's hair / in his left hand, his right hand sweeping forth his sword – / a flash of steel – he buries it hilt-deep in the king's flank" (2.683–685). Likewise, Marlowe's narrative describes Priam, collapsed under the weight of his own wielded sword, promptly disemboweled by Pyrrhus: "Then from the navel to the throat at once / He ripp'd old Priam" (2.1.255–256). Hamlet's verbal pause, which stylistically punctuates the conversion of the Virgilian original into the sable-armed Pyrrhus, therefore, parallels Priam's murder in symbolic potency: rhetorically, his figuration of a Murderous Black Man type is as momentous for the future of English theater and culture as Priam's death for the fate of imperial Troy. Blackness, one might say, is the new early modern epic subject.

The dramatic narrative of black Pyrrhus is Hamlet's choice, but, importantly, this speech that he has memorized already belonged in the players' repertory. The Violent or Murderous Black Man is not Hamlet's invention, as has been established in the dramatic literature, dating back eleven years earlier, to Peele. Shakespeare, in making it clear that this figure already exists in the itinerant players' catalog, helps us understand something about the cultural history of the theater and the growing popularity of the black man type. Black Pyrrhus now belongs to the roster of theatrical types Hamlet articulates. This particular figure is interesting because it had not previously existed in the English theater nor had the dramatic ubiquity of the Adventurous Knight or the Lover in the preceding centuries. *Hamlet* helps us understand, however, that it is now a recurring figure and sign of early modernity, one that is poised to extend beyond the narrative limits of character type to pose serious and culturally transformative questions about personal and national identity mediated through blackness and race.

Lucianus and the Traveling Company's Black Repertory

Hamlet's collaboration with the players on *The Murder of Gonzago* brings into focus the company's dramatic repertory in which recurring black roles of the Violent Black Man type have prominence. Inquiring after the identity of the players who are reportedly coming specifically to offer Hamlet their service, the theater-aficionado prince is informed by Rosencrantz, "Even those you were wont to take such delight in, the tragedians of the city" (2.2.304–305). Hamlet welcomes them collectively as "good friends," and the First Player as "my old friend" (2.2.386) who has grown a beard since their last encounter. To the young male actor who plays female roles, Hamlet observes that "your ladyship is nearer to heaven than when I saw you last by the altitude of a chopine" (2.2.388–389), as a commentary on some inches gained in height. Having patronized their entertainments on multiple previous occasions, Hamlet is intimately acquainted with the troupe, the actors, their likely roles, and, importantly, their standard play offerings including the company's little-known Pyrrhus extract that he has heard recited, but the play itself "was never acted, or if it was, not above once" (2.2.395–396) since it failed to garner popular success despite being lauded by the intelligentsia. Thus, when Hamlet makes his request for the royal performance, he references a second work that is already part of the company's repertory: "Dost thou hear me old friend, can you play *The Murder of Gonzago*?" (2.2.490–491).

Hamlet's query concerns the players' readiness to perform the *Murder*, especially considering their current touring status that requires an economy of equipment and properties, comparable to what Arthur F. Kinney describes as the "reduced repertory" of London traveling companies.[55] Given a company's business and artistic infrastructure – in-house playwrights as well as individually purchased plays; actors in specialist tragic, comedic, or female roles; costumes and properties re-used from one production to another – some overlap among groups of plays is likely to pertain. Roslyn L. Knutson argues for such filiation when she subjects the albeit incomplete evidence of theater companies' repertories to analysis: "theater historians are looking within and across lines of company ownership and giving new attention to repertory items that share such issues as politics, international trade and exploration, social governance, gender and sexuality, labor, religion, science, and/or domestic relations."[56] For Hamlet, the local expert looking within the traveling company's repertory, the overlapping issue is blackness and race. He is that early modern theater historian, to use Knutson's frame, who perceives significant racial content within and across the Pyrrhus speech and *The Murder of Gonzago*. To this play that "is the image of a murder done in Vienna" (3.2.216–217), Hamlet's addition of "a speech of some dozen or sixteen lines" (2.2.493–494) of his own invention highlights the collaborative congruency that sets in relief the racial symmetry between the two pieces from the players' catalog of works.

During Hamlet's staged performance of *Murder*, the Player Queen's protestations of eternal fidelity deliberately target Gertrude, but the entry of Lucianus – Claudius's stage alter ego – replays the ideology of a black Pyrrhus in this second black murderer's menacing opening lines: "Thoughts black, hands apt, drugs fit, and time agreeing, / Confederate season, else no creature seeing" (3.2.231–232). My critical assessment offered here is that Lucianus is not an unraced murderer, a mere plot feature of Hamlet's staged, heuristic tragedy, and Shakespeare's choice of the word "[c]onfederate" has conceptual value for early modern race. The evocation of midnight as a season confederate with acts so evil that they are suitably obscured by darkness complements the familiar racial marker of Lucianus's blackness. In *All's Lost by Lust* Mulymumen, we recall, is denounced as "base African, / Thine inside's blacker then thy sooty skin," while in *Titus Andronicus* Shakespeare's Moor declares about himself: "Aaron will have his soul black like his face" (3.1.206). The unitarian construct of Africans that equates black skin with what lies within, positing a dubious moral equivalence of outside and inside, extends to evil acts and antisocial behavior, as in Muly Hamet's descriptor in *Alcazar*: "Black in his look and bloody in his deeds." Shakespeare embeds in Lucianus's opening words what is, in effect, a tripartite paradigm propagated by English playwrights: "Thoughts black, hands apt"; the latter phrase "hands apt" already the external referent to an internal state, also connoting the additional idea of black deeds. Lucianus fits the pattern of black men on the stage whose internality and physical appearance are confederate with their immoral acts.

Consider that in her analysis of the Pyrrhus speech, Gail Paster argues that bodies have a reciprocal relationship to the world, that internality and environmental reality are modeled on similar metaphorical systems resulting in "mutual permeation."[57] The ontological effect is "one of *transumption*, a rhetorical figure that designated both the actual transfer of qualities from one place to another and the metaphorical transfer of the terms."[58] Paster, however, does not make the important next move, which is to consider the implications for the externality of skin, the median in the repeated early modern tripartite construction of blackness. Shakespeare does, and the particularities of the poison Lucianus transports onstage immediately build on his opening words ("Thoughts black, hands apt") to evoke a somatic *transumption*: "Thou mixture rank, of midnight weeds collected, / With Hecat's ban thrice blessed, thrice infected" (3.2.233–234). Signaling the ecology or external environment of action, the "weeds" gathered at midnight, the darkest hour, are also "infected" – from the Latin *inficere* meaning "dark" or "black" – to mirror Lucianus's internal, corporal, and environmental conditions – as the play states, "thrice infected." Not only is Lucianus dramaturgically conceived as black, I submit, but Shakespeare's chiastic linguistic patterning further argues for a parallel between Pyrrhus's "sable arms, / Black as his purpose" and Lucianus's "Thoughts black, hands apt" to highlight the symmetry between the two black characters that Hamlet selects from the players' repertory.

Discussion of a black repertory requires an understanding of the material means of theatrical personation. In Kinney's historical reconstruction of traveling theater companies, players carried "costumes, properties, and playscripts, covering perhaps 25 miles a day."[59] But performing blackness also required transporting specialized properties and cosmetics for disguising white skin. Immediately before Lucianus arrives onstage, Hamlet addresses him from the sidelines, urging the actor in language that constitutes a critical piece of racial evidence that has gone largely unnoticed: "Begin, murderer. Pox, leave thy damnable faces and begin" (3.2.228–229). Addressing the growth of performance studies, Cherrell Guilfoyle remarks that in "modern criticism much attention has been paid to the problem of how Shakespeare's plays were staged in his own time, and how this might illumine our understanding of the works." Guilfoyle continues, "it is apparent that Shakespeare used stagecraft as well as poetry to gain his dramatic effects."[60] Robert Lublin argues, in fact, that "stagecraft" is often implied in the language that serves as a performance blueprint for *Hamlet*: "Apparel, cosmetics, color, and accoutrements appear in the dialogue and stage directions of virtually every scene in Shakespeare's longest play. These references are more than literary allusions. They are also markers that hint at the way Shakespeare's original production was staged, seen, and understood in the early modern English theater."[61]

It is noteworthy, therefore, that modern editors including Philip Edwards, G. R. Hibbard, and Robert S. Miola have avoided glossing the statement, "Begin, murderer. Pox, leave thy damnable faces and begin," thereby eliding or ignoring its racially performative import.[62] Hamlet is a notoriously fastidious stage manager, offering sharp directives to the players about actorly comportment, diction, and gestural style: "Speak the speech I pray you as I pronounced it to you, trippingly on the tongue, but if you mouth it as many of our players do, I had as lief the town-crier spoke my lines. Nor do not saw the air too much with your hand thus, but use all gently" (3.2.1–4). So, Hamlet's charge to the actor playing Lucianus to cease making "damnable faces," that is, stop rehearsing the exaggerated stock-in-trade stage looks, is of a piece with his mandates on acting decorum. Shakespeare's use of the racially resonant "damnable faces" makes it clear that the actor's rehearsed facial set-pieces belong to the specific category of the overwrought facial contortions of the stage Moor that relies on the widespread assumption of devils as proto-racial Moors. The phrase "damnable faces" thus denotes the exaggerated expressions of the white actor that would be magnified through the application of face-blackening agents.

From medieval acting traditions that required white men to impersonate black devils and damned souls to the early modern human types like Aaron and Othello, stage practice demanded various skin-darkening methods. The first and probably most intuitively recognizable prosthetic effect of racialization in the early modern theater is the direct application of substances to the skin. Thus, the use of charcoal or soot is conveyed in Aaron's well-known description as a "coal-black Moor." Even more pertinent here is the denigration of Eleazar in Dekker's *Lust's Dominion* as having "damnation dy'd upon his flesh" (5.2.19–20) and, from the same play, two white men, Philip and Hortenzo, the enemies of the Eleazar, who apply the "oil of hell" (*S.D.* 5.3.22) to their skins to disguise as Moors. The metaperformative language, "damnation dy'd upon his flesh," substantively echoes Lucianus's "damnable faces," and awareness of this performative tradition allows modern students of the play to know that Lucianus, like his analog Pyrrhus, is black. Add to this a range of terms throughout the play suggesting sullying, rubbing, daubing, smudging, and smirching, as Patricia Parker has meticulously detailed for *Hamlet*,[63] and a highly visible, dramaturgically infused vocabulary of skin-coloring appears. Earlier, we are told that Pyrrhus "Hath now this dread and black complexion smeared / With heraldry more dismal," where the term "smeared" in conjunction with the somatic referent "complexion" is consistent with technologies of racial mimicry. The First Player's description of Pyrrhus as the "painted tyrant," therefore, takes on additional meaning, evoking the language of metatheater to make legible the company's practice of skin painting to effect racial imitation in performance. *Hamlet* enforces the inseparability of narrative, performance, and prosthetic realization in Hamlet's and the company's imagining of blackness and race.

The examples from *Lust's Dominion* are, indeed, very useful for the theater historian insofar as they dramatize, quite self-consciously, the challenges and solutions of white actors impersonating Africans: dyeing, staining, or applying topical ointments to the body to create the effect of black skin condemned as damned. The name Lucianus in *Hamlet* provokes a similar set of effects: meaning light, it calls out the irony of a white or light-skinned actor who is blackened to play a murdering Moor and activates the deep cultural reference to the fall of Lucifer, the prelapsarian son of light, into the darkness that early modern racial ideology assigns Moors. Given Hamlet's plan to entrap Claudius through the staged performance, audiences anticipate the theatrical excitement of the moment that will replay the rumored experiences of guilty spectators who spontaneously "proclaimed their malefactions" (2.2.545). The difference in Hamlet's production for modern readers and playgoers is that Claudius is forced to confront his own blackness in a striking stage image. Lucianus's emblematic theatrical function – white name/black deeds and skin – accords with the duality Hamlet attaches to Claudius, the white uncle, turned black "Moore." By having a black Lucianus murder the sleeping duke, Hamlet uses the racial spectacle not only to pique Claudius's conscience, but also to materialize the ideological argument he has nursed throughout: Claudius is the murdering "Moore." Criminality and racial blackness conflate dangerously, making African identity, signaled in the category "Moore," the baseline for moral depravity.

Black Hamlet

Hamlet's strategic staging of the black murderer Lucianus is consistent with his revenge agenda to expose the king's guilty conscience. But why is he equally drawn to a black Pyrrhus? Why, after all this time since Hamlet's earlier encounter with the players, has this particular figure made such an impression on him? I have already suggested that Pyrrhus's impetuosity resonates deeply for the stalled prince, but in Hamlet's further probing of his own cowardly delay, he advances a racial rationalization that materializes inwardness and explains his incorporation of a black subjectivity.[64] Immediately after the players take their momentary leave after the initial exchange, Hamlet balks at his own failure to be roused to passionate action in comparison to the First Player, who tearfully recites Hecuba's grief at the sight of Priam's mutilated body. His soliloquy, "O what a rogue and peasant slave am I" (2.2.502), reeks of self-recrimination, in which he asks bluntly: "Am I a coward" (2.2.523)? His tolerance for invective, a barrage of common insults, and a father's murder without retaliating would justify such a conclusion. "But I am pigeon-livered and lack gall / To make oppression bitter" (2.2.529–530), he confesses, alluding to the liver as the organ traditionally associated with courage, in addition to the fact that adult pigeons lack a gall bladder, and hence the bitterness that would feed Hamlet's resentment.[65] Had he not been incapacitated by a dove-like timidity, he would have fed Claudius's entrails to kites, making these black-colored birds confederates in his vengeance (2.2.530–532). But this description of cowardice is related to an even more fully racialized unfolding of his fear.

In the play's best-known soliloquy, "To be, or not to be" (3.1.56), Hamlet argues that,

> conscience does make cowards of us all,
> And thus the native hue and resolution
> Is sicklied over with the pale cast of thought,
> And enterprises of great pitch and moment
> With this regard their currents turn awry
> And lose the name of action.
>
> (3.1.83–88)

With striking dramatic irony, Hamlet's central argument pits reflection, which animates conscience, as the enemy of action in a soliloquy that, like all the other six major soliloquies for which this play is famous, is itself the quintessence of reflection. The argument is fairly straightforward, despite most editors' lack of a racial frame of analysis that results in partial commentary. Cowardice, the consequence of reflection or "the pale cast of thought," produces physical effects that mimic an unhealthy or sickly whiteness; cowardice degenerates "the native hue and resolution," that is, one's normal, healthy, fair complexion, until that somatic condition appears paler, whiter, and sickly. By contrast, "enterprises of great pitch and moment" are synonymous with "the name of action," but cowardice can be a deterrent to such enterprises by weakening resolve. Since cowardice manifests as a form of whiteness, it comes as no surprise that Hamlet construes action as having a contrasting color designated by the blackness of "great pitch" that is diminished by cowardice and thereby lose the hue and name of action.[66] While "great pitch" is typically glossed as the peak of a hawk's flight in falconry, in Hamlet's ratiocinative universe of pallid embodiment, the allusion to "currents" is also suggestive of the popular emblem asserting the impossibility of "washing the Ethiop white," to represent instead the erosive depth of Hamlet's cowardice leaving him a drained, limp figure of whiteness unfit for the pitch and color of action.[67] According to Hamlet's reasoning, his penchant for reflection means that every soliloquy represents a weak act of performative whiteness in need of blackness-as-action to satisfy the mandate for revenge. In a play notable for its soliloquies, the racial argument encapsulated in cowardly reflection is deeply embedded in the dramaturgic fabric.

Audiences can already begin to appreciate better the structural significance of Hamlet's white cowardice and the role it plays in his recollective affinity with a black Pyrrhus. Blackness has become the sign for action, the antithesis of pallid embodiment generated by enervating reflection. In Pyrrhus, Hamlet has made a specific and considerable investment in a racially black foil whose quick and unrelenting sense of duty, impulsivity, and ferocity throw into sharp relief Hamlet's self-described "pigeon-livered" cowardice. Consistent with his logic, Hamlet must move toward a form of perverse identification that will amount to the declaration: "I am a black man." Once the performance of *Murder* is abruptly interrupted by Claudius's hasty departure, Hamlet believes he has his necessary proof of guilt; now, he can take the requisite action unconstrained by white cowardice, as he explains in yet another soliloquy:

> 'Tis now the very witching time of night,
> When church yards yawn, and hell itself breathes out
> Contagion to this world. Now could I drink hot blood,
> And do such bitter business as the day
> Would quake to look on.
>
> (3.2.349–353)

The grim and, by now, highly recognizable atmospheric architecture of revenge tragedy is fully evoked to announce the revenger's assumption of his bloody role, enhanced and enabled by forces that breathe hellish contagion. Of particular interest, however, is Shakespeare's diction, which brings ingested blood and bitterness into rhetorical proximation.

Among the theories addressing the early modern fascination with blackness in humans, Sir Thomas Browne in *Pseudodoxia Epidemica* (1646) explains blackness as a result of "a chemical compound in the blood."[68] In investigating this riddle of human blackness, Browne posits its cause among early modern culture's most commonly held beliefs. Browne argues that the "way whereby bodies become black is an Atramentous condition or mixture," stipulating a metaphoric precedent to be found in the chemistry of ink, "Atramentous" meaning "inky, ink-like, black as ink."[69] It matters, therefore, that Browne pinpoints the "infusion of galls," and its association with bitterness, as the reactive agent in the chemistry of black ink: "for so is *Atramentum Scriptorium*, or writing Ink commonly made by copperose cast upon a decoction or infusion of galls."[70] The "galls" identified by Browne are oak galls, outgrowths on trees "largely used in the manufacture of ink and tannin, as well as in dyeing and in medicine."[71] Shakespeare relies on this ink-making commonplace, which would have been familiar to working writers, in lines from *Twelfth Night*, "Let there be gall enough in thy ink" (3.2.38); *Cymbeline*, "Though ink be made of gall" (1.1.116); and *King John*, "Thou wert better gall the devil, Salisbury" (4.3.99), that is, make the devil blacker with rage, where the addition of gall as an ingredient is synonymous with blackening.[72]

Trying to narrow the gap between the ink metaphor and hematological conjecture, Browne maintains that "an atramentous condition there is to be found sometime in the blood" whereby light-skinned "Moors might possibly become Negroes."[73] More dramatically Hamlet contemplates himself, a white man, becoming black, a "Negro" in Browne's vocabulary, to assert his total and complete embrace of heedlessly violent action. Hamlet's words, "Now could I drink hot blood / And do such bitter business" build on the metaphoric precedent of ink-making, with which Shakespeare is familiar, and extends it to the commonly held theory of racial causation in humans. The infusion of bitterness mimics the unique blood chemistry by which Hamlet acquires access to being a "Negro" filled with rage of the kind imputed to black persons by a white culture Hamlet represents. In addition to merely finding inspiration for his own retaliatory action, therefore, Hamlet reflexively turns to the construct of a black Pyrrhus as if violence was, in fact, the chronic disposition of black men. Examining Hamlet as a man contemplating what racialized blackness means presents a singular challenge to the play's conventional assessments. Hamlet's denigrating imputation of racialized blackness to his murdering uncle undergoes a radical adaptation as he rationalizes his own unseemly accommodation of a violent, black subjectivity.

Dressed in Black: Hamlet and White Violence

Hamlet's assumption of an essential, racialized black violence is by itself deeply disturbing and made more so by the degree to which it was in the process of becoming the norm through the instrumentality of the early modern English theater in evolving the Violent Black Man type. Hamlet's inscription in a racialized inky discourse is already underway in the play's opening scenes, where Shakespeare articulates the premises of this carefully calibrated race play to foster and test readers' racial literacy in interrogating a black Hamlet. Polonius's advice, "apparel oft proclaims the man" (1.3.72), has no greater dramaturgic relevance than in Hamlet's black clothing, which the court takes as an ostensible sign of melancholy and mourning over King Hamlet's death. "Good Hamlet cast thy nighted colour off" (1.2.68), Gertrude implores, reasoning that death's universality should mitigate his seemingly keen and excessive sadness. Hamlet responds:

> Seems madam? nay it is, I know not seems.
> 'Tis not alone my inky cloak, good mother,
> Nor customary suits of solemn black,
> Nor windy suspiration of forced breath,
> No, nor the fruitful river in the eye,
> Nor the dejected haviour of the visage,
> Together with all forms, moods, shapes of grief,
> That can denote me truly. These indeed seem,
> For they are actions that a man might play,
> But I have that within which passes show –
> These but the trappings and the suits of woe.
>
> (1.2.76–86)

The tearful eye, the dejected look, and formal mourning dress are familiar, external, but only partial expressions of grief; he touts a much deeper sense of internal loss, incomprehensible to Gertrude and the others, that stands as a critique of their "o'erhasty" (2.2.57) forgetting of the deceased king. Moreover, Hamlet contends that these external "forms, moods, shapes of grief" belong to the actor's toolkit because "they are the actions a man might play." What still remains partial in Hamlet's own analysis, but Shakespeare highlights through the detailed lexical items, is that the discourse of performance Hamlet employs is specific to staging blackness in the early modern theater.

While the application of ointments or rubbing sooty substances on the actor's white skin constituted one form of early modern blackface, the use of black cloth to cover the extremities formed another that included the actual practice and rhetoric of dyeing.[74] Hamlet's later insistence on the word "sable," for example, suggests his performative identification with black Pyrrhus through the real and linguistic prosthetics of dress: "I'll have a suit of sables" (3.2.115–116). Here in the opening, Hamlet's black or "inky cloak" is already immersed in the racial discourse of black skin, as explained in Browne, that found real theatrical employment in the dyed black fabrics used to imitate skin. The "suits of solemn black," along with "the suits of woe," double their performative value in verbally overlaying the cosmetic use of "soot" and the tailored fabrics of dyed cloth to consolidate the prosthetic technologies of conjuring and fashioning racialized bodies to make possible the image of Hamlet as the white actor in racial drag. Consistent with the evolution of the prince's thinking, Hamlet in black stands out in the newly assembled court in the way a black man might in a room full of white persons.

Claudius's estimate of melancholy and mourning proves equally insufficient to the racial case Shakespeare presents:

> Claudius: But now my cousin Hamlet, and my son –
> Hamlet (*Aside*): A little more kin, and less than kind.
> Claudius: How is it that the clouds still hang on you?
> Hamlet: Not so my lord, I am too much i'th'sun.
>
> (1.2.64–67)

While Hamlet's opening aside has already been discussed, I set out his first words in full here to highlight Shakespeare's deliberate verbal stacking of the play's framing racial content. Because Claudius focuses on Hamlet's melancholy, he, too, misses the racial potential of that condition. For instance, melancholy, referencing more than an emotionally depressive state, had its own physiology that argued a causal connection between black bile and black skin. About melancholics, Timothy Bright's *Treatise of Melancholy* (1586) notes: "Of colour they be black, according to the humour whereof they are nourished, and the skinne always receauing the blacke vapors which insensible do pass from the inward parts, taketh die and staine thereof."[75] Still, Shakespeare's specific language supplies another reading and frame of reference. Hamlet challenges his stepfather's trope of mourning, "Not so, my lord," and offers a reply that indicates sunburn, the result of being too much in the sun. From Ovid into the Renaissance, the climatological narrative of the origins of blackness, due to Phaeton's accident driving the sun god's chariot too close to the earth and singeing the population below, is memorialized in the name Ethiop, synonymous with African, meaning a sunburnt face of a sunburnt race: "It was then, according to some folks, / that the inhabitants of Ethiopia / turned black when blood was drawn up to their skins."[76] From Claudius's query about hanging clouds and Hamlet's discontent with being too much in the sun to the famed "inky cloak" and black vestments, Shakespeare elaborates the racial argument in ways that consistently shift the discourse from mourning to Mooring – the art of becoming a Moor, impersonating a black man through clothing on the stage, and, eventually, Hamlet's appropriation of a violent black racial identity.

An important function of Shakespeare's introductory sequence featuring Hamlet, therefore, is to implant for audiences and readers a specific, governing narrative. Whatever the subsequent scenes, Shakespeare has ensured that the definitive stage image of Hamlet dressed in black is sustained over the course of the action as a constant visual reminder requiring audiences to factor race into our conception and reading of the play. Shakespeare's dramaturgic prefiguration early in the play, in fact, lays the foundation of Hamlet's unstable relationship to blackness. On the one hand, Hamlet shows contempt for the person and idea of the Moor through an act of projection that condemns Claudius's murderous acts and reputation conceived as the product of race. Demeaning a white man through the use of a highly racialized term constitutes a de facto denigration of black persons that debases them as a class entirely serviceable to white interests. On the other hand, the revenge paradox of resemblance and repetition finds Hamlet imitating and embracing blackness as a counterpoise to weakness and betraying a grotesque naïveté in his ideation and appropriation of black violence. For Hamlet, agency in the revenge mode devolves into a horrendous stereotype of the Violent Black Man as a form of compensatory will to action.

Examining Hamlet as a man contemplating the meaning of racialized blackness presents a singular challenge to the play's traditional critical assessments. The legacy of the Violent Black Man type is, without question, devastatingly consequential to modernity, resulting in the usability and disposability of black life in the interests of white power. Let us recall that beginning in the Enlightenment, the elevation of inwardness in *Hamlet* criticism occurred against a series of interlocking events in a program of *white violence*: European colonialism, the transatlantic slave trade, and the wealth revolution of the plantation economy in the Americas. These vast, systemic operations of white violence were built on the everyday torture and discipline of black bodies. In Orlando Patterson's account, for example, slavery is defined as a relationship of domination enabled and sustained by various technologies of power such as the emblematic and ubiquitous whip: "Whipping was not only a method of punishment. It was a conscious device to impress upon the slaves that they were slaves; it was a crucial form of social control particularly if we remember that it was very difficult for slaves to run away successfully."[77] The salient horrors of plantation slavery – domination, the instrumentality of violence, forced submission, erasure of the will – conjured the black body as the cultural totem across which histories of violent acquisition of power and economic success were written. The 1829 decision of South Carolina judge Thomas Ruffin articulated the consequence of corporal violence, abject submission, and the unnatural surrender to labor without hope for happiness or personal economic improvement: "There is nothing else which can operate to produce the effect. The power of the master must be absolute, to render the submission of the slave perfect."[78]

Importantly, early modern scholars have granted that "the rhetoric of inwardness is highly developed in the English Renaissance, but maintain that these terms inevitably refer to outward, public, and political factors."[79] Their concession to externality notwithstanding, what these scholars share is a general blind spot for the racial import of these "outward, public, and political factors."[80] Where white violence – enslavement, subjugation, control through physical discipline, death – is muted in the critical turn to inwardness in the post-Enlightenment history of *Hamlet* criticism, that insistence on looking away leads to the failure to recognize the play's complicity in constructing the damaging myth of the Violent or Murderous Black Man of early and, subsequently, late modernity through the cultural institution of the theater. Such a type lends itself all too readily to the dictum: "To plunder a people of everything, you must plunder their humanity first."[81] To be clear, white Enlightenment violence has often been mitigated over time through strategies of forgetting and displacement that, in turn, construct persons of African descent as dangerous and, therefore, deserving of suitable punishment and corporal containment. According to this egregious logic of projection, if the black man is a priori a threat, his preemptive erasure is a morbid justification for the health of civil society. Yet this pattern of projection, evident in the post-Enlightenment period, has a prehistory that is exemplified in *Hamlet*'s circulation of the Violent Black Man type.

The Burden of Reading *Hamlet* Today

Hamlet's Pyrrhus extract is taken from a play that bears the notable distinction of being performed not more than once because it "pleased not the million: 'twas caviary to the general" even though the theatrical elite judged it "an excellent play, well digested in the scenes, set down with as much modesty as cunning" (2.2.396–397, 399–400). In the self-consciously metatheatrical drama that is *Hamlet*, the dismal performance history of the black Pyrrhus play contrasts with Shakespeare's own challenge to create a black drama that would escape the same fate of flagging popular reception. Of course, Shakespeare's *Hamlet* experiment was from its inception "an unqualified success in the theatre" and acquired a virtually unmatched reputation among critics.[82] But *Hamlet*, like *Othello*, is a black play, and Shakespeare's Hamlet is a white man navigating his complicated relationship to blackness through a uniquely theatrical prism. Moreover, his passion for theater results in vitally important historical evidence about the theatrical modalities of representing blackness: questions of repertory, new literary and dramatic types, blackface prosthetics, the gestural and facial expression of blackface performance, didascalia or linguistically embedded stage directions, and the rhetoric of black identity and racial ontology. *Hamlet* is, therefore, conscious of its historical placement not just in the revenge tragedy genre, but at the outset of an emerging black drama that, over time, has been obscured from view by the pressures exerted by systemic whiteness on canonical formation. From our historical perspective, *Hamlet* does, in fact, rival the "late innovation" reportedly causing a stir in the city theaters, but the real disturbance for the modern Shakespeare industry is the unsettling of conventional approaches that have caused us to ignore or forget the substantial evidence of blackness and race in the play.

At his return to Denmark, Hamlet happens upon the gravedigger tossing skeletal parts as he prepares a new burial plot, in a scene that has yielded the iconic image of the prince contemplating Yorick's skull.[83] What is this graveyard scene if not a symbolic reminder for the audience of missing skin and flesh, the racialized elements of which have preoccupied the prince throughout the play? This scene has been read as an example of the *memento mori* tradition of remembering the dead: "it is, therefore, a reminder of every man's death, a reminder to Hamlet of his own death as well as that of his father."[84] *Memento mori* figures, in reminding the observer of death's ubiquity, urged moral stocktaking and readiness in this life. However, *memento mori* also means "remember the Moor," and in the case of Hamlet, the scene is a startling visual provocation, urging readers and audiences to remember the uses to which the Moor's skin and flesh have been put that require intense moral reflection and reckoning. The commentary on this play has invested in the idea of remembrance and resemblance to an unusual degree whereby critics have hailed Hamlet as their own: "What one of us does not say with a mixture of pity, comradeship, admiration, and horror, Goodnight, sweet Prince!"[85] Approaching *Hamlet* from a critical race studies frame challenges this body of commentary, asking for a reconsideration of the centuries-old proposition of identifying with Hamlet. Certainly, modern readers of this play must seriously question their "comradeship, admiration, and horror" in embracing the racist views propagated by Hamlet. In light of Hamlet's deeply flawed attitudes toward blackness, readers must rethink what it means to maintain their esteem for this prince as literary hero. Should scholars and critics finally confront the play's racist content, it remains to be seen how such a recognition will affect the type of responsive and responsible scholarship that might follow, and how it will challenge scholars and readers themselves. *Hamlet* tests our capacity to reckon with and remember the Moor.

One of the important trends we find in contemporary popular culture is the increased consumption of blackness. In the United States we have witnessed a cultural evolution that brought blackness into the contemporary musical mainstream and touched a significant swath of white America.[86] A similar impact can be seen in specific segments across other areas of the entertainment industry, including sports. But what has been the broad, positive social impact of hip-hop and rap flowing through the earphones of young white listeners, or of sport-jersey-wearing grown men proudly identifying with and ritualistically cheering for their favorite black basketball or football stars either in person or during weekly televised games? That is, has sports fans' identification with black athletes or music lovers' sustained decades-long self-directed contact with black culture made any positive difference in creating racial proximity and lessening the racial divide that continues to undermine the grand social contract that is America? I am, of course, drawing a cultural parallel with the advent, evolution, and response to early modern critical race studies in a predominantly white Shakespeare industry. What has been the impact of more exposure to critical race readings of texts, conferences, and symposia? And, should critics and scholars adopt a race-critical framework of analysis, how will this awareness truly change the work of reading and teaching Shakespeare in an engaged commitment toward racial literacy? In short, how will critics and scholars remember the Moor?

Mass commercial consumption of blackness does not appear to have moved the dial forward in promoting and revolutionizing racial consciousness among its primarily white consumers or in laying the foundation for racial rapprochement. The oversimplification and misrepresentation of American black life in certain segments of popular music are accompanied by the lurid attraction of dangerous, violent, stereotypes of black men whose obscene machismo appeals to its predominantly white, male American audience.[87] Four hundred years ago, the packed London theaters too circulated similar representations of black men for the entertainment and pleasure of white audiences. Hamlet, in particular, stands as a precursor to the modern white consumer of a curated idea of violent black culture, for whether proffered by contemporary musicians or Hamlet the theater artist, that idea of blackness does not fully equate to real persons but to a usable commercial formula of race and masculinity. Greg Tate's formulation of the failed responsibilities attendant on white appropriation is relevant: *Everything but the Burden: What White People Are Taking from Black Culture*.[88] Whites' conspicuous consumption of black culture has too often adroitly sidestepped, or been oblivious to, the burden of the systemic obstructions to constitutional provisions, human rights, equal opportunity, and economic dignity for black Americans.

Hamlet's vision of blackness as a kind of histrionic endeavor, comparable to his putting "an antic disposition on," imagines the actor putting on and taking off the "inky cloak" of blackface performance. Hamlet's dabbling in blackface is the structural prefiguration of his all too easy self-serving dalliance with race as a white man seeking to bolster his courage without any due concern for the political and historical realities of black persons' existence and lives. Hamlet has the improvisational and racial liberty as a white man to choose black Pyrrhus in his quest throughout the play to find the courage to set Denmark right. The responsibility is grave, no doubt, but his investment in blackness, recalling his prosthetic profligacy, is entirely self-serving, aimed at resolving his crisis, and undertaken with the entertainment consumer predicate of race. Hamlet's example is a stark reminder of the superficiality, privilege, and dangers of racial tourism. Ironically, the declaration "[i]t is *we* who are Hamlet" lands with astonishingly revealing candor, since the traditional resistance, denial, and blindness to race among general readers and scholars have left the racist agenda that suffuses Hamlet's thinking firmly intact. In reality, race is evident everywhere in Shakespeare and early modern drama; it resides in plain sight. But what has this meant to our profession, what must it mean today for our own critical investments in early modern texts? Is blackness "still something to be consumed but not necessarily anything to engage with"?[89] Is the destiny of early modern race studies codified in the popularity of the broader field's favorite, canonical text and its hero's apparent stance: everything but the burden? Here, then, is an opportunity to consider the work of racial literacy which countermands the big lie, "the idea that in America white lives have always mattered more than the lives of others," and involves learning to read oneself through the process of reading texts, discovering who we are and *how we are* in relation to others.

Racial literacy is understanding the "racism structured" into every aspect of our society and "accepting the equality of others," their experiences and lives as part of the democracy we build.[90] Reading *Hamlet* critically, and taking on the burden of race, can be a rewarding investment as we contemplate the intersection of literary studies and an antiracist politics and future.

Notes

1 Eddie Glaude Jr., *Begin Again: James Baldwin's America and Its Urgent Lessons for Our Own* (New York: Crown, 2020), 7.
2 Ibid., 8–9.
3 Jamaica Kincaid, "On Seeing England for the First Time," *Transition* 51 (1991): 32–40 (34).
4 Ibid., 39.
5 The main exceptions are Patricia Parker, "Black *Hamlet*: Battening on the Moor," *Shakespeare Studies* 31 (2003): 127–164; Peter Erickson, "Can We Talk about Race in *Hamlet*?" in *"Hamlet": New Critical Essays*, ed. Arthur F. Kinney (New York: Routledge, 2002); and David Sterling Brown, "Code Black: Whiteness and Unmanliness in *Hamlet*," in *Hamlet: The State of Play*, ed. Sonia Massai and Lucy Munro (London: Bloomsbury, 2021), 101–128. For some observations about race in *Hamlet*, see also Urvashi Chakravarty, "More Than Kin, Less Than Kind: Similitude, Strangeness, and Early Modern English Homonationalisms," *Shakespeare Quarterly* 67.1 (2016): 14–29.
6 The notable exception is Patricia Parker, who discusses a range of civic theatrical practices that employed face-blackening in relation to the language of *Hamlet* in "Black *Hamlet*," 128–129.
7 William Shakespeare, *Hamlet: Prince of Denmark*, ed. Philip Edwards, The New Cambridge Shakespeare (Cambridge: Cambridge University Press, 2003). All citations from this play will follow this edition. Citations from other works by Shakespeare will follow David Bevington, ed., *The Complete Works of Shakespeare*, 4th ed. (New York: Longman, 1997).
8 Stephen Greenblatt, *Will in the World: How Shakespeare Became Shakespeare* (New York: Norton, 2004), 299; for an argument concerning the inaccessibility of Hamlet's inwardness, see Susan Baker, "Hamlet's Bloody Thoughts and the Illusion of Inwardness," *Comparative Drama* 21.4 (1987–88): 303–317.
9 G. R. Hibbard, ed., *Hamlet* (Oxford: Oxford University Press, 1998), 1.
10 Margreta de Grazia, *"Hamlet" Without Hamlet* (Cambridge: Cambridge University Press, 2007), 1.
11 Ibid., 4.
12 Mbembe, *Critique*, 55.
13 Quoted in Edwards, introduction to *Hamlet*, 33.
14 Chakravarty, "More Than Kin," 14.

15 See "race," n.6 1.a: "A group of people belonging to the same family and descended from a common ancestor; a house, family, kindred." *OED Online*, Oxford University Press, March 2022, www.oed.com/view/Entry/157031. On the early modern word "race" signifying lineage and family, see Hendricks, "Race," 16–17.

16 Unlike some modern editions, like the Oxford Shakespeare or the New Cambridge Shakespeare used for this chapter (3.4.67), The Second Quarto and First Folio both use the capitalized spelling "Moore," identifying the racial signifier for an African. The Second Quarto and First Folio are cited from *The Three-Text Hamlet: Parallel Texts of the First and Second Quartos and First Folio*, ed. Paul Bertram and Bernice W. Kliman (New York: AMS Press, 1991), 168, 169. Further citations will reference this edition as *TTH*.

17 *TTH*, 167, 168.

18 Ronald Broude, "Revenge and Revenge Tragedy in Renaissance England," *Renaissance Quarterly* 28.1 (1975): 36–58 (38–39).

19 James J. Condon, "Setting the Stage for Revenge: Space, Performance, and Power in Early Modern Revenge Tragedy," *Medieval and Renaissance Drama in English* 25 (2012): 62–82 (62).

20 Tanya Pollard, "Tragedy and Revenge," in Emma Smith and Garret Sullivan Jr., eds., *The Cambridge Companion to English Renaissance Tragedy* (Cambridge: Cambridge University Press, 2010), 59.

21 Broude, "Revenge and Revenge Tragedy," 38; Fredson Bowers, *Elizabethan Revenge Tragedy, 1587–1642* (Princeton: Princeton University Press, 1940).

22 On the critical tendency to see revenge tragedy as inferior to Renaissance achievements, see Stevie Simkin, ed., *Revenge Tragedy* (New York: Palgrave, 2001), 3–4. Building on the work begun in Bowers, several critics, including Simkin, have explored further the tensions surrounding the political evolution of more centralized state bureaucracies. See especially Wendy Griswold, *Renaissance Revivals: City Comedy and Revenge Tragedy in the London Theatre, 1576–1980* (Chicago: University of Chicago Press, 1986), esp. 90–100.

23 Griswold, *Renaissance Revivals,* 71.

24 Simkin, *Revenge Tragedy,* 9.

25 Marston's *Antonio's Revenge* is included in Emma Smith, ed., *Five Revenge Tragedies* (New York: Penguin, 2012). All quotations of this play will be taken from this edition.

26 In addition to Bowers and Simkin, notably the range of approaches exemplified in the latter's collection of essays, *Revenge Tragedy,* see also the introductions to Smith, *Five Revenge Tragedies,* and Katharine Eisaman Maus, ed., *Four Revenge Tragedies* (Oxford: Oxford University Press, 1995).

27 Peter Erickson, "Representations of Blacks and Blackness in the Renaissance," *Criticism* 35 (1993): 499–527; and his "Representations of Race in Renaissance Art," *The Upstart Crow: A Shakespeare Journal* 18 (1998): 2–9.

28 Thomas Middleton's civic pageants are particularly revealing on this point. See his *The Collected Works.*

29 George Peele, *The Battle of Alcazar*, in *The Stukeley Plays*, ed. Charles Edelman (Manchester: Manchester University Press, 2005), 1.Prol.7, 16–18.

30 Barthelemy, *Black Face, Maligned Race*, 1–17, 72–146. *Lust's Dominion* adapted by Aphra Behn as *Abdelazar, or the Moor's Revenge* (1676); *All's Lost by Lust* adapted by WC as *The Rape Revenged, or the Spanish Revolution* (1690); and *Titus Andronicus* adapted by Edward Ravenscroft as *Titus Andronicus, or the Rape of Lavinia* (1678), and multiple other times.

31 Thomas Dekker, *The Dramatic Works of Thomas Dekker*, vol. IV, ed. Fredson Bowers (Cambridge: Cambridge University Press, 1961). All quotations from *Lust's Dominion* follow this edition.

32 William Rowley, *All's Lost by Lust in All's Lost by Lust, and A Shoemaker, a Gentleman*, ed. Charles Wharton Stork (Philadelphia: University of Pennsylvania, 1910).

33 Barthelemy, *Black Face, Maligned Race*, 91.

34 In addition to Barthelemy, *Black Face, Maligned Race*, Tokson, *The Popular Image of the Black Man*, and D'Amico, *The Moor in English Renaissance Drama;* see Eldred Jones, *Othello's Countrymen: The African in English Renaissance Drama* (London: Oxford University Press, 1965).

35 Maynard Mack, "The World of Hamlet," *The Yale Review* 41 (1952): 502–523 (512). "Metatheater" was coined by Lionel Abel in 1960, so I am referring to the concept and not suggesting that Mack used the term itself. On the history of the term and its relevance for early modern theater studies, see Sarah Dustagheer and Harry Newman, "Metatheatre and Early Modern Drama," *Shakespeare Bulletin* 36.1 (2018): 3–18. See also Anne Barton, *Shakespeare and the Idea of Play* (New York: Penguin Books, 1967).

36 Lyell Asher, "Gertrude's Shoes," *ELH* 83.4 (2016): 959–987 (974, 963).

37 Louis Montrose, *The Purpose of Playing: Shakespeare and the Cultural Politics of the Elizabethan Theatre* (Chicago: University of Chicago Press, 1996), 42.

38 Hibbard, the Arden editor, notes this rivalry, *Hamlet*, 220–222.

39 Roslyn Knutson challenges this widely held reading about the war of the theaters. She argues instead that the "eyrie of children, little eyases that cry out on the top of question" (2.2.315–316) that appears only in the 1623 First Folio refers to a revival of *Hamlet* between 1606 and 1608 that criticizes the satirical excesses of the boy actors at the Blackfriars, which could lead to unwanted political scrutiny. The passage's singular appearance in the first Folio, and neither the 1601 nor 1604/5 Quartos, bolsters her argument. For an engaging and thorough account of the textual and stage history of the passage concerning the boy actors see Roslyn L. Knutson, "Falconer to the Little Eyases: A New Date and Commercial Agenda for the 'Little Eyases' Passage in *Hamlet*," *Shakespeare Quarterly* 46.1 (1995): 1–31; on the passage's relevance to the political sensitivities of the Essex rebellion in 1601, referenced in the "inhibition" (2.2.308) that sent the troupe out of the city, see Montrose, *The Purpose of Playing*, 103–105.

40 Andrew J. Green, "The Cunning of the Scene," *Shakespeare Quarterly* 4.4 (1953): 395–404 (396).
41 Arthur Johnston, "The Player's Speech in *Hamlet*," *Shakespeare Quarterly* 13.1 (1962): 21–30 (21); see also Michael Taylor, "A Note on the 'Pyrrhus Episode' in *Hamlet*," *Shakespeare Quarterly* 21.1 (1970): 99–103.
42 Christopher Marlowe, *The Complete Plays, ed.* J. B. Steane (London: Penguin, 1986). The 1594 first edition identifies Christopher Marlowe and Thomas Nashe as authors.
43 Homer, *The Odyssey*, trans. Emily Watson (New York: Norton, 2018), Book 11.519–520, 527–528.
44 Ibid., ll.536–537.
45 Euripides, *Andromache*, trans. David Kovacs, Loeb Classical Library (Cambridge, MA: Harvard University Press, 1995), 337.
46 Jonathan Bate, *How the Classics Made Shakespeare* (Princeton: Princeton University Press, 2019); Timothy D. Crowley, "Arms and the Boy: Marlowe's Aeneas and the Parody of Imitation in *Dido, Queen of Carthage*," *English Literary Renaissance* 38.3 (2008): 408–438; Andy Mousley, *Re-Humanising Shakespeare: Literary Humanism, Wisdom and Modernity* (Edinburgh: Edinburgh University Press, 2007), 33–45; Martin Mueller, "Hamlet and the World of Ancient Tragedy," *Arion: A Journal of Humanities and the Classics*, third series 5.1 (1997): 22–45; James Black, "Hamlet Hears Marlowe; Shakespeare Reads Virgil," *Renaissance and Reformation/Renaissance et Réforme* 81.4 (1994): 17–28; Joseph Westlund, "Ambivalence in the Player's Speech in *Hamlet*," *Studies in English Literature, 1500–1900* 18.2 (1978): 245–256; Avi Erlich, *Hamlet's Absent Father* (Princeton: Princeton University Press, 1977), esp. 99–151. Several critics have also commented on Hamlet's ironic identification with Pyrrhus as an avenger figure, but the failure to account for the racial implications limits severely the scope of the scene's purpose.
47 De Grazia, *"Hamlet" Without Hamlet*, 94.
48 Ibid.
49 See "sable," A. n2.1, "Black, one of the heraldic colors"; and B. adj. 2, "gen. Black." *OED Online*, Oxford University Press, March 2022, www.oed.com/view/Entry/169362.
50 Mary Floyd-Wilson has argued the importance of early modern humoralism and its effect on producing different body types in *English Ethnicity and Race in Early Modern Drama* (Cambridge: Cambridge University Press, 2003), 38–41.
51 Mueller, "Hamlet and the World of Ancient Tragedy," 37.
52 Virgil, *The Aeneid*, trans. Robert Fagles (New York: Penguin, 2008), 2.584–589.
53 Westlund, "Ambivalence in the Player's Speech," 249–250. See also Hibbard in his introduction to *Hamlet* (228), who summarizes Marlowe's Hyrcanian citation from later in Book 4 of *The Aeneid*. Westlund references the epic simile, but neither he nor Hibbard broaches the racial significance or the

innovation in theatrical convention. Shakespeare has pointedly re-articulated both Virgil and Marlowe.

54 Bate, *How the Classics Made Shakespeare*, 141.

55 Arthur F. Kinney, *Shakespeare by Stages: An Historical Introduction* (Malden: Blackwell, 2003), 55.

56 Roslyn L. Knutson, "The Repertory," in *A New History of Early English Drama*, ed. John D. Cox and David Scott Kastan (New York: Columbia University Press, 1997), 472.

57 Gail Kern Paster, *Humoring the Body: Emotions and the Shakespearean Stage* (Chicago: University of Chicago Press, 2004), 34.

58 Ibid., 35.

59 Kinney, *Shakespeare by Stages*, 53.

60 Cherrell Guilfoyle, "The Beginning of *Hamlet*," *Comparative Drama* 14.2 (1980): 137–158 (137).

61 Robert I. Lublin, "'Apparel oft proclaims the man': Visualizing *Hamlet* on the Early Modern Stage," *Shakespeare Bulletin* 32.4 (2014): 629–647 (629).

62 Robert S. Miola, ed., *Hamlet*, 2nd ed. (New York: Norton 2019); Edwards and Hibbard are cited above. The Arden editors, Ann Thompson and Neil Taylor, *Hamlet* (London: Bloomsbury, 2016), gloss the line as "execrable faces," overlooking the racial and performative significance.

63 See Parker, "Black *Hamlet* ".

64 In his discussion of the Pyrrhus speech, Westlund argues that Hamlet wishes to renounce his passivity and sees in Pyrrhus a figure of action, taken from classical literature and fictionalized further into drama; however, like other scholars, he ignores the racial dimension of the speech and its subsequent impact. See Westlund, "Ambivalence in the Player's Speech," 245–246.

65 On the gall bladder as it relates to pigeons and doves, see C. F. W. Illingworth, "The Gall-Bladder in Animals," *Edinburgh Medical Journal* 43.7 (1936): 458–461, esp. 460.

66 Modern editorial choices vary between "pitch" (Q2) and "pith" (F).

67 For Thomas Palmer's rendition of the emblem titled "Impossible Things," see Loomba and Burton, *Race in Early Modern England*, 98–99.

68 Scott Oldenburg, "The Riddle of Blackness in England's National Family Romance," *Journal of Early Modern Cultural Studies* 1.1 (2001): 46–62 (46).

69 Sir Thomas Browne, *Pseudodoxia Epidemica: Or, Enquiries into Commonly Presumed Truths* (1672) (Oxford: Benediction Classics, 2009), 496. For this definition of "Atramentous," see *OED Online*, Oxford University Press, March 2022, www.oed.com/view/Entry/12637. Importantly, Browne offers two theories: one based on blood compound, the "atramentous" theory discussed here, and another concerning heat and the release of a black or "fuliginous" substance that affects skin color (494–496).

70 Browne, *Pseudodoxia Epidemica*, 496. On the manufacture of ink, especially printer's ink, see Mitchell M. Harris, "The Expense of Ink and Wastes of Shame: Poetic Generation, Black Ink, and Material Waste in Shakespeare's Sonnets," in *The Materiality of Color: The Production, Circulation, and*

Application of Dyes and Pigments, 1400–1800, ed. Andrea Feeser, Maureen Daly Goggin, and Beth Fowkes Tobin (Burlington: Ashgate, 2012), esp. 68–72.

71 See "gall," n.3. *OED Online*, Oxford University Press, March 2022, www.oed.com/view/Entry/76231.

72 In "Sir Thomas Browne's Chemistry," *Journal of the Faculty of Arts* 2.3 (1964): 217–228, W. G. H. Edwards points out that although Browne was aware of the ferrous component in the reaction he describes, Browne downplays the role of iron in this chemistry of blackening effects. However, it is clear that Shakespeare, like Browne, fixates on what could only be described as the common view of gall's chemical agency.

73 Browne, *Pseudodoxia Epidemica,* 498.

74 For example, for Edward VI's Christmas festivities of 1548, the ledger records the purchase of black velvet for actors to cover their arms: "black vellet for gloves abouve thelbow for mores," indicating that black velvet gloves were prosthetic devices intended to imitate the color and texture of black skin; see Albert Feuillerat, ed., *Documents Relating to the Office of the Revels in the Time of King Edward VI and Queen Mary* (Louvain: A. Uystpruyst, 1914), 30.

75 Quoted in Parker, "Black *Hamlet,*" 138.

76 Ovid, *Metamorphoses*, trans. Charles Martin (New York: Norton, 2004), 11.314–316.

77 George P. Warwick, quoted in Orlando Patterson, *Slavery and Social Death: A Comparative Study* (Cambridge, MA: Harvard University Press, 1982), 3; on "natal alienation" and submission of the enslaved persons, see Ibid., 5–10.

78 Quoted in Ibid., 4.

79 Katharine Eisaman Maus, *Inwardness and Theater in the English Renaissance* (Chicago: University of Chicago Press, 1995), 2.

80 See Paster, *Humoring the Body,* 25–76. Paster demonstrates how internality and environmental externality echo and mirror each other, since both are modeled on similar metaphorical systems. In her chapter on *Hamlet* and *Othello*, however, she hesitates to see externality as skin color.

81 Ta-Nehisi Coates, "The Great Fire," *Vanity Fair*, August 24, 2020, www.vanityfair.com/culture/2020/08/ta-nehisi-coates-editor-letter.

82 Hibbard, introduction to *Hamlet*, 14; for a full discussion, see 14–28.

83 John Drakakis, "Yorick's Skull," in *Gothic Renaissance: A Reassessment*, ed. Elisabeth Bronfen and Beate Neumeier (Manchester: Manchester University Press, 2014); Aimée Ross-Kilroy, "'The Very Ragged Bone': Dismantling Masculinity in Thomas Middleton's *The Revenger's Tragedy*," *Renaissance and Reformation/Renaissance et Réforme* 33.4 (2010): 51–71; David Willbern, *Poetic Will: Shakespeare and the Play of Language* (Philadelphia: University of Pennsylvania Press, 1997), esp. 160–171.

84 Marjorie Garber, "'Remember Me': *Memento Mori* Figures in Shakespeare's Plays," *Renaissance Drama*, New Series, 12 (1981), 3–25 (4); Roland Mushat Frye, *The Renaissance Hamlet: Issues and Responses in 1600* (Princeton: Princeton University Press, 1984), 206–253.

85 Anatole France, quoted in Mack, "The World of Hamlet," 520.

86 For an engaging history of the cooptation of black music and culture in America, see Baruti N. Kapano, "Soul Thieves: White America and the Appropriation of Hip Hop and Black Culture," in *Soul Thieves: The Appropriation and Misrepresentation of African American Popular Culture*, ed. Tamara Lizette Brown and Baruti N. Kopano (New York: Palgrave Macmillan, 2014).

87 Tom Barnes, "How Music Executives Created 'Black' Hip Hop for White Suburban Kids," *Mic*, January 9, 2014, www.mic.com/articles/78487/how-music-executives-created-black-hip-hop-for-white-suburban-kids#.YxAIV4pf8.

88 I am taking the notion of "burden" from Greg Tate, ed., *Everything but the Burden: What White People Are Taking from Black Culture* (New York: Harlem Moon, 2003).

89 Hannah J. Davies, "Culture's Race Problem: 'For White Hipsters, Blackness is a Thing to Consume but not Engage With,'" *The Guardian*, March 16, 2019, www.theguardian.com/culture/2019/mar/16/cultures-race-problem-for-white-hipsters-blackness-is-a-thing-to-consume-but-not-engage-with.

90 Though he is not speaking about "racial literacy," I find some of the language relevant for my definition: Timothy Snyder, "The American Abyss," *The New York Times Magazine*, January 9, 2021.

CHAPTER 5

We Are Othello

> Speak of me as I am; nothing extenuate,
> Nor set down aught in malice.
>
> *Othello*, 5.2.341–342[1]

Beyond the Postracial Myth

The previous chapter presented Hamlet's ambivalent investment in the threatening Violent Black Man type that was singled out for moral condemnation and aggressive containment. The reception of this newly emergent, popular theatrical figure spoke to its entertainment value as well as the incipient culture of retaliation against racialized blackness that would, in time, be revealed for what it was: the projection of a white cultural imaginary. Suppression of a black threat engendered the early modern theater's thesis of the disposability of black life that would replicate itself with devastating consequence in subsequent history. Over time, the myth-turned-specter of the Violent Black Man justified a plethora of actions targeting and subverting black humanity in the real world to, once again, insist on "the idea that in America white lives have always mattered more than the lives of others." This chapter explores the deadly consequence of such a wildly persistent attitude today. Recently, numerous reports of police killings of unarmed black persons have dominated the media and initiated a public debate that has largely split along racial lines.[2] The disposability of black life, the legacy of the Violent Black Man type, has erupted in fatalities that have sparked calls for social justice in an era of renewed civil rights activism in the United States.

The explosion of black deaths into the dialogue of the public sphere came at a time, notably in the aftermath of the Obama election, when the thesis of a postracial, color-blind America had inserted itself into mainstream thinking as evidence of a growing sentiment to move beyond race and erase its explicit and violent history.[3] The postracial claim professes social progress in the form of a race-free society; it deems race an archaic holdover of bad science and an outmoded category of critical reflection. In this new dispensation, the reasoning holds, any barrier to black advancement or obstacle to black success is entirely self-inflicted, the fault of black people themselves, and whites are absolved from any sins of the racist past. W. J. T. Mitchell remarks, however, that "one would have to suffer from a very deep form of blindness to ignore" the virulence of today's racism.[4] The postracial desire to transcend race comes up against the brutal reality of multiple deaths of unarmed black civilians, forcing an inquiry into its very premise as complicit with the politics of white privilege. "White privilege," challenges Paula S. Rothenberg, "is the other side of racism."[5] The serious charge here is that white privilege, the open secret of dominant white culture, including academia, is anything but benign.[6] Given the attitudinal formation around blackness as inherently menacing and dangerous, this chapter explicitly pursues the issue that resides at the center of this book's concerns, and one that I have been formulating over the course of this study: How can one navigate current ideas of blackness and tell the black person's story? How can a largely white Shakespeare industry tell the story of race?

Earlier, in Chapter 2, I argued that Shakespeare deliberately calls out the audience's white identity and epistemology. I return to *Othello* to confront specifically the realization that this audience is not simply a historically removed entity; it is also the modern spectator and reader, for whom the legacy of centuries of reckoning with racialized blackness has come full circle. In addition *Othello* asks, therefore: How can today's reader tell the story of a black man, putting us directly in Hamlet's position of having to wrestle with *our* perceptions of blackness? Othello, the "noble Moor" (2.3.121), is often regarded as the exception to the Violent Black Man type, yet the full unfolding of his story produces a complicated human picture to which the audience is expressly set up to respond. This is the challenge Shakespeare poses in *Othello*, and it represents a profound ethical self-inquiry that far surpasses mere scholarly production, dutiful analysis, or skillful performance as we navigate the modern, worldly equivalents of racial distortion and delegitimating of black life represented in *Hamlet*. In the process, I am engaging further in a dialogue about making Shakespeare not just relevant but immediate and accessible for our time and using Shakespeare's own work to generate the terms of that investigation.[7]

Telling a Black Man's Story

Toward the end of *Hamlet*, the prince, with the knowledge that he has been poisoned and is running out of time, asks Horatio to "tell my story" (5.2.302). Hamlet exclaims, "Things standing thus unknown, I leave behind me!" (5.2.298), and Horatio understands that it is his job to explain the obscure, murderous in-house drama that has national political significance. Hamlet intends that personal vindication will follow if Horatio will "report me and my cause aright / To the *unsatisfied*" (5.2.292–293, emphasis added). His actions, mysteriously hidden behind a public veil of madness, are to be made legible and his reputation preserved with dignity. So critical and memorable is the prince's request that Jonathan Gil Harris remarks that "surviving Hamlet is Horatio's fate," one that extends to "making Hamlet live on in future narrations, a project that anticipates how *Hamlet* also survives."[8] Within humanist ideals of balance and equality in male friendship, both men represent congruency in age, upbringing, and education so that Horatio is the capable and perfect narrator of Hamlet's life.[9] The play posits, therefore, an important conjunction between Horatio and Hamlet, narrator and narrative subject, friends. By the play's end, despite the bloody period of "unnatural acts, / Of accidental judgements, casual slaughters" (5.2.334–335), Fortinbras joins a collaborative effort of character rehabilitation. Hamlet is borne away to be given a soldier's funeral: "For he was likely, had he been put on" (5.2.350). Hamlet is accorded privileges without any tangible proof of valiant, soldierly behavior that would earn him military rites.[10] This presumption of achievement ("had he been put on") has outpaced even the dying prince's desire for narrative clarification to initiate an entirely different program of Hamlet's biographical whitewashing and protection.

Over the centuries, the Horatian assignment to tell Hamlet's story has become the business of scholars producing literary criticism, and, despite the drama's singularities, Hamlet the man has long found a place among the critically satisfied. Philip Edwards asserts what most critics will likely grant: "It is probably safe to say that in the world's literature no single work has been so extensively written about as *Hamlet Prince of Denmark*."[11] This considerable critical attention functions as a vast collective bid to tell Hamlet's story and, at the same time, suggests the popularity of the play's male protagonist with generations of scholars. Hazlitt, as I noted earlier, memorably claimed that Hamlet's speeches are "as real as our own thoughts ... It is *we* who are Hamlet."[12] Critics identify with Hamlet personally and see in his doubt and skepticism a philosophy that resonates with their world view and points toward a modern social ethos.[13] The pattern of identification continues in the Oxford editor's assessment: "Spectators and readers alike feel drawn to identify themselves with Hamlet."[14] Even more recently, Marjorie Garber reiterates this theme: "Readers, scholars, and actors have over the years consistently identified with the character of Hamlet, finding in his gifts and his foibles an image of themselves."[15] Importantly, therefore, Marcellus's affirmation of Horatio as an intellectual – "Thou art a scholar" (1.1.42) – underwrites a compelling attraction to Horatio that leads to a neat symmetry: the critic as intellectual telling, in effect, a story of one's own deeply rooted identification with Hamlet. As a "just" man, (3.2.49), Horatio is adjudicated to be balanced, fair, equitable, and honorable in his dealings, the man suited to the responsibility Hamlet delegates and the very type of the literary critic implicated in the play's cultural afterlife.[16]

Michael Neill has argued, however, that at the turn of the twenty-first century, *Hamlet* has ceded its place of favor and prominence to *Othello* because of the global political shifts that have overtaken contemporary life. "Critics and directors alike," he writes, "began to trace in the cultural, religious, and ethnic animosities of its Mediterranean setting, the genealogy of the racial conflicts that fractured their own societies."[17] What connects these two plays for the purposes of this chapter, is that Othello, like Hamlet, issues an appeal to have his story told and his actions explained. Within such a comparative framework, pressure must be applied to the "we" in Hazlitt's "It is *we* who are Hamlet" to explore what is at stake in the identification so habitually assumed among critics even today. Who are the subjects of this collective "we," and what is its institutional power? One obvious but too often underappreciated answer is that this claim of identification has been nurtured by an academic industry in which white, male interests were historically epitomized, reflected, and affirmed in this much celebrated, cerebral prince. Hamlet is not only a male protagonist, but he is also white, his iconic black clothing serving to contrast with his pale northern European complexion. The failure among critics to routinely remark whiteness as a fully realized racialized category in all-white plays – that is, where all the characters are presumed to be white, unless otherwise noted – enables the normative invisibility of whiteness, which is a sign of its hegemony. This critical failure is a form of protectionism, precluding scrutiny of racialized whiteness, refusing to make it visible and subject to critique, and foreclosing self-inquiry into the nature and purpose of critics' own identification with Hamlet. Hazlitt's privileged category, "we," has, therefore, multiple referents, including of course a male academic elite but also, most centrally for the purposes of this book, a white literary intelligentsia whose investments in the project of white invisibility – that is, its hegemonic ubiquity – require attention. And as I have argued in Chapter 4, white identification with Hamlet runs the risk of complicity in misconstruing blackness while it entertains playing in the dark.

Consequently, the following question assumes particular significance: Despite *Othello*'s potent political relevance for today, where are the voices proclaiming, "It is *we* who are Othello"? Further, what might such a general absence reveal about our scholarly practices and profession as literary critics? The unavoidably simple yet pertinent response to the lack of overt statements of identification with Othello is that Othello is black, while the cadre of critics in Shakespeare studies has been predominantly white. That is, in a color-conscious society, blackness often functions too easily as the mark of unassailable difference. Blackness, however, registers far more than a deceptively simple superficial barrier, for it represents a body that bears within its material corporeality histories of domination, claims of illegitimacy, and dispossession, from black slavery and Jim Crow up to the present when institutional practices seek to maintain an inherited racial status quo.[18] The black body produced within these histories has consistently been exposed to threat and subjected to various forms of physical assault and psychological brutality. Ta-Nehisi Coates recognizes this body as the deliberate consequence of sanctioned human choice: "How do I live free in this black body? It is a profound question because America understands itself as God's handiwork, but the black body is the clearest evidence that America is the work of men."[19] The notion of collective cultural innocence ("God's handiwork") crumbles against the stark reality of motivated human action ("the work of men") to reveal the production of an alien black body enmeshed in a sharply contested racial history.

Importantly, knowledge within America's racial divide is asymmetrical: blacks have always needed to know whiteness, its rules, discipline, and various forms of corporal punishments, while whiteness has been free of the burden of knowing anything about the cultural intimacies of blackness. "While people of color understand the necessity of being able to read the white system and to know what life for white people is like," Frances E. Kendall argues, "those of us who are white are able to live our lives knowing very little of the experiences of people of color."[20] The disinterest in knowing is further complicated by strategically willed ignorance. These discrepancies in knowledge affect the capacity and will for a predominantly white class of critics to declare, "It is *we* who are Othello." At the same time, the absence of general critical identification with Othello rests on a broadly instituted disaffection and cultural desire to distance oneself from the abjection that is blackness – resulting in an epistemic assault on the black body – and to repress knowledge of the necessary complicity of whiteness in the seemingly unending manufacture of blackness as a peculiar institution.[21]

Hamlet and Othello – one white, the other black – desire to have their stories told, and it is perhaps this singular racial distinction that affects the telling, offering an insight into contemporary critical practice as it relates to matters of race and racial experience. Hamlet appears to have generated a good deal of critical satisfaction; thus, it is my intent to focus more sharply on Othello in order to engage speculatively the dissatisfaction swirling around race, whiteness, and critical reading in early modern studies.

Racial Ethics and the (Un)reliable White Critic

Othello's first Act is replete with verbal assaults targeting the play's titular black man that amount, in Edward Berry's words, to an "overt and vicious racism."[22] Importantly, these attacks against the Moor, a salacious mix of claims about monstrous blackness and barbaric sexual conquest, achieve additional meaning within the larger political context of the invading Ottoman forces and situate Othello as the corresponding black threat within. The metaphor of war thus hangs over the play's action. After the apparent resolution of the very public racial conflict that explodes in the Senate scene, Othello departs in his role as general of the Venetian military. Then, something peculiar happens: at the beginning of the second act, inclement weather intervenes, the Turkish fleet is devastated by a powerful storm, and the military crisis that was to play a significant role in the action disappears. What, as a result, must we make of the remainder of the play? The answer lies in Shakespeare's use of structural analogy. Shakespeare's suspension of the Turkish aggression forces us to recognize that conflict continues as a major issue but in the form of an internal "race war" initiated by the play's resident racist, Iago. In place of the violent clash of military warfare, the audience is treated instead to Iago's more covert but no less destructive operations that generate Othello's racial anxiety and self-hate.[23] One war replaces another.

To speak of racial conflict today risks being met with disapproval, wariness, or skepticism since the notion might suggest disturbance or upheaval of a kind that is antithetical to the desire for social stability. But Shakespeare's notion of a "race war" as expressed in *Othello* primarily educates us about the correlation of race and violence, indeed, about racism as a form of violent interaction that leaves the targeted individual sensing an assault on his or her humanity. A "race war" also suggests a desired outcome of winning so that Othello's mounting internalized racism, especially evident beginning in the temptation scene in Act 3, is the necessary correlate for the firm establishment of white racial superiority.[24] Othello's embarrassed confession of blackness as a stigmatized identity coincides with Iago's growing control over his black victim's self-perception, thus reinforcing the dynamic of power between white mastery and racialized blackness that degrades black persons at every level of social interaction. The play dramatizes two different kinds of racial tactics – one explicit and direct, the other covert and invisible – that operate as complementary forms of active racial aggression. Shakespeare's bold assertion of racial hostility by way of structural analogy constitutes a major political statement about the *already* evident and unresolved racial conflict in the early modern period for which the play serves as a provocative meditation extending into the modern world.

Throughout the action, in response to perceived racial animosity, Othello resorts to narrative explanation in order to evade entrapment and to achieve exoneration. Specifically, Othello is dramatically presented as telling stories with urgency when his life depends on it, most famously in the Senate scene. Indicted for the social inappropriateness of his dark skin as Desdemona's husband, Othello deploys narrative as a counteroffensive in this attack on the legitimacy of his black body (1.3.91). Whether in Brabantio's explicit appeal to Othello's black skin and the racial disgust it elicits (1.3.99) or later in Iago's callously quotidian reference to "black Othello" (2.3.29), Venice's racial climate consistently puts Othello on the defensive. At the play's conclusion, however, Othello experiences another narrative moment, this time with a notable difference. Because death will soon rob Othello of the power of speech, he will have to rely on his immediate audience to be collaborators in telling his story. Speaking or writing about race is central to Othello's penultimate speech that begins, "Soft you, a word or two before you go" (5.2.337) and ends with his suicide. This speech is typically regarded by critics as exemplifying Othello's divided self, epitomized by his split loyalties between Christian and Muslim, European and Moor, and white and black identities.[25] Despite this generally accepted and entirely accurate reading of an internal conflict, "turbaned Turk" versus

"Venetian" (5.2.352–353), I would emphasize Othello's stated chief concern regarding a posthumous biography: "Speak of me as I am."[26] Finally grasping the horror of Iago's deception, which led to Desdemona's murder, Othello wants the world to know the full complexity of "these unlucky deeds" (5.2. 340). Othello is, in effect, sensitive not only to the fact of murder, that casts him in the recognizable role of reckless black killer like Aaron his stage predecessor, but also to the perception of the black, racial stereotype of being "easily jealous" (5.2.344) as the precipitating factor in his behavior.[27] Additional references to himself as "the base Indian" (5.2.344) or the embodied, tear-dropping "Arabian trees" (5.2.349) multiply images of otherness to suggest how steeped Othello's language is in racial self-awareness. His act of self-slaughter, an attack on his own body, is designed to punish a racialized self who, like the "turbaned Turk," has committed the heinous assault on Venice in the person of Desdemona. Framed within the brutal cultural logic of a racist hegemony, the ruination that Iago promised is here fulfilled through a series of lies and machinations that leads Othello to become the agent of his own destruction.

Othello presents a classic Shakespearean tragic conceit: the master storyteller undone by a rival storyteller, Iago, whose baseless fictions are the intended "pestilence" (2.3.341) poured into Othello's ear. After learning about Iago's manipulations, Othello is even more anxious about narration, audience, and credibility. Othello understands that, given the play's imperial geopolitics, the members of his immediate audience will revert to seeing in his blackness the enemy "Turk" within, an identity and status that will require rigorous unpacking and thoughtful explanation. In the play's closing moments, therefore, unable to ultimately exercise his own narrative agency, Othello will have to delegate and entrust that responsibility elsewhere. Letters and official reports will be "set down" (5.2.342) or written to the Venetian hierarchy, but Othello's attendant concerns about racial stereotyping that undermines his felt loyalty to Venice leave him doubtful about the final impressions and judgments to be made. What, Othello questions, will be the reports from the military outpost in Cyprus now turned into the fatal scene of his racial undoing? The uncertainty driving Othello's forthright request for an explanatory story of his actions is, therefore, the matter of the unreliable narrator. That is, among his white, Christian auditors, whom can he trust to tell his story or speak of him in a balanced way? Even more pointedly, who among Othello's listeners is sufficiently free of racial bias, stemming from stereotyping, to allow for fair representation? Speaking "of" Othello thus has multiple overlapping meanings: speaking for him or on his behalf; speaking about him; and, because of the Othello's blackness, speaking about race.

Like Hamlet, Othello also needs a Horatio-like figure who will disentangle the complex racially inspired machinations that have drawn him into an unbearably murderous conundrum. Horatio the "just" man is imagined as Hamlet's friend with the added implication of shared class perspectives, cultural backgrounds, and values that are integral to the Renaissance male ideal. Shakespeare's omission of this figure in *Othello* or, rather, the deliberate negation of this ideal partner in the person of the false friend, Iago, produces the explicit effect of leaving Othello culturally adrift, alienated, and alone – without a firm conviction that, as a dying black man, he will receive the racially sensitive and responsible representation that he deserves. Othello is justifiably concerned with identifying a reliable narrator who exhibits shared commonalities or the Horatian "just" racial sensitivity suitable for the job. Locating such a person is a consideration that extends beyond the immediate dramatic scenario, with its questions about unreliable narrators, to include contemporary scholars and literary critics, the trustees of Othello's dying request to tell his story. Can we, contemporary critics, reliably tell his story? At this juncture the full scope of the play's intellectual demand on us becomes clear, especially given the co-optation of Shakespeare within high culture, specifically elite, white culture, whose authorities include literary critics steeped in systemic whiteness and constitute an overwhelmingly white demographic.[28] Othello's speech registers another kind of bifurcation or division, not within himself but for literary critics who are obliged to speak or write across a racial divide emblematized in the black body. Shakespeare probes a divided self that represents literary critics' white racial and epistemological investments – investments that might impede the ability to become the kind of reliable cultural narrators and race thinkers Othello envisions. The play ends with a disturbing crime, the murder of Desdemona, and relates it to the question of moral responsibility. But part of the play's genius is to prolong that moral reflection and extend it to the matter concerning audiences and literary critics as reliable narrators in order to question our complicity in reifying racial divisions as insurmountable.

Dead, Black Persons

Shakespeare's metaphor of race as "war" captures the inherent violence of unresolved social division that ensues. The 400-year history of the United

States, as Joe R. Feagin reminds us, is deeply implicated in precisely such an antagonistic racial reality. "It was exactly 350 years from 1619 [the year of the first purchase of Africans in Jamestown] to 1969," he writes, "the year the last major civil rights law went into effect officially ending legal segregation. Few people realize that for most of our history we were a country grounded in, and greatly shaped by, extensive slavery and legal segregation," whose reality was brutal and severe.[29] The white abolitionist Harriet Beecher Stowe concluded from contemporary evidence that "legal power of the master amounts to an absolute despotism over body and soul; and that there is no protection for the slave's life and limb, his family relations, his conscience, nay, more his eternal interests, but the character of the master."[30] This arbitrary subjection of the black slave's body to the will of the master sustained the ideological program of white supremacy that justified the idea of blacks as inferior to whites within a transatlantic, colonial trade that enriched Europe and became the bedrock of the United States economy.[31] It was in the service of a flourishing plantation economy that Thomas Jefferson perceived and argued a racial division "fixed in nature" that reinforces black inferiority "to the whites in the endowments both of body and mind" and advertises the superiority or supremacy of whites.[32] The open exploitation of black bodies not only fueled the nation's economic enterprise and made manifest the cultural ideology of white supremacy, but it was also reified in the institutional biases of a white slaveholding elite who shaped the provisions of the Constitution and populated the United States Senate and Supreme Court.[33] In truth, following Feagin, we are not far removed in time from the physical harms endured, the social constraints suffered, and the legal proscriptions levied against blacks under slavery and Jim Crow, especially when we consider the legacy of institutional and systemic racism in unfair housing practices, with its impact on wealth accrued over time, and the current startling rate of mass incarceration of blacks.[34] In Coates's words, "Whiteness and blackness are not a fact of providence, but of policy – of slave codes, black codes, Jim Crow, redlining, GI Bills, housing covenants, New Deals."[35] Race, therefore, with its history of violation of black bodies, stigmatization of inferiority, economic exploitation, legal excesses, and wide-ranging expropriation must be understood as a "thick description," not merely a "thin" or superficial reference to decontextualized skin color, which can disrupt and deter dialogue and understanding.[36]

The place names Ferguson, Baltimore, and Cleveland have been reconfigured by recent history as flash points in a longer national drama of race in America. The fatal shooting of unarmed teenager Michael Brown by a white police officer in Ferguson, Missouri on August 9, 2014 sparked nationwide, headline-grabbing protests for months and fueled wide-ranging debates about anti-black bias, state violence, and social justice.[37] Other names of unarmed black males have been added to a still growing gallery of the dead. Among the most widely reported, John Crawford III was mistakenly shot and killed in an Ohio retail store by law enforcement, and three weeks before that on Staten Island, New York, Eric Garner died at the hands of yet another police officer using an illegal chokehold.[38] In the following months, Akai Gurley in Brooklyn and twelve-year-old Tamir Rice in Cleveland lost their lives.[39] A grand jury's failure to indict the officer involved in the Brown killing further inflamed public passions, strained municipal relations, and exacerbated national perceptions of police brutality. The introduction of cell-phone video helped secure otherwise rare charges or indictments for officers involved in these kinds of incidents and seared horrific images permanently into the digital public consciousness: a lumbering Walter Scott in South Carolina shot from behind by an officer who fired eight times, and a screaming, limp Freddie Gray in Baltimore being taken by police to a transport van and thereafter found to be suffering from fatal spinal injuries.[40] Still, these gruesome incidents continued to mount. Alton Sterling, shot dead by two police officers, July 5, 2016; Philando Castile, shot five times and killed by a police officer, July 6, 2016; Stephon Clark, shot fatally by two police officers, March 18, 2018; Botham Jean, shot and killed by an off-duty officer who entered the wrong apartment, September 6, 2018; Ahmaud Arbery, chased while jogging by three armed white men in vehicles and fatally shot, February 23, 2020.[41]

While media attention has largely focused on African American men, the Say Her Name project advocates for justice for African American women in similarly violent situations.[42] The names Sandra Bland, who died in a jail cell after a pretextual traffic stop on July 13, 2015, and Breonna Taylor, killed in a barrage of bullets as officers forced their way into the sleeping woman's home on March 13, 2020, join the annals of the dead. May 25, 2020, a stunned worldwide audience watched in disbelief and horror as George Floyd lay on a public street in Minneapolis, with the now convicted white officer, Derek Chauvin, kneeling on his neck for nine-and-a-half minutes, his life slowly ebbing away as he gasped, "I can't breathe." Floyd's words reiterated the grim cycle of police killings and racial abuse, echoing those of Eric Garner as he, too, struggled in vain to breathe in a fatal, police chokehold. I take the time to repeat a mere fraction of the names of black lives taken to remind us not to forget and to allow the accounting of the dead to approximate numerically the emotional weight of loss and the historical measure of injustice. In this context of multiple deaths and unresolved legal outcomes for the perpetrators – Chauvin's is a notable exception, given the global publicity of Floyd's public murder – one person's discomfort with the notion of Shakespeare's construction of racial conflict as a war contrasts with another's frustrated acceptance of its experiential accuracy.

The Black Lives Matter movement, born in the wake of seventeen-year-old Trayvon Martin's murder on February 26, 2012, has emerged to agitate vigorously for accountability and more comprehensive approaches to address racial inequality, possibly signaling "a new era of civil rights activism."[43] The shocked reaction to the wanton disregard for Floyd's life has led some cautiously to hope that the multiracial uprising that followed in the summer of 2020 might predict "for the first time in American history, a legitimate anti-racist majority."[44] At the same time, the insurrection on Capitol Hill of January 6, 2021 stunned the nation, as multiple white supremacist groups forced the language of domestic terrorism into the public lexicon. The troubling undercurrent to the killings of black persons is the specter of a long, shameful history of white violence and abused, slain black bodies from the era of violent slave patrols deployed in southern states through the Black Codes and the Jim Crow era: "Early municipal departments in growing US cities were overwhelmingly white, and brutalized vulnerable communities routinely. Thousands of lynchings of black Americans by white vigilantes went unpunished by the judicial system. And during the civil rights era and well beyond, peaceful protest has been harshly suppressed by officers sworn to protect and serve."[45] It is no wonder, then, that the public reaction has been visceral, given this visitation in the form of media reports and images of a haunting history revived. The authors of "Unarmed and Black" note that for the first seven months of 2015, "24 unarmed black men have been shot and killed by police – one every nine days, according to a *Washington Post* database of fatal police shootings" and conclude that "black men were seven times more likely than white men to die by police gunfire while unarmed."[46] More recently, researchers from the University of Pennsylvania's Perelman School of Medicine, Yale University, and Drexel University have found that shootings by police "of unarmed Black people in the United States were three times higher than that of white people between 2015 and the beginning of 2020."[47] When black lives appear to be under threat, especially from representatives of state power, the stakes are immediately increased, and public concern is, understandably, high.

Among the most striking findings was the significant difference in the public reaction to the conversations generated around black killings, a split predicated on racial identity, cultural location, and perception. Established in 1968 by President Lyndon B. Johnson to study the race riots of 1967, the Kerner Commission was unqualified in its summary conclusion: "Our nation is moving toward two societies, one black, one white – separate and unequal."[48] Several studies have since confirmed a continued, growing division exacerbated by the 2008 recession, which generated a mortgage crisis and high unemployment.[49] A snapshot of the public reaction to the black deaths involving police in the period following Michael Brown's death has been captured by polls that show a persistent separation of opinion and experience that is marked by race. The Pew Research Center reports that "by about four-to-one (80% to 18%), African Americans say the shooting in Ferguson raises important issues about race that merit discussion. By contrast, whites, by 47% to 37%, say the issue of race is getting more attention than it deserves."[50] The numbers concerning trust in the police and the criminal justice system show a similar divergence: "About three-fourths of blacks said they thought that the system was biased against African-Americans, and that the police were more likely to use deadly force against a black person than a white person. Only 44 percent of whites felt that the system was biased against blacks."[51] Police officers generally believe that fatal "encounters are isolated incidents and not signs of broader problems between police and the black community," but a closer examination within the ranks show a marked racial contrast: "A majority of black officers (57%) said that such incidents were evidence of a broader problem, but only 27% of white officers and 26% of Hispanic officers said so."[52] Taken at different points and by various agencies since the Brown killing in Ferguson, the polls nevertheless reveal a consistent pattern of racial divergence in opinion. Pioneering research conducted over the last decade in the field of social psychology corroborates the disparities in the polls' stark racial findings. Research on perceived black aggression and the tendency for whites to misread objects associated with blacks as weapons helps to explain the idea of the perennial black criminal in a white-dominant society.[53] As noted earlier, researchers have also found that a substantial majority of those tested (almost 75 percent) showed "automatic White preference" that is consistent with "racially discriminatory behavior."[54] The public's ability to perceive and speak coherently about black persons is fundamentally undermined by the kind of racial disjunction Othello intuits and that has become even more socially, economically, and perceptually "thick" and pronounced with time.

Robert P. Jones alleges that self-segregation – whites having little routine, daily contact with blacks and other racial and ethnic groups – plays a significant role in the current state of divided perceptions. Using "social networks" theory, he explains: "The social networks of whites are a remarkable 91 percent white. White American social networks are only one percent black, one percent Hispanic, one percent Asian or Pacific Islander, one percent mixed race, and one percent other race. In fact, fully three-quarters (75 percent) of whites have entirely white social networks without any minority presence."[55]

Offering a broader historical and theoretical framework, Charles W. Mills describes a "racial contract" wherein a white polity seeks to maintain the security of its vested social and political interests in a forced and unequal agreement between races.[56] Adam Serwer, drawing on Mills, observes:

> If the social contract is the implicit agreement among members of a society to follow the rules – for example, acting lawfully, adhering to the results of elections, and contesting the agreed-upon rules by nonviolent means – then the racial contract is a codicil rendered in invisible ink, one stating that the rules as written do not apply to nonwhite people in the same way.[57]

In this intense climate of separatism and contest, Judith Butler perceives a destructive racial logic at work. Whites regard blacks "as threats even when they do not threaten, when they have no weapon, and the video footage that shows precisely this is taken to be a ratification of the police's perception."[58] Because blacks threaten, according to this thinking, one can justify the disposal of life in such an anxious, perpetual state of self-defense. The devastation of black bodies by state authorities, moreover, does not register the same measure of alarm for whites as it does for blacks since such destruction works offensively to protect white interests and privilege: "But those whose lives are not considered to matter, whose lives are perceived as a threat to the life that embodies white privilege can be destroyed in the name of that life."[59] This brutal mix of physical violence in the service of ideology elicits the phrase "race war" from Butler who, like Shakespeare, seems to understand the profoundly violent nature of the callous exploitation of blackness. Butler's assessment of racial violence linked to white privilege allows for a transition to the undercurrent of tension that circulates in predominately white academic disciplines.

Race: No One Is Immune

Literary scholars, specifically Shakespeareans, are not impervious to the cultural biases and strategies deployed within white dominance that set up a contentious relationship between diverse racial groups. Structural inequality as the legacy of sanctioned racism – whether in the form of black slavery or a discriminatory criminal justice system – continues to be reinforced by its progenitors: white supremacy and white privilege, the latter being a less explicit form of domination but no less consequential and harmful.[60] As subjects working and writing under the historical legacy and contemporary circumstances of a divided society I described earlier, it would be nearly impossible not to be affected. Barbara Trepagnier's observation, "No one is immune to ideas that permeate the culture in which he or she is raised," must extend to the professional culture within which one experiences intellectual gestation and growth.[61] Thus, the pertinence and urgency of Othello's request for us to tell his story must be restated as a major disciplinary concern. In the current state of racially divided American society, how might literary scholars responsibly tell Othello's story or, more broadly, speak and write reliably about race? Given race's deep historical roots, it does not appear that the subject can be avoided altogether – nor should it. The task is made more difficult when forms of denial set in.

A few years ago, at a Shakespeare Association of America (SAA) meeting in Boston, a seminar participant declared with intensity that "*Othello* is not about race."[62] The seminar was devoted to a discussion of the play, and, not surprisingly, some of the contributors, including me, had proceeded with the assumption that *Othello* constitutes a major intervention in the emergence of a racial discourse and examination of the attendant asymmetries of power in the early modern period. Several minutes later, still dissatisfied with the flow of the discussion, the same participant reiterated the claim, insisting yet again that "*Othello* is not about race." The remark was to serve as a corrective, an attempt to stem the critical tide of a misguided and erroneous enterprise that identified *Othello* with race. The speaker's strong denial appealed to the fantasy of historical accuracy that would banish race talk as a dangerous anachronism. Indeed, Michael Neill reports that "the most striking thing about the very earliest responses to the tragedy is that they pay no attention to what, from a modern perspective, seems its most conspicuous feature – the interracial love affair."[63] But Kim F. Hall points out that for over two centuries white actors blackened their skins. They did so up until the 1814 Drury Lane performance by Edmund Kean in which he instituted the so-called "Bronze Age" of Othello in performance because a lighter skin tone appeared requisite to suit a public taste that had grown to associate blackness with the denigration of slavery.[64] I understand Hall's statement as confirmation that the play's attention to color differential was significant and consequential from the earliest performances.

To dismiss race in *Othello* as anachronistic and misplaced, therefore, constitutes an appeal to historical accuracy that recalls the old debates of the 1990s, when early modern race studies was in its emergent period. Fetishizing historical accuracy is to claim the high moral ground of sound scholarship, a position from which to disguise resistance to race work, from which to promote a singular perspective and methodology as acceptable while placing firm restrictions on others. Two panel sessions at the 2013 SAA conference in Toronto – "Race: Medieval and Early Modern" and "Race: Early Modern and Transatlantic" – seemed poised to serve as major platforms to investigate the state of the art in race studies and reflect on the future of the field. Instead, a few panelists, some more attenuated in their views than others, seemed mired in the kind of skepticism that gave rise to the same arguments about anachronism and hence questioning of the legitimacy of the early modern race project altogether. About anachronism and the disputed term "race," Ania Loomba and Jonathan Burton observe that racial constructs have taken multiple, different modes over time, so "it makes less sense to try and settle upon a precise definition or indeed to locate a precise moment of origin for racial ideologies than to delineate the ways in which they order and delimit human possibilities through a wide range of conjoined discourses and practice."[65] Indeed, more is at stake in the acts of resistance in my cited examples, where a driving ideology limits and places constraints on "human possibilities through a wide range of conjoined discourse and practice."

My experience sitting in that room directly across from the speaker demanding that "*Othello* is not about race" was akin to Tim Wise's description of the effect of white privilege and power in social intercourse: "That which keeps people of color off-balance in a racist society is that which keeps whites in control: a truism that must be discussed if whites are to understand our responsibility to work for change."[66] As a result of the heated declaration, was I, as well as other like-minded members of the seminar, supposed to recuse myself from the conversation, return to silence, and abandon the project of race in the early modern period because I had been duly chastised about a gross error in scholarship? Was I, as a result, supposed to yield control over the proceedings to the bearer of the claim? On my part, such withdrawal, imposed silence, and delegitimization within an academic and professional arena would epitomize the "off-balance" racial experience, discussed by Wise, from which whiteness draws its superiority and power. I would suggest that the assertive claim, "*Othello* is not about race," is contextually, in Adrienne Rich's words, an example of "White solipsism: To think, imagine, and speak as if whiteness described the world."[67] For the injunction would drain the proceedings of all critical race analysis, mute the significance of Othello's skin color differential, remove all trace of intersectional politics, and mark a return to broad humanistic discourse, while producing a strategically bland white-washed text whose primary goal is evasion.

At the 2011 gathering of the SAA in Bellevue, Washington, Margo Hendricks delivered a panel presentation paper titled "'I saw him in my visage': Problems with Race Studies in Early Modern English Literature."[68] In an impassioned address, Hendricks lamented what she saw as the growing metaphorization of race among the already large number of publications that took race as their ostensible subject or wore it as an ornamental label betraying a fashionable gesture to the topic's trendiness. Drawing on Desdemona's famous admission, "I saw Othello's visage in his mind" (1.3.250), Hendricks called attention to Desdemona's looking away from the fact of Othello's blackness to focus on her own mental construct or imagining of Othello's reality.[69] In this reading, Othello's mind is only accessible as a projection of the observer's fantasy. Like Desdemona, Hendricks argues, contemporary Shakespearean scholarship, especially as practiced by white scholars, she implies, has made race into whatever it wishes, "envisioning race everywhere but the body."[70] Hendricks's insistence on the black body is meant to challenge what she sees as the erosion of the materiality of race and to check the negation at the heart of much recent race scholarship that "has served to de-politicize the politics of race in Shakespeare studies as well as Renaissance and early modern studies."[71] What is at stake in Hendricks's reading, I would argue, is a critique of systemic whiteness and white privilege in the practice of literary criticism, where whiteness is a position from which one speaks and writes, an ideological location grounded in membership in the majority culture.[72] With such an investment in one's own privilege, how reliable might one be as a narrator speaking across the social boundaries of racial difference?

Unpacking White Positionality

I conclude by considering the possible implications of Othello's request to "Speak of me" by distinguishing among "speaking of," "speaking for," and "speaking about." "Speaking of" Othello, that is, speaking and writing about race within the discipline of English studies, requires unpacking one's white positioning to reach toward new forms of racial knowledge. Speaking of Othello is an invitation to see and engage from a conscious, racialized perspective (whiteness is a race too) in order to better understand race, its dependence on contested categories of difference, and the contractual complicity exercised by the dominant culture in sustaining white innocence and a strategically requisite ignorance of oppression. Barbara Applebaum submits that, "whites have a positive interest in remaining ignorant because this serves to sustain their moral self-image" without having to contend with the cognitive disturbance of burdensome racial knowledge.[73] Such recognition will require the reconsideration of one's own part in this destructive, parasitic construct of power that is race and racism, especially important in a dominant culture where white privilege enables intellectual stasis, political inaction, and selective professional disaffection. To speak of Othello will also include listening to members of nondominant groups in order to expand awareness that might lead to effective change and introduce relevant perspectives that can better facilitate speaking of others.[74]

At the same time, feminist and postcolonial critics have interrogated the gesture of "speaking for" another as an act of ownership and erasure that reinstalls a privileged subject and strengthens existing hierarchies.[75] Speaking for another, some maintain, is a form of imperialism that ensures mastery over the one spoken for.[76] A radical formulation would suggest that one could only speak for oneself in order to avoid various forms of expropriation. Despite the claim to ethical responsibility as the rationale for this stance, that is too easy a way out. Drawing on Foucault's notion of "rituals of speaking," Linda Alcoff understands speech acts as embedded within discursively dense communication networks that do not permit any simple peeling away or unique separation.[77] It is futile to think

> that one *can* retreat into one's discrete location and make claims entirely and singularly based on that location that do not range over others, that one can disentangle oneself from the implicating networks between one's discursive practices and others' locations, situations, and practices.[78]

Alcoff further argues that the retreat option, by its own design, "allows the continued dominance of current discourses and acts by omission to reinforce their dominance."[79] This would mean that in the instance of race, not speaking for those subjected to its marginalizing and alienating effects might further negate its problems through neglect and gradually erase it from our social agenda through practiced ignorance, at the same time leaving intact white-dominant frameworks.

I would suggest that we approach Othello's request for a responsible, explanatory narrator as an invitation to make legible the "continued dominance" of the forms of racial discourse that misread Othello's social location as a black man. Through the heuristic construct of the critic's divided self – racially white but having to tell a black man's story – the play positions its audience to have its racial knowledge and intelligence tested. Feminist and postcolonial critiques notwithstanding, the proposition *Othello* offers concerning white auditors speaking for a black man engages the question of responsibility to others through a rigorous self-examination. Moreover, the refusal to speak for another might, in specific contexts, result in ignoring the mandate for coalition building toward social justice and equity, in abjuring the responsibility to speak for others who sometimes lack the resources to speak for themselves (quite literally, Othello will be dead), and in protecting the interests of a white racial status quo. Patricia J. Williams insightfully affirms that "the solution to racism lies in our ability to see its ubiquity but not to concede its inevitability."[80] The goal of an inclusive, plural society involves precisely the issue of successfully bridging the racial divide that *Othello* proposes: the "imaginary exercise of taking to mind and heart the investment of oneself in another, indeed the investment of oneself as that other."[81] That is, in Shakespearean shorthand, the articulation of a self-interrogating critical credo, "We are Othello." To "speak of" Othello demands the informed self-inquiry embedded in the assertion, "We are Othello."

Finally, "speaking about" race means positioning whiteness in relation to other social identities and classes, exchanging exceptionality for the collective solidarity of antiracist coalition building. Rather than preserve whiteness as a protected category, one understands and accepts the shared intersectional interests that speaking race requires.[82] Framing the recent killings of blacks within a renewed vision of the civil rights movement for contemporary America, the hip-hop artist and actor Common, who renounced homophobia in his own lyrics in 2007, reflects in a recent speech, "I realize that I am the hopeful black woman who was denied her right to vote; I am the caring white supporter killed on the front lines of freedom; I am the unarmed black kid who maybe needed a hand but instead was given a bullet; I am the two fallen police officers, murdered in the line of duty."[83] Here is a voice giving a modern take on "It is *we* who are Othello." Speaking race enlightened by this level of intersectional identity and real-world awareness can do justice to Othello's request, "Speak of me as I am," and inform our disciplinary endeavors as responsible, reliable scholars, committed to antiracist practices, working in a real twenty-first century world of change for Shakespeare in our time. Shakespeare, a figure who already unites us in a broad collaborative scholarly endeavor, can prove instrumental in helping us recognize and talk about the barriers that divide us and suggest how we can rethink and improve on our collective responsibility of living together in a plural society.

Notes

This chapter is an expanded version of a piece first published in *Shakespeare in Our Time: A Shakespeare Association of America Collection*, ed. Dympna Callaghan and Suzanne Gossett, Bloomsbury Arden Shakespeare (London: Bloomsbury Publishing, 2016).

1 *Othello*, ed. Michael Neill (Oxford: Clarendon, 2006), 1. All further references are taken from this edition and are cited parenthetically.

2 Sandhya Somashekhar, Wesley Lowery, Keith L. Alexander, Kimberly Kindy, and Julie Tate, "Black and Unarmed," *Washington Post*, August 8, 2015, www.washingtonpost.com/sf/national/2015/08/08/black-and-unarmed/.

3 For a critique of the post-race concept, see Mitchell, *Seeing Through Race*; on the related concept of colorblindness, see Lani Guinier and Gerald Torres, *The Miner's Canary: Enlisting Race, Resisting Power, Transforming Democracy* (Cambridge, MA: Harvard University Press, 2002), esp. 32–66.

4 Mitchell, *Seeing Through Race*, xi.

5 Rothenberg, *White Privilege*, 1.

6 Shannon Sullivan, *Revealing Whiteness: The Unconscious Habits of Racial Privilege* (Bloomington: Indiana University Press, 2006); Rothenberg, *White Privilege*; Frances E. Kendall, *Understanding White Privilege: Creating Pathways to Authentic Relationships Across Race*, 2nd ed. (New York: Routledge, 2013); Moon-Kie Jung et al., eds., *State of White Supremacy: Racism, Governance, and the United States* (Stanford: Stanford University Press, 2011).

7 For a wide-ranging study of this kind, see Brett Stockdill and Mary Yu Danico, *Transforming the Ivory Tower: Challenging Racism, Sexism, and Homophobia in the Academy* (Honolulu: University of Hawai'i Press, 2012).

8 Jonathan Gil Harris, "Surviving *Hamlet*," *Shakespeare Quarterly* 62.2 (2011): 145–147 (146). Harris writes as the editor of a special issue on the topic of "Surviving *Hamlet*."

9 On the humanist ideal of male friendship, as well as its value for social advancement and self-definition, see Elizabeth Hanson, "Fellow Students: Hamlet, Horatio, and the Early Modern University," *Shakespeare Quarterly* 62.2 (2011): 205–229, esp. 207–208; Tom MacFaul, *Male Friendship in Shakespeare and His Contemporaries* (Cambridge: Cambridge University Press, 2009); and Michael Neill, "'He that thou knowest thine': Friendship and Service in *Hamlet*," in *A Companion to Shakespeare's Works, vol. 1: The*

Tragedies, ed. Richard Dutton and Jean E. Howard (Malden: Blackwell, 2003), 319–338.

10 In "Fellow Students," Hanson remarks that Ophelia's description of Hamlet as courtier, soldier, and scholar (3.1.151–52) recycles "a Renaissance ideologeme," an ideal that hardly fits Hamlet since "he utterly lacks the attributes of courtier and soldier" (207).

11 Phillip Edwards, ed., Introduction to *Hamlet, Prince of Denmark*, The New Cambridge Shakespeare (Cambridge: Cambridge University Press, 2003), 32.

12 Quoted in Ibid., 33.

13 Ibid., 34–35, where he discusses a range of opinions from A. W. Schlegel to Friedrich Nietzsche.

14 Hibbard, introduction to *Hamlet*, 1.

15 Marjorie Garber, *Shakespeare and Modern Culture* (New York: Anchor Books, 2008), 201.

16 On the emergence of Horatio as a figure for the literary critic, see Christopher Warley, "Specters of Horatio," *ELH* 75.4 (2008): 1023–1050, esp. 1024; and Harris, "Surviving *Hamlet*," 145.

17 Neill, introduction to *Othello*, 1.

18 See Alexander, *The New Jim Crow*. In "White Privilege/White Complicity: Connecting 'Benefiting From' to 'Contributing To,'" *Philosophy of Education Yearbook* (2008): 292–300, Barbara Applebaum notes, "The understanding of racism has shifted from a focus on individual people and prejudiced attitudes to an awareness of institutional and cultural practices that generate and maintain it" (292). On institutional or structural racism, see also Eduardo Bonilla-Silva, *Racism without Racists: Color-Blind Racism and the Persistence of Inequality in America* (New York: Rowman and Littlefield, 2014).

19 Ta-Nehisi Coates, *Between the World and Me* (New York: Spiegel and Grau, 2015), 12.

20 Kendall, *Understanding White Privilege*, 65. See n. 6.

21 On the complex issue of racial complicity, see Barbara Applebaum, *Being White, Being Good: White Complicity, White Moral Responsibility, and Social Justice Pedagogy* (Lanham: Lexington Books, 2010); and Sandra Lee Bartky, "Race, Complicity, and Culpable Ignorance," in her *"Sympathy and Solidarity" and Other Essays* (Lanham: Rowan & Littlefield, 2002).

22 Edward Berry, "Othello's Alienation," *Studies in English Literature 1500–1900* 30.2 (1990): 315–333 (319); on the question of racism in the play, see also Martin Orkin, "Othello and the 'plain face' of Racism," *Shakespeare Quarterly* 38.2 (1987): 166–188.

23 See, for example , Janet Adelman, "Iago's Alter Ego: Race as Projection in *Othello*," *Shakespeare Quarterly* 48.2 (1997): 125–144. Berry observes, "Although Iago's notorious artistry is usually linked to his capacity to shape a plot, it extends as well to characterization, for the Othello he in many ways creates comes to see himself as his own stereotype" ("Othello's Alienations," 319).

24 Othello suddenly confesses a highly racialized self-image because of Iago's manipulations: "Haply, for I am black" (3.3.266).

25 Loomba, *Shakespeare, Race, and Colonialism*, 97; and Ambereen Dadabhoy, "Two Faced: The Problem of Othello's Visage," in *Othello: The State of Play*, ed. Lena Cowen Orlin (New York: Bloomsbury, 2014), 121–147, esp. 142.

26 The installation artist Fred Wilson intuited the significance of this crucial moment in his 2003 Venice Biennale exhibit; see Peter Erickson, "Respeaking Othello in Fred Wilson's 'Speak of Me as I Am,'" *Art Journal* 64.2 (2005): 4–19.

27 In addition to stereotypes that could have been learned from repeated visits to the early modern theater, where stage Moors were represented as violent, dangerous, and criminal, the designation "Moor" by itself signified foreigner, non-Christian (and, therefore, un-English), and black. Barthelemy examines the negative black stereotypes in *Black Face, Maligned Race*, esp. 72–146.

28 The ascendancy of Shakespeare to elite cultural status has accelerated the debate over the inherent tension in the appropriations and adaptations of Shakespeare within popular culture; see Lanier, *Shakespeare and Modern Popular Culture*, and Paul Prescott, "Shakespeare and Popular Culture," in *The New Cambridge Companion to Shakespeare*, ed. Margreta de Grazia and Stanley Wells (Cambridge: Cambridge University Press, 2010), 269–284.

29 Joe R. Feagin, *The White Racial Frame: Centuries of Racial Framing and Counter-Framing*, 2nd ed. (New York: Routledge, 2013), 1.

30 Quoted in Ibid., 35.

31 On the convergence of "colonialism, capitalism, modernity and global exploitation," see Ibid., 24–28, esp. 24. See also Edward E. Baptist, *The Half Has Never Been Told: Slavery and the Making of American Capitalism* (New York: Basic Books, 2014).

32 Thomas Jefferson, "Laws" from *Notes on the State of Virginia*, in *Race and the Enlightenment: A Reader*, ed. Emmanuel Chukwudi Eze (Malden: Blackwell, 2000), 97, 102. On the European side, David Hume insisted in "Of National Characters" that blacks are "naturally inferior to the whites. There never was a civilized nation of any other complexion than white," in Eze, *Race and the Enlightenment*, 33.

33 On the white slaveholding elite and the protection of their interests in our founding institutions and legal documents, see Feagin, *The White Racial Frame*, 30–34.

34 In *The Possessive Investment in Whiteness*, Lipsitz notes, for example, the role of the Homestead Act of 1863 and the management of the Federal Housing Act (FHA) loans between 1932 and 1962 in creating white wealth at the expense of blacks; in the case of the FHA loans, appraisers funneled 98 percent of loans to whites (107).

35 Coates, "The Case for Reparations."

36 On the concept of "thick description," see Clifford Geertz, "Thick Description: Toward an Interpretive Theory of Culture," in *The*

Interpretation of Cultures: Selected Essays by Clifford Geertz (New York: Basic Books, 1973), 3–32.

37 Somashekhar et al., "Black and Unarmed."

38 Mark Berman, "No Indictments after Police Shoot and Kill Man at an Ohio Wal-Mart; Justice Dept. Launches Investigation," *Washington Post*, September 24, 2014, www.washingtonpost.com/news/post-nation/wp/2014/09/24/no-indictments-after-policeshoot-and-kill-man-at-an-ohio-wal-mart-justice-dept-launches-investigation/; Al Baker, J. David Goodman, and Benjamin Mueller, "Beyond the Chokehold: The Path to Eric Garner's Death," *New York Times*, June 13, 2015.

39 J. David Goodman and Vivian Yee, "Officer Charged in Akai Gurley Case Debated Reporting Gunshot, Officials Say," *New York Times*, February 11, 2015; Michael Muskal and Lauren Raab, "Cleveland Blames Tamir Rice, 12, for His Own Death Then Apologizes," *Los Angeles Times*, March 2, 2015, www.latimes.com/nation/la-na-tamir-rice-lawsuit-blame-cleveland-20150302-story.html.

40 Michael S. Schmidt and Matt Apuzzo, "South Carolina Officer is Charged with Murder of Walter Scott," *New York Times*, April 7, 2015; Sheryl Gay Stolberg, "Baltimore Suspends 6 Police Officers in Inquiry in Death of Freddie Gray," *New York Times*, April 20, 2015.

41 Other incidents that barely made the news allegedly involved the victims having guns: 2-year-old E. J. Bradford, shot three times in the back, November 22, 2018; 20-year-old Willie McCoy, shot at 55 times while asleep in his car, February 9, 2019.

42 Sarah Lazare, "Say Her Name: In Expression of Vulnerability and Power, Black Women Stage Direct Action with Chests Bared," *Common Dreams*, 22 May 2015, www.commondreams.org/news/2015/05/22/say-her-name-expression-vulnerability-and-power-blackwomen-stage-direct-action. The article cites Kimberlé Williams Crenshaw who remarks that, "inclusion of Black women's experiences in social movements, media narratives and policy demands around policing and police brutality is critical to effectively combating racialized state violence for Black communities and other communities of color."

43 Black Lives Matter was created in 2013 after the death of seventeen-year-old Trayvon Martin at the hands of a civilian who was acquitted of the charge, but it has become a visible national movement in the years following with the multiple deaths of unarmed persons at the hands of the police.

44 Ta-Nehisi Coates, "The Great Fire."

45 Oliver Laughland, "US Police Have a History of Violence Against Black People. Will It Ever Stop?" *The Guardian*, June 4, 2020, www.theguardian.com/us-news/2020/jun/04/american-police-violence-against-black-people.

46 Somashekhar et al., "Black and Unarmed."

47 Penn Medicine News. "Fatal Police Shootings Among Black Americans Remain High, Unchanged Since 2015," *Penn Medicine News*, October 28, 2020, www.pennmedicine.org/news/news-releases/2020/october/fatal-police-shootings-among-black-americans-remain-high-unchanged-since-2015.

48 "The Kerner Commission Report," *Social Service Review* 42.2 (1968): 261–263 (261).

49 Samuel Walker, Cassia Spohn, and Miriam DeLone, *The Color of Justice: Race, Ethnicity and Crime in America*, 5th ed. (Belmont: Wadsworth, 2012), 99. See also Andrew Hacker, *Two Nations: Black and White, Separate, Hostile, Unequal* (New York: Scribner, 2003); Donald R. Kinder and Lynn M. Sanders, *Divided by Color: Racial Politics and Democratic Ideals* (Chicago: University of Chicago Press, 1996).

50 "Stark Racial Divisions in Reactions to Ferguson Police Shooting," Pew Research Center, Washington, DC, August 18, 2014, https://www.pewresearch.org/politics/2014/08/18/stark-racial-divisions-in-reactions-to-ferguson-police-shooting/. Other surveys support the stated findings of the Pew Research Center polls; see "Gallup Review: Black and White Differences in Views on Race," Gallup, Washington, DC, December 12, 2014, www.gallup.com/poll/180107/gallup-review-black-white-differences-views-race.aspx.

51 Kevin Sack and Megan Thee-Brenan, "Poll Finds Most in U.S. Hold Dim View of Race Relations," *New York Times*, July 23, 2015. Another poll observes, "There are substantial differences in the confidence that blacks and whites have in their local police forces. For instance, whites are twice as likely as blacks to express at least a fair amount of confidence in police officers in their communities to treat blacks and whites equally (72% of whites vs. 36% of blacks)." See "Few Say Police Forces Nationally Do Well in Treating Races Equally," Pew Research Center, Washington, DC, August 25, 2014, www.people-press.org/2014/08/25/few-say-police-forces-nationally-do-well-in-treating-races-equally/.

52 Drew Desilver, Michael Lipka, and Dalia Fahmy, "10 Things We Know about Race and Policing in the U.S.," Pew Research Center, Washington, DC, June 3, 2020, www.pewresearch.org/fact-tank/2020/06/03/10-things-we-know-about-race-and-policing-in-the-u-s/.

53 Kurt Hugenberg and Galen V. Bodenhausen, "Facing Prejudice: Implicit Prejudice and the Perception of Facial Threat," *Psychological Science* 14.6 (2003): 640–643; Anthony G. Greenwald et al., "Targets of Discrimination: Effects of Race on Responses to Weapon Holders," *Journal of Experimental Social Psychology* 39.4 (2003): 399–405.

54 Banaji and Greenwald, *Blindspot*, 47.

55 Robert P. Jones, "Self-Segregation: Why It's So Hard for Whites to Understand Ferguson," *Atlantic*, August 21, 2014, www.theatlantic.com/national/archive/2014/08/self-segregation-why-its-hard-for-whites-to-understand-ferguson/378928/. Jones adds, "This level of social-network racial homogeneity among whites is significantly higher than among black Americans (65 percent) or Hispanic Americans (46 percent)."

56 Charles W. Mills, *The Racial Contract* (Ithaca, NY: Cornell University Press, 1997), 12.

57 Adam Serwer, "The Coronavirus Was an Emergency Until Trump Found Out Who Was Dying," *Atlantic*, 8 May 2020, www.theatlantic.com/ideas/archive/2020/05/americas-racial-contract-showing/611389/.

58 Judith Butler, interview by George Yancy, "What's Wrong with 'All Lives Matter?,'" *New York Times*, January 12, 2015.
59 Judith Butler, interview by George Yancy, "What's Wrong with 'All Lives Matter?'"
60 Sullivan remarks that, in contrast to white supremacy's "conscious, deliberate forms of white domination," today "white domination tends to prefer silent tiptoeing to loud stomping" (*Revealing Whiteness,* 5).
61 Barbara Trepagnier, *Silent Racism: How Well-Meaning White People Perpetuate the Racial Divide* (Boulder: Paradigm, 2007), 15.
62 "*Othello,* Part One" seminar, Shakespeare Association of America meeting, Boston, MA, April 2012. The discussion that follows seeks to extend the argument in practical terms but must not be taken as a criticism of the Shakespeare Association of America, a professional association that has been institutionally supportive of addressing matters of race and racial politics.
63 Neill, introduction to *Othello,* 1.
64 Kim F. Hall, "*Othello* and the Problem of Blackness," in *A Companion to Shakespeare's Works, vol.* 1*: The Tragedies*, ed. Richard Dutton and Jean E. Howard (Malden: Blackwell, 2003), 357–374, esp. 358. In his introduction to *Othello,* Neill admits that "from the end of the seventeenth century [. . .] the hero's colour was capable of generating the most intense anxiety amongst viewers and critics alike" (2).
65 Loomba and Burton, *Race in Early Modern England,* 2; see also Espinosa, *Shakespeare and the Shades of Racism,* 1–9.
66 Tim Wise, "Membership Has Its Privileges: Thoughts on Acknowledging and Challenging Whiteness," in Rothenberg, *White Privilege,* 133–136 (133).
67 Adrienne Rich, *On Lies, Secrets, and Silence: Selected Prose 1966–1978* (New York: Norton, 1979), 299.
68 Margo Hendricks, "'I saw him in my visage': Problems with Race Studies in Early Modern English Literature," paper delivered as part of the panel presentation "Black Studies in the English Renaissance" at the Shakespeare Association of America meeting, Bellevue, WA, April 2011. Hendricks generously shared this paper with me.
69 My reference here is to Frantz Fanon, "The Fact of Blackness," in *Black Skin, White Masks.*
70 Hendricks, 'I saw him in my visage,' 5.
71 Ibid., 4.
72 See also Margo Hendricks's address, "Coloring the Past, Rewriting Our Future: RaceB4Race," Race and Periodization Symposium, September 2019, www.folger.edu/institute/scholarly-programs/race-periodization/margo-hendricks.
73 Applebaum, "White Privilege/White Complicity," 297.
74 In *Being White, Being Good,* Applebaum notes that although listening to others for counteractive knowledge is crucial, not "all members of oppressed groups automatically have such knowledge" (40). See n. 23.
75 Linda Alcoff, "The Problem of Speaking for Others," *Cultural Critique* 20 (1991–1992): 5–32, esp. 6–7.

76 Applebaum, *Being White, Being Good*, 96.
77 Alcoff, "The Problem of Speaking for Others," 12.
78 Ibid., 20. In the real social spaces of our dynamic communities, she adds, "there is no neutral place to stand free and clear in which one's words do not prescriptively affect or mediate the experience of others."
79 Ibid.
80 Patricia J. Williams, *Seeing a Color-Blind Future: The Paradox of Race* (New York: Farrar, Straus, and Giroux, 1997), 68.
81 Ibid., 69.
82 On intersectionality, see Vivian M. May, *Pursuing Intersectionality, Unsettling Dominant Imaginaries* (New York: Routledge, 2015); and Richard Delgado and Jean Stefancic, *Critical Race Theory: An Introduction* (New York: New York University Press, 2012), 57–62.
83 My transcription from Common's acceptance speech at the Golden Globes awards ceremony on January 11, 2015.

Epilogue
Forms of Whiteness

The story woven through American history is one of a persistent trauma of dispossession. Racial discrimination, inequality, and the erosion of civil rights all have as their motivating force the animating instauration of whiteness and the abridgment of freedoms for the many classified as nonwhite. Casting his reflective gaze across the turbulent American landscape in 1920, W. E. B. DuBois observes this complex of social effects in "The Souls of White Folk." "Wave on wave, each with increasing virulence, is dashing this new religion of whiteness on the shores of our time," he writes, employing "soul" in the sense of whiteness's attitude of voraciousness and appetite for dominion. Thus, with bewildered exasperation, he asks: "But what on earth is whiteness that one should so desire it? Then always, somehow, some way, silently but clearly, I am given to understand that whiteness is the ownership of the earth, forever and forever, Amen!"[1] For DuBois, the advent of European imperialism is the culmination of extravagant flights of ownership, already visible, I would argue, in the early modern slide from exploration to conquest. Published in the aftermath of the Red Summer of 1919 that unleased riots, lynching, and white terrorist attacks against African Americans, DuBois's essay compels us with the prescience of its rhetoric for the modern day: "Is not this the record of present America? Is not this its headlong progress? Are we not coming more and more, day by day, to making the statement 'I am white,' the one fundamental tenet of our practical morality?"[2]

That "practical morality" has governed our social and political life with a seemingly unrelenting grip, yet I would like to explore, in this Epilogue, the need and possibility for reparative hope in breaking up this monolith of whiteness that has become our legacy. Several years ago, during a class where students were naming or explaining their understanding of their racial identities, one student proposed the following: "I am white, but not *white*, white." I do not believe he was consciously citing DuBois's thesis of whiteness as dispossession. Yet setting the student's statement against

DuBois's work points to a veiled recognition of the kind of whiteness DuBois describes and at the same time allows for alternative intuitions or *forms of whiteness.* Here was an attempt to distinguish among whiteness as skin color ("I am white in physical appearance"); whiteness as ideology ("I am not *white*, white in a systemic, proprietary sense"); and, finally, whiteness as a renegotiated category ("I identify with alternate versions to being *white*, white"). The student's straightforward, incisive response fragments the one, singular form of dispossessing whiteness or, in DuBois's words, resists the pressure to "so desire" its monolithic heritage. I situate my appeal to *forms of whiteness* within Ta-Nehisi Coates's definition of "reparations," which requires close self-scrutiny and self-reckoning. For Coates, "white supremacy is . . . a force so fundamental to America that it is difficult to imagine the country without it. And so we must imagine a new country. Reparations – by which I mean the full acceptance of our collective biography and its consequences – is the price we must pay to see ourselves squarely."[3]

Today, the power of race and the devastation it can cause, when left unchecked precisely because of denialism, have made any pretense of a postracial agenda seem curiously out of touch. The nation has suffered seismic emotional shocks from a series of violent racial incidents. The shooting of nine African Americans in a church in Charleston, South Carolina in 2015; the brazen tiki-torchlit marches by neo-Nazi and white extremist sympathizers intoning anti-Semitic chants in Charlottesville, Virginia, followed by the murder of an antiracist demonstrator in 2017; the largest mass murder of Latinos in United States history in El Paso, Texas in 2019; and the dramatic spike in hate crimes against Asian Americans and Pacific Islanders in 2020–21 driven by the ghastly presidential rhetoric about the origins of the pandemic virus have all assaulted our collective sense of sanctity and safety.[4] The effects have filtered deep into everyday American life and generated much debate and anxiety. "It's quite a transition from being invisible to being visible in a lethal way. It's something new to my community. We are used to the basic darkness of racism, not this," a Mexican American lawyer remarked ominously in response to the El Paso massacre.[5] The assertion of property ownership is replayed in the racial volatility of Trump-era immigration policies determined to erect a permanent structure along the southern border that would enforce legitimate dweller status based primarily on skin color demonized as the external sign of threatening immoralities eagerly enumerated and publicized by presidential tweet.

In the 2020 post-election period, the insurrectionist assault on the US Capitol by groups with white extremist ties on January 6, 2021, delivered a wrenching blow to a plural democracy. At the same time, ironically, concepts like white privilege are aggressively being queried, while the latest in multiple schemes in the culture wars involves a sustained, outlandish assault on Critical Race Theory (CRT), deemed "anti-American,"[6] that relies on a combination of ignorance and an automatic negative association of the keyword "race" with blackness. One self-described "panicked" US senator emitted the rallying call against teaching CRT in the bellicose cause of white re-appropriation: "Take back our school boards, our county boards, our city councils. We will take back our culture."[7] With a renewed assault on banned curricula and loyalty testing of school board nominees, the schoolroom has become once again embroiled in centuries-old battles over racial denialism in education to ensure the primacy of whiteness.[8] Still, a public reeducation has begun with the launch of the 1619 Project, followed by the summer of reckoning in 2020 in the wake of the George Floyd murder protests, revitalizing little-known historic events like the 1921 Tulsa race massacre, during which white mobs blazed and bombed the homes and businesses of black residents of the town's Greenwood district, leaving hundreds dead.[9] Talking about race is not the cause or problem; ignoring the destructive behaviors and actions perpetrated in its name will only create a false sense of security while human damage is done. Blatant forms of white supremacy, outright violence, and injustice have flourished while denial, detachment, and a penchant for white racial gatekeeping have become major motifs in America's national narrative and sustained an earnest devotion to its "practical morality."

The strain of white "racial dictatorship" across US history, stretching back to Shakespeare's time, in his late sixteenth and early seventeenth-century works like *The Merchant of Venice*, *Othello*, and *Hamlet*, and the 1607 founding of Jamestown followed some twelve years later by the enslavement of Africans arriving at Point Comfort, Virginia, is traceable into the challenging decades of the twenty-first century.[10] Of course, this pronounced streak of whiteness has its worldwide counterpart. Achille Mbembe recognizes this repeated pattern in the political manufacture of "Whiteness" as a global phenomenon: "Fantasy, we know, seeks to anchor itself in the real in the form of an effective truth. In this, the fantasy of Whiteness succeeded, for, in the end, it became the mark of a certain mode of Western presence in the world, a certain figure of brutality and cruelty, a singular form of predation with an unequaled capacity for the subjection and exploitation of foreign peoples."[11] Given its role in modern global capitalism, the United States' contribution to this phenomenon of "Whiteness" cannot be underestimated. Here, however, I would like to focus, not so much on whiteness's global reach as on a historically specific character or attitude – a form of whiteness – that has played such a defining role in our elective, economic, and cultural politics. In plain terms, the central question remains embedded in the very interrogation of the racialized reader: What kind of person (reader, scholar, teacher, student, theater practitioner) am I committed to being? Am I prepared to inhabit and reproduce *the* form of whiteness, that is, invest in its unique character and attitude, that has for so long controlled and shaped our collective enterprise of living together?

I have employed the term systemic whiteness throughout to identify a cultural and epistemological formation contingent on a history of violent, custodial white rule. The foregoing review of the persistent manifestations of that quality and attitude of whiteness in our recent elective, economic, and cultural politics is meant to underscore, yet again, the congruence between aggressive white proprietorship and the historically informed positionality of the racialized reader. The two are inseparable and urge important reflection on the enterprise of Shakespeare scholarship and criticism whose persistent, sometimes subtle, patterns of indifference to race fly in the face of modern worldly reason. Because we are situated in history and culture, a connective line must be drawn between the character of whiteness, which Mbembe argues has considerable Western purchase, and the cultural practices engaged, like reading, scholarship, criticism, and teaching. However, to acquiesce to only one form of whiteness locks the racialized reader into a narrow, overdetermined praxis aligned with proprietary aggression that distorts and obfuscates through epistemological truculence.

Instead, I argue for the concept of *forms of whiteness*, alluded to in the introduction, and I return to it because of its ultimate importance to the arc of this book's argument. While I have tried to diagnose and describe the source of racial hesitancy, denial, or indifference in the formula of systemic whiteness, this study is rooted in a creative and emancipatory set of antiracist possibilities. As a remedy, racial literacy, as I have used it, is a dynamic practice signaling an active, conscious commitment to acquire awareness and knowledge of the cultural and political work of race. However, racial literacy is more than the acquisition of a set of reading, learning, and knowledge skills. Racial literacy represents an epistemological competence that works hard to resist the pressures of the learned habits that inculcate erasure, denial, and ambivalence in matters of race. It envisages a reorientation in attitude and a commitment to alternate antiracist possibilities of reckoning with systemic whiteness. To these alternate possibilities – what Coates describes as the reparative "revolution of the American consciousness" – I assign the term *forms of whiteness* as a reimagining of the reader's positionality in the culture and the world, a resolve to grapple with the multiple ways of disassociating from the tired, malignant monopoly of systemic whiteness, and a determination to undo patterns and practices of denial and discrimination within literary studies.[12] "Form" should not be construed as "merely superficial," even as it evokes the racial aspect of "appearance"; rather, it suggests racial construction, the ethical and individual reimagining of the manifestation of whiteness that has persisted within the broad sweep of US history in an intransigent, recalcitrant guise. The indices of one's positionality – including gender, age, sexuality, class, ability, and geographic location – will inform the situated nuances and possibilities for change and evolve dynamic, complex, accountable forms of whiteness. *Forms of whiteness* are, therefore, not absolute, nor do they have a predetermined scope although they bend toward an ethical outcome of antiracist practice for reading and living productively.

The work toward enacting and inhabiting different forms of whiteness poses real challenges, to be sure. The resilience of what I have described earlier in the book as the property of whiteness, a historical tendency toward nocuous dispossession, continues to shape and direct individual and institutional behavior. The growth and impact of the Black Lives Matter movement, which received a positive boost in its global public reception over the summer of 2020, is a current example of the potential for change in racial awareness. Decades earlier, the civil rights movement, characterized by historian C. Vann Woodward as the second Reconstruction, produced landmark victories that altered the legal landscape, fulfilling some of the promise of the first Reconstruction. The work is often slow in its constant adjustment to multiple variables of resistance to change, but incremental achievement has proven factually and substantively real. Nevertheless, reaction to civil rights legislation of the 1960s popularized the word *backlash*, "signifying a virulent counterreaction to all manner of social movements and cultural transformations."[13] White backlash, argues Jonathan Chait, set the stage for the present racial partisanship in the United States that opposes black advancement.[14] Lawrence Glickman explains: "*Backlash* may have burst onto the scene as 'the word of the year in American politics' in 1964, but it described one of the oldest and deepest patterns in American politics," white backlash expressing resentment toward black achievement with a resolve to claw back equitable gains.[15] While the pattern of denial and dispossession perpetuates its ruinous cycle, I caution against its reappearance in Shakespeare and early modern studies as a reactionary pushback to the changes initiated by race studies, including this book's urgent, heartfelt call for racial literacy. Should frustration, impatience, or fear morph into our own intra-disciplinary backlash, we stand to inherit and reproduce the historically proven legacy of debilitating opposition.

As an alternative, *forms of whiteness* can be understood within the context of an ethics of worldly care as articulated by Ella Myers, which comprehends "the complex, extrasubjective 'web' that constitutes the conditions of our lives."[16] Though Myers does not focus on race, her ethics of "care for worldly things" is acutely pertinent to the goals of racial literacy and the potential for the awareness of forms of whiteness to follow.[17] "To attest to care about something," Myers writes, "is at the most basic level, to indicate that the something in question has a claim on our attention; if we care in this sense, we are interested, not indifferent."[18] In my view, race matters as a worldly interest as "some particular feature of that world that becomes a site of mobilization."[19] One should not mistake caring for a soft ethics and politics. A commitment to caring is not about sentimentalizing others, which can be regarded as patronizing and self-authorizing; it also rejects attacking others following the increasing polarization in our society. In Myers's account, caring is not reducible to mere feeling, but is the agent for coaction in "the world, understood as the array of material and immaterial conditions under which human beings live."[20] In short, she is advocating for "a special kind of care enacted by citizens in association" that can be described as "a worldly ethics for democracy."[21]

Racial literacy can evolve material, worldly coaction in the practice of scholarship and classroom instruction. It provides opportunities for a reflective pedagogy and an engaged learning experience; values discovery as a cherished enterprise in an inclusive, outward-looking humanist tradition; and maintains a rigorous commitment to an ethics of self and other in the world that translates from scholarly inquiry and classroom examination into public life. In literary studies, however, legitimate considerations are often raised regarding uncertainty about how to approach and address race in an instructional environment. First, not to attempt to address race is to forego an opportunity to fulfill our responsibility to prepare students for life beyond the classroom and engage them in ways that encompass worldly care. I believe this to be true for all levels of tertiary education, where pedagogic investments in racial literacy might encounter fewer structural barriers. High school, despite the curricular controls in place, presents the widest student audience, and opportunities abound given the universality of Shakespeare's texts in that curriculum. Second, the primacy of expertise as part of professional development and identity can work against surrendering to the felt or perceived lack of expertise in teaching race. This is, however, a temptation that would otherwise have us settle back into the epistemological routines of the systemic status quo and hold on to the emotional, psychological, and political comfort of our current expertise in ways that stymie renovative learning. The critical vision of *forms of whiteness* is exploratory, disengaging from the monopoly of the dispossessing iteration of whiteness to effect discoveries of other modalities of knowing and being that can unite readers, researchers, teachers, and students as ethical learners about self, others, texts, and the world.

As a space of accountable collective endeavor and scholarship in action, the classroom enables the inquiries and discoveries of racial literacy. The coaction and collaborative endeavor toward "a worldly ethics for democracy" can – dare I say *must* – define the investment among early modern scholars, theater practitioners, audiences, students, and readers of Shakespeare in the practical and engaged work of race. The "thing" in Myers's phrase, "the care for worldly things," does double duty in referencing the material and political conditions of race as well as envisioning the substantive, *care*ful scholarship it requires. A "thing," Myers observes, "originally meant 'a gathering, and specifically gathering to deliberate a matter under discussion, a contested matter.' *Thing* designated precisely an associative activity by which participants collectively addressed a matter of importance."[22] Race, as a worldly thing, not only denotes a complex of institutional, cultural, and intersubjective processes, but also the collective exchanges and deliberations – the dialogues and conversations pursuant to racial literacy whether through reading, scholarship, conference deliberations, classroom learning, or theatrical performance – that envision fully invested participation, mobilization, and change.

Notes

1 W. E. B. DuBois, *The Souls of Black Folk with 'The Talented Tenth' and 'The Souls of White Folk'* (New York: Penguin, 2018), 228.

2 Ibid., 231.

3 Coates, "The Case for Reparations."

4 Joe Hernandez, "Hate Crimes Reach the Highest Level in More than a Decade," *NPR*, September 1, 2021, www.npr.org/2021/08/31/1032932257/hate-crimes-reach-the-highest-level-in-more-than-a-decade.

5 Simon Romero et al., "'It Feels Like Being Hunted': Latinos Across U.S. in Fear After El Paso Massacre," *The New York Times*, August 6, 2019.

6 Matthew S. Schwartz, "Trump Tells Agencies To End Trainings on 'White Privilege' and 'Critical Race Theory,'" *NPR*, September 5, 2020, www.npr.org/2020/09/05/910053496/trump-tells-agencies-to-end-trainings-on-white-privilege-and-critical-race-theor.

7 Jessie Opoien, "At WI Convention, Ron Johnson Calls for GOP to 'take back our culture,'" *The Capital Times*, June 26, 2021, https://madison.com/ct/news/local/govt-and-politics/election-matters/at-wi-convention-ron-johnson-calls-for-gop-to-take-back-our-culture/article_46b93b52-ed0d-5f90-b0ed-d5347e12563a.html.

8 Olivia B. Waxman, "'Critical Race Theory is Simply the Latest Bogeyman.' Inside the Fight Over What Kids Learn About American History," *Time*, July 16, 2021, https://time.com/6075193/critical-race-theory-debate/.

9 For a quick primer on other incidents of white terror and African Americans slaughtered over having access to vote (Wilmington, NC 1898) or black farmers murdered for unionizing to circumvent the oppressive sharecropping laws (Elaine, AR 1919), see Gillian Brockell, "Tulsa Isn't the Only Race Massacre You Weren't Taught in School. Here Are Others," *Washington Post*, June 1, 2021, www.washingtonpost.com/history/2021/06/01/tulsa-race-massacres-silence-schools/.

10 The phrase "racial dictatorship" is used by Omi and Winant in *Racial Formation*, 65.

11 Mbembe, *Critique*, 45.

12 Coates, "The Case for Reparations."

13 Lawrence Glickman, "How White Backlash Controls American Progress," *The Atlantic*, May 21, 2020, www.theatlantic.com/ideas/archive/2020/05/white-backlash-nothing-new/611914/.

14 Jonathan Chait, "Bill Clinton, O. J. Simpson, Clarence Thomas, and the Politics of 1990s Racial Backlash," *Intelligencer*, July 4, 2016, http://nymag.com/intelligencer/2016/06/clinton-and-the-politics-of-90s-racial-backlash.html.

15 Glickman, "How White Backlash Controls American Progress."

16 Ella Myers, *Worldly Ethics: Democratic Politics and Care for the World* (Durham: Duke University Press, 2013), 87.

17 Ibid., 85–110.

18 Ibid., 87.

19 Ibid., 93.

20 Ibid., 86.

21 Ibid., 88.

22 Ibid., 92.

Works Cited

Ad Herennium. Translated by Harry Caplan. Loeb Classical Library (Cambridge, MA: Harvard University Press, 1981).

Adelman, Janet. "Iago's Alter Ego: Race as Projection in Othello." *Shakespeare Quarterly* 48.2 (1997): 125–44.

Adelman, Janet. *Blood Relations* (Chicago: University of Chicago Press, 2008).

Akhimie, Patricia. *Shakespeare and the Cultivation of Difference: Race and Conduct in the Early Modern World* (New York: Routledge, 2018).

Alcoff, Linda. "The Problem of Speaking for Others." *Cultural Critique* 20 (1991–1992): 5–32.

Alcoff, Linda Martin. *The Future of Whiteness* (Cambridge: Polity Press, 2015).

Alexander, Michelle. *The New Jim Crow: Mass Incarceration in the Age of Colorblindness* (New York: The New Press, 2012).

Allen, Theodore W. *The Invention of the White Race*. 2 vols (New York: Verso, 1994, 1997).

Allen, Theodore W. *The Invention of the White Race: Volume 1: Racial Oppression and Social Control*. 2nd ed. (New York: Verso, 2012).

Althusser, Louis. *Lenin and Philosophy and Other Essays*. Translated by Ben Brewster (New York: Monthly Review Press, 2001).

Altman, Joel B. *The Improbability of "Othello": Rhetorical Anthropology and Shakespearean Selfhood* (Chicago: University of Chicago Press, 2010).

Amussen, Susan Dwyer. *Caribbean Exchanges: Slavery and the Transformation of English Society, 1640–1700* (Chapel Hill: University of North Carolina Press, 2007).

Andersen, Jennifer, and Elizabeth Sauer, eds. *Books and Readers in Early Modern England: Material Studies* (Philadelphia: University of Pennsylvania Press, 2002).

Andersen, Margaret L. "Whitewashing Race: A Critical Perspective on Whiteness." In *Whiteout: The Continuing Significance of Racism*, edited by Ashley W. Doane and Eduardo Bonilla-Silva (New York: Routledge, 2003), 21–34.

Appiah, Anthony. "The Uncompleted Argument: DuBois and the Illusion of Race." *Critical Quarterly* 12.1 (1985): 21–37.

Applebaum, Barbara. *Being White, Being Good: White Complicity, White Moral Responsibility, and Social Justice Pedagogy* (Lanham: Lexington Books, 2010).

Applebaum, Barbara. "White Privilege/White Complicity: Connecting 'Benefiting From' to 'Contributing To.'" *Philosophy of Education Yearbook* (2008): 292–300.

Aristotle. *Politics*. Translated by H. Rackham. Loeb Classical Library (Cambridge, MA: Harvard University Press, 1977).

Aristotle. Metaphysics. In *Introduction to Aristotle*, edited by Richard McKeon. Translated by W. D. Ross (New York: Random House, 1947).

Asher, Lyell. "Gertrude's Shoes." *ELH* 83.4 (2016): 959–987.

Babb, Valerie. *Whiteness Visible: The Meaning of Whiteness in American Literature and Culture* (New York: New York University Press, 1998).

Bailey, Amanda. *Of Bondage: Debt, Property, and Personhood in Early Modern England* (Philadelphia: University of Pennsylvania Press, 2013).

Baird, Robert P. "The Invention of Whiteness: The Long History of a Very Dangerous Idea." *The Guardian*, April 20, 2021. www.theguardian.com/news/2021/apr/20/the-invention-of-whiteness-long-history-dangerous-idea.

Baker, Al, J. David Goodman, and Benjamin Mueller. "Beyond the Chokehold: The Path to Eric Garner's Death." *New York Times*, June 13, 2015.

Baker, Steven. "Sight and a Sight in *Othello*." *Iowa State Journal of Research* 61.3 (1987): 301–309.

Baker, Susan. "Hamlet's Bloody Thoughts and the Illusion of Inwardness." *Comparative Drama* 21.4 (1987–88): 303–317.

Baldwin, James. *Nobody Knows My Name* (New York: Vintage, 1993).

Banaji, Mahzarin R., and Anthony G. Greenwald. *Blindspot: Hidden Biases of Good People* (New York: Delacorte Press, 2013).

Baptist, Edward E. *The Half Has Never Been Told: Slavery and the Making of American Capitalism* (New York: Basic Books, 2014).

Barnes, Tom. "How Music Executives Created 'Black' Hip Hop for White Suburban Kids." *Mic*, January 9, 2014. www.mic.com/articles/78487/how-music-executives-created-black-hip-hop-for-white-suburban-kids .

Barnett, Timothy. "Reading 'Whiteness' in English Studies." *College English* 63.1 (2000): 9–37.

Barthelemy, Anthony Gerard. *Black Face, Maligned Race: The Representation of Blacks in English Drama from Shakespeare to Southerne* (Baton Rouge: Louisiana State University Press, 1987).

Barthes, Roland. "The Death of the Author." In *The Rustle of Language*. Translated by Richard Howard (New York: Hill & Wang, 1986), 49–55.

Bartky, Sandra Lee. "Race, Complicity, and Culpable Ignorance." In her *"Sympathy and Solidarity" and Other Essays* (Lanham: Rowman & Littlefield, 2002), 151–167.

Bartolovich, Crystal. "Humanities of Scale: Marxism, Surface Reading – and Milton." *PMLA* 127.1 (2012): 115–121.

Barton, Anne. *Shakespeare and the Idea of Play* (New York: Penguin Books, 1967).

Bate, Jonathan. *How the Classics Made Shakespeare* (Princeton: Princeton University Press, 2019).

Bazerman, Max H., and Ann E Tenbrunsel. *Blind Spots: Why We Fail to Do What's Right and What to Do about It* (Princeton: Princeton University Press, 2011).

Bearman, Robert. *Shakespeare's Money: How Much Did He Make and What Did this Mean?* (Oxford: Oxford University Press, 2016).

Berman, Mark. "No Indictments after Police Shoot and Kill Man at an Ohio Wal-Mart; Justice Dept. Launches Investigation." *Washington Post*, September 24, 2014. https://www.washingtonpost.com/news/post-nation/wp/2014/09/24/no-indictments-after-police-shoot-and-kill-man-at-an-ohio-wal-mart-justice-dept-launches-investigation/.

Berry, Daina Ramey. *The Price for Their Pound of Flesh: The Value of the Enslaved, from Womb to Grave, in the Building of a Nation* (Boston: Beacon Press, 2017).

Berry, Edward. "Othello's Alienation." *Studies in English Literature, 1500-1900* 30.2 (1990): 315–333.

Bertram, Paul, and Bernice W. Kliman. *The Three-Text Hamlet: Parallel Texts of the First and Second Quartos and First Folio* (New York: AMS Press, 1991).

Best, Stephen M. *The Fugitive's Properties: Law and the Poetics of Possession* (Chicago: University of Chicago Press, 2004).

Best, Sharon, and Stephen Marcus. "Surface Reading: An Introduction." *Representations* 108.1 (2009): 1–21.

Bevington, David, ed. *The Complete Works of Shakespeare*. 4th ed. (New York: Longman, 1997).

Black, James. "Hamlet Hears Marlowe; Shakespeare Reads Virgil." *Renaissance and Reformation/Renaissance et Réforme* 81.4 (1994): 17–28.

"Black Like Me, Past, Present and Future: Behind the Stratford Festival Curtain." Video, June 6, 2020. www.youtube.com/watch?v=xJK85IRtzYM.

Blackmon, Douglas A. *Slavery by Another Name: The Re-Enslavement of Black Americans from the Civil War to World War II* (New York: Anchor Books, 2009).

Bloom, Harold. *Shakespeare: The Invention of the Human* (New York: Riverhead Books, 1999).

Bonilla-Silva, Eduardo. *Racism Without Racists: Color-Blind Racism and the Persistence of Inequality in America* (New York: Rowman and Littlefield, 2014).

Bourdieu, Pierre. *Outline of a Theory of Practice*. Translated by Richard Nice (Cambridge: Cambridge University Press, 1977).

Bowers, Fredson. *Elizabethan Revenge Tragedy, 1587–1642* (Princeton: Princeton University Press, 1940).

Bray, Alan. "Homosexuality and the Signs of Male Friendship in Elizabethan England." *History Workshop* 29 (1990): 1–19.

Britton, Dennis Austin. *Becoming Christian: Race, Reformation, and Early Modern English Romance* (New York: Fordham University Press, 2014).

Britton, Dennis Austin. "Recent Studies in English Renaissance Literature." *English Literary Renaissance* 45.3 (2015): 459–478.

Britton, Dennis Austin, and Melissa Walter, eds. *Rethinking Shakespeare Source Study* (New York: Routledge, 2018).

Brockell, Gillian. "Tulsa Isn't the Only Race Massacre You Weren't Taught in School. Here Are Others." *Washington Post*, June 1, 2021. www.washingtonpost.com/history/2021/06/01/tulsa-race-massacres-silence-schools/.

Bronstein, Herbert. "Shakespeare, the Jews, and *The Merchant of Venice*." *Shakespeare Quarterly* 20.1 (1969): 3–10.

Brooks, C. W. *Pettyfoggers and Vipers in the Commonwealth: The Lower Branch of the Legal Profession in Early Modern England* (Cambridge: Cambridge University Press, 1986).

Broude, Ronald. "Revenge and Revenge Tragedy in Renaissance England." *Renaissance Quarterly* 28.1 (1975): 36–58.

Brown, David Sterling. "Code Black: Whiteness and Unmanliness in *Hamlet*." In *Hamlet: The State of Play*, edited by Sonia Massai and Lucy Munro (London: Bloomsbury, 2021), 101–128.

Browne, Thomas. *Pseudodoxia Epidemica: Or, Enquiries into Commonly Presumed Truths* (Oxford: Benediction Classics, 2009).

Bryson, Norman. "The Gaze in the Expanded Field." In *Vision and Visuality*, edited by Hal Foster (Seattle: Bay Press, 1988), 87–108.

Bullough, Geoffrey, ed. *Narrative and Dramatic Sources of Shakespeare*. Vol. 1 (New York: Columbia University Press, 1977).

Butler, Judith. "What's Wrong with 'All Lives Matter?'" *New York Times*, January 12, 2015.

Calmore, John O. "Jews and the Problem of Whiteness." *Race, Racism, and the Law*, August 26, 2011. http://racism.org/index.php/articles/race/66-defining-racial-groups/white-european-american/370-white01a2.

Castle, Gregory. *The Blackwell Guide to Literary Theory* (Malden: Blackwell, 2007).

Chait, Jonathan. "Bill Clinton, O. J. Simpson, Clarence Thomas, and the Politics of 1990s Racial Backlash." *Intelligencer*, July 4, 2016. http://nymag.com/intelligencer/2016/06/clinton-and-the-politics-of-90s-racial-backlash.html.

Chakrabarti, Lolita. *Red Velvet* (New York: Bloomsbury Methuen Drama, 2012).

Chakravarty, Urvashi. "More Than Kin, Less Than Kind: Similitude, Strangeness, and Early Modern English Homonationalisms." *Shakespeare Quarterly* 67.1 (2016): 14–29.

Chakravarty, Urvashi. "The Renaissance of Race and the Future of Early Modern Race Studies." Special Issue: The State of Renaissance Studies II. *English Literary Renaissance* 50.1 (2019): 17–24.

Chamberlin, J. Edward. *Come Back to Me My Language: Poetry and the West Indies* (Chicago: University of Illinois Press, 1993).

Chapman, Matthieu. *Anti-Black Racism in Early Modern English Drama: The Other "Other"* (New York: Routledge,2016.)

Clark, Stuart. *Vanities of the Eye: Vision in Early Modern European Culture* (Oxford: Oxford University Press, 2007).

Clarke, Simon, and Steve Garner. *White Identities: A Critical Sociological Approach* (New York: Pluto Press, 2010).

Coates, Ta-Nehisi. *Between the World and Me* (New York: Spiegel and Grau, 2015).

Coates, Ta-Nehisi. "The Case for Reparations." *The Atlantic*, June 2014. www.theatlantic.com/magazine/archive/2014/06/the-case-for-reparations/361631/.

Coates, Ta-Nehisi. "The First White President." *The Atlantic*, October 2017. www.theatlantic.com/magazine/archive/2017/10/the-first-white-president-ta-nehisi-coates/537909/.

Coates, Ta-Nehisi. "The Great Fire." *Vanity Fair*, August 24, 2020. www.vanityfair.com/culture/2020/08/ta-nehisi-coates-editor-letter.

Cobb, Keith Hamilton. *American Moor* (New York: Methuen, 2020).

Cohen, Shaye J. D. "The Matrilineal Principle in Historical Perspective." *Judaism* 34.1 (1985): 5–13.

Cohen, Walter. "*The Merchant of Venice* and the Possibilities of Historical Criticism." *ELH* 49.4 (1982): 765–789.

Coles, Kimberly Anne, Kim, F. Hall, and Ayanna Thompson, "BlacKKKShakespearean: A Call to Action for Medieval and Early Modern Studies." *Profession*, Fall 2019. https://profession.mla.org/blackkkshakespearean-a-call-to-action-for-medieval-and-early-modern-studies/.

Condon, James J. "Setting the Stage for Revenge: Space, Performance, and Power in Early Modern Revenge Tragedy." *Medieval and Renaissance Drama in English* 25 (2012): 62–82.

Corredera, Vanessa. "'Not a Moor exactly': Shakespeare, *Serial*, and Modern Constructions of Race." *Shakespeare Quarterly* 61.1 (2016): 30–50.

Critchley, Simon, and Tom McCarthy. "Money and Morality in *The Merchant of Venice.*" *Diacritics* 34.1 (2004): 2–17.

Croll, Paul R. "Modeling Determinants of White Racial Identity: Results from a New National Survey." *Social Forces* 86.2 (2007): 613–642.

Crowley, Timothy D. "Arms and the Boy: Marlowe's Aeneas and the Parody of Imitation in *Dido, Queen of Carthage.*" *English Literary Renaissance* 38.3 (2008): 408–438.

Cutler, Brian, ed. *Expert Testimony on the Psychology of Eyewitness Identification* (Oxford: Oxford University Press, 2009).

Cutler, Brian, and Margaret Bull Kovera. *Evaluating Eyewitness Identification* (Oxford: Oxford University Press, 2010).

D'Amico, Jack. *The Moor in English Renaissance Drama* (Tampa: University of South Florida Press, 1991).

Dadabhoy, Ambereen. "Two Faced: The Problem of Othello's Visage." In *Othello: The State of Play*, edited by Lena Cowen Orlin (New York: Bloomsbury, 2014), 1–20.

Dalton, Harlon. "Failing to See." In *White Privilege: Essential Readings on the Other Side of Racism*, edited by Paula S. Rothenberg (New York: Worth Publishers, 2012), 15–18.

Darnton, Robert. "First Steps Toward a History of Reading." *Australian Journal of French Studies* 23.1 (1986): 5–30.

Darnton, Robert. "What is the History of Books?" *Daedalus* 3.3 (1982): 65–83.

Davies, Hannah J. "Culture's Race Problem: 'For White Hipsters, Blackness is a Thing to Consume but not Engage With.'" *The Guardian*, March 16, 2019. www.theguardian.com/culture/2019/mar/16/cultures-race-problem-for-white-hipsters-blackness-is-a-thing-to-consume-but-not-engage-with.

De Certeau, Michel. *The Practice of Everyday Life*. Translated by Steven Rendall (Berkeley: University of California Press, 1984).

De Grazia, Margreta. *"Hamlet" Without Hamlet* (Cambridge: Cambridge University Press, 2007).

De Grazia, Margreta, and Peter Stallybrass. "The Materiality of the Shakespearean Text." *Shakespeare Quarterly* 44.3 (1993): 255–283.

Dekker, Thomas. *The Dramatic Works of Thomas Dekker*. Vol. IV. Edited by Fredson Bowers (Cambridge: Cambridge University Press, 1961).

Delgado, Richard, and Jean Stefancic. *Critical Race Theory: An Introduction* (New York: New York University Press, 2012).

Desilver, Drew, Michael Lipka, and Dalia Fahmy. "10 Things We Know about Race and Policing in the U.S." Pew Research Center, Washington, DC, June 3, 2020. www.pewresearch.org/fact-tank/2020/06/03/10-things-we-know-about-race-and-policing-in-the-u-s/.

Diehl, Huston. *Staging Reform, Reforming the Stage: Protestantism and Popular Theater in Early Modern England* (Ithaca: Cornell University Press, 1997).

Doane, Woody. "Rethinking Whiteness Studies." In *Whiteout: The Continuing Significance of Racism*, edited by Ashley W. Doane and Eduardo Bonilla-Silva (New York: Routledge, 2003), 3–18.

Dobson, Michael. *The Making of the National Poet: Shakespeare, Adaptation, and Authorship, 1660–1769* (Oxford: Clarendon Press, 2001).

Dollimore, Jonathan, and Alan Sinfield, eds. *Political Shakespeare: New Essays in Cultural Materialism* (Ithaca: Cornell University Press, 1985).

Dollimore, Jonathan. *Radical Tragedy: Religion, Ideology, and Power in the Drama of Shakespeare and His Contemporaries* (Chicago: University of Chicago Press, 1984).

Drakakis, John, ed. *The Merchant of Venice*. The Arden Shakespeare (London: Bloomsbury, 2010).

Drakakis, John. "Yorick's Skull." In *Gothic Renaissance: A Reassessment*, edited by Elisabeth Bronfen and Beate Neumeier (Manchester: Manchester University Press, 2014), 17–31.

DuBois, W. E. B. *Black Reconstruction in America*. Edited by Henry Louis Gates Jr. (Oxford: Oxford University Press, 2007).

DuBois, W. E. B. *The Souls of Black Folk with "The Talented Tenth" and "The Souls of White Folk."* Introduced by Ibram X. Kendi (New York: Penguin, 2018).

Dustagheer, Sarah, and Harry Newman. "Metatheatre and Early Modern Drama." *Shakespeare Bulletin* 36.1 (2018): 3–18.

Dyer, Richard. "The Matter of Whiteness." In *White Privilege: Essential Readings on the Other Side of Racism*, ed. Paula S. Rothenberg (New York: Worth Publishers, 2012), 9–14.

Dyer, Richard. *White: Essays on Race and Culture* (New York: Routledge, 1997).

Dyson, Michael Eric. "Foreword." In *White Fragility: Why It's So Hard for White People to Talk about Racism*, by Robin DiAngelo (Boston: Beacon Press, 2018), ix–xii.

Eagleton, Terry. *Literary Theory: An Introduction*. 3rd ed. (Minneapolis: Minnesota University Press, 2008).

Earle, T. F. and K. J. P. Lowe, eds. *Black Africans in Renaissance Europe* (Cambridge: Cambridge University Press, 2005).

Edelman, Charles. *The Merchant of Venice*. Shakespeare in Production. (Cambridge: Cambridge University Press, 2002).

Edwards, Paul. "The Early African Presence in the British Isles." In *Essays on the History of Blacks in Britain: From Roman Times to the Mid-Twentieth Century*, edited by Jagdish G. Gundera and Ian Duffield (Aldershot: Avebury, 1992), 9–29.

Edwards, Phillip, ed. "Introduction." In *Hamlet, Prince of Denmark*. The New Cambridge Shakespeare (Cambridge: Cambridge University Press, 2003), 1–82.

Edwards, W. G. H. "Sir Thomas Browne's Chemistry." *Journal of the Faculty of Arts* 2.3 (1964): 217–228.

Ender, Evelyne, and Deidre Shauna Lynch, eds. Special Topic: Cultures of Reading. Double Issue. *PMLA* 133.5 (2018) and *PMLA* 134.1 (2019).

Engle, Lars. "'Thrift is Blessing': Exchange and Explanation in *The Merchant of Venice*." *Shakespeare Quarterly* 37 (1986): 20–37.

Ephraim, Michelle. "Jephthah's Kin: The Sacrificing Father in *The Merchant of Venice*." *Journal for Early Modern Cultural Studies* 5.2 (2005): 71–93.

Erasmus, Desiderius. *On Copia of Words and Ideas*. Translated by Donald B. King and H. David Hix (Milwaukee: Marquette University Press, 1963).

Erickson, Peter, and Clark Hulse, eds. *Early Modern Visual Culture: Representation, Race, and Empire in Renaissance England* (Philadelphia: University of Pennsylvania Press, 2000).

Erickson, Peter, and Kim F. Hall, "'A New Scholarly Song': Rereading Early Modern Race." *Shakespeare Quarterly* 67.1 (2016): 1–13.

Erickson, Peter. "Can We Talk about Race in *Hamlet*?" In *"Hamlet": New Critical Essays*, edited by Arthur F. Kinney (New York: Routledge, 2002), 207–213.

Erickson, Peter. "Invisibility Speaks: Servants and Portraits in Early Modern Visual Culture." *Journal of Early Modern Cultural Studies* 9 (2009): 23–61.

Erickson, Peter. "Representations of Blacks and Blackness in the Renaissance." *Criticism* 35 (1993): 499–527.

Erickson, Peter. "Representations of Race in Renaissance Art." *The Upstart Crow: A Shakespeare Journal* 18 (1998): 2–9.

Erickson, Peter. "Respeaking Othello in Fred Wilson's 'Speak of Me as I Am.'" *Art Journal* 64.2 (2005): 4–19.

Erlich, Avi. *Hamlet's Absent Father* (Princeton: Princeton University Press, 1977).

Espinosa, Ruben. *Shakespeare and the Shades of Racism* (New York: Routledge, 2021).

Espinosa, Ruben, and David Ruiter, eds. *Shakespeare and Immigration* (New York: Routledge, 2016).

Euripides. *Andromache*. Translated by David Kovacs. Loeb Classical Library (Cambridge, MA: Harvard University Press, 1995).

Eze, Emmanuel Chukwudi, ed. *Race and the Enlightenment: A Reader* (Oxford: Blackwell, 2000).

Fanon, Frantz. *Black Skin, White Masks*. Translated by Charles Lam Markmann (New York: Grove Press, 1967).

Feagin, Joe R. *Racist America: Roots, Current Realities, and Reparations*. 4th ed. (New York: Routledge, 2019).

Feagin, Joe R. *The White Racial Frame: Centuries of Racial Framing and Counter-Framing*. 2nd ed. (New York: Routledge, 2013).

Felski, Rita. *The Limits of Critique* (Chicago: University of Chicago Press, 2015).

Feuillerat, Albert, ed. *Documents Relating to the Office of the Revels in the Time of King Edward VI and Queen Mary* (Louvain: A. Uystpruyst, 1914).

"Few Say Police Forces Nationally Do Well in Treating Races Equally." Pew Research Center, Washington, DC, August 25, 2014. www.people-press.org/2014/08/25/few-say-police-forces-nationally-do-well-in-treating-races-equally/.

Fish, Stanley. *Is There a Text in This Class?: The Authority of Interpretive Communities* (Cambridge, MA: Harvard University Press, 1980).

Fiske, John. "Cultural Studies and the Culture of Everyday Life." In *Cultural Studies*, edited by Lawrence Grossberg et al. (New York: Routledge, 1992), 154–173.

Flaherty, Colleen. "Professors Still More Likely Than Students to be White." *Inside Higher Ed*, August 1, 2019. www.insidehighered.com/quicktakes/2019/08/01/professors-still-more-likely-students-be-white.

Fletcher, Catherine E. *The Black Prince of Florence: The Spectacular Life and Treacherous World of Alessandro de' Medici* (Oxford: Oxford University Press, 2016).

Floyd-Wilson, Mary. *English Ethnicity and Race in Early Modern Drama* (Cambridge: Cambridge University Press, 2003).

Fontaine, Laurence. *The Moral Economy: Poverty, Credit, and Trust in Early Modern Europe* (Cambridge: Cambridge University Press, 2014).

Frankenberg, Ruth. "The Mirage of an Unmarked Whiteness." In *The Making and Unmaking of Whiteness*, edited by Birgit Brander Rasmussen et al. (Durham: Duke University Press, 2001), 72–96.

Frankenberg, Ruth. *White Woman, Race Matters: The Social Construction of Whiteness* (Minneapolis: University of Minnesota Press, 1993).

Freeman, Lisa. "Why We Argue about the Way We Read: An Introduction." *The Eighteenth Century* 54.1 (2013): 121–124.

Frye, Roland Mushat. *The Renaissance Hamlet: Issues and Responses in 1600* (Princeton: Princeton University Press, 1984).

Fudge, Erica, Ruth Gilbert, and Susan Wiseman, eds. *At the Borders of the Human: Beasts, Bodies and Natural Philosophy in the Early Modern Period* (New York: Palgrave 2002).

Gallup. "Gallup Review: Black and White Differences in Views on Race." Washington, DC, December 12, 2014. https://news.gallup.com/poll/180107/gallup-review-black-white-differences-views-race.aspx.

Garber, Marjorie. "'Remember Me': *Memento Mori* Figures in Shakespeare's Plays." *Renaissance Drama* n.s. 12 (1981): 3–25.
Garber, Marjorie. *Shakespeare and Modern Culture* (New York: Anchor Books, 2008).
Garrett, Lauren. "True Interest and the Affections: The Dangers of Lawful Lending in *The Merchant of Venice*." *Journal for Early Modern Cultural Studies* 14.1 (2014): 32–62.
Geertz, Clifford. "Thick Description: Toward an Interpretive Theory of Culture." In *The Interpretation of Cultures: Selected Essays by Clifford Geertz* (New York: Basic Books, 1973), 3–30.
Geisst, Charles R. *Beggar Thy Neighbor: A History of Usury and Debt* (Philadelphia: University of Pennsylvania Press, 2013).
Gilman, Sander. "Are Jews White?" In *Theories of Race and Racism: A Reader*, edited by Les Black and John Solomon (New York, Routledge, 2009), 229–237.
Glaser, Judith E. *Conversational Intelligence: How Great Leaders Build Trust and Get Extraordinary Results* (New York: Bibliomotion, 2014).
Glaude, Eddie, Jr. *Begin Again: James Baldwin's America and Its Urgent Lessons for Our Own* (New York: Crown, 2020).
Glickman, Lawrence. "How White Backlash Controls American Progress." *The Atlantic*, May 21, 2020. www.theatlantic.com/ideas/archive/2020/05/white-backlash-nothing-new/611914/.
Goldstein, Eric L. *The Price of Whiteness: Jews, Race, and American Identity* (Princeton: Princeton University Press, 2008).
Goodell, William. *The American Slave Code in Theory and Practice* (London: Forgotten Books, 2018).
Goodman, J. David, and Vivian Yee. "Officer Charged in Akai Gurley Case Debated Reporting Gunshot, Officials Say." *New York Times*, February 11, 2015.
Graeber, David. *Debt: The First 5,000 Years* (New York: Melville House, 2011).
Green, Andrew J. "The Cunning of the Scene." *Shakespeare Quarterly* 4.4 (1953): 395–404.
Greenblatt, Stephen J. *Learning to Curse: Essays in Early Modern Culture* (New York: Routledge, 1990).
Greenblatt, Stephen. *Renaissance Self-Fashioning: From More to Shakespeare* (Chicago: University of Chicago Press, 1980).
Greenblatt, Stephen. *Will in the World: How Shakespeare Became Shakespeare* (New York: Norton, 2004).
Greenwald, Anthony G., et al. "Targets of Discrimination: Effects of Race on Responses to Weapon Holders." *Journal of Experimental Social Psychology* 39.4 (2003): 399–405.
Griswold, Wendy. *Renaissance Revivals: City Comedy and Revenge Tragedy in the London Theatre, 1576–1980* (Chicago: University of Chicago Press, 1986).
Grossberg, Lawrence. "Cultural Studies and/in New Worlds." *Critical Studies in Mass Communication* 10 (1993): 1–22.
Guilfoyle, Cherrell. "The Beginning of *Hamlet*." *Comparative Drama* 14.2 (1980): 137–158.

Guinier, Lani, and Gerald Torres. *The Miner's Canary: Enlisting Race, Resisting Power, Transforming Democracy* (Cambridge, MA: Harvard University Press, 2002).

Habib, Imtiaz. *Black Lives in the English Archives, 1500–1677: Imprints of the Invisible* (Burlington: Ashgate, 2008).

Hackel, Heidi Brayman. "'Boasting of silence': Women Readers in a Patriarchal State." In *Reading, Society and Politics in Early Modern England*, edited by Kevin Sharpe and Steven N. Zwicker (Cambridge: Cambridge University Press, 2003), 101–121.

Hackel, Heidi Brayman. *Reading Material in Early Modern England: Print, Gender and Literacy* (Cambridge: Cambridge University Press, 2005).

Hacker, Andrew. *Two Nations: Black and White, Separate, Hostile, Unequal* (New York: Scribner, 2003).

Hall, Kim F. "*Othello* and the Problem of Blackness." In *A Companion to Shakespeare's Works: Volume I, The Tragedies*, edited by Richard Dutton and Jean E. Howard (Malden: Blackwell, 2003), 357–374.

Hall, Kim F. "'Troubling Doubles': Apes, Africans, and Blackface in Mr. Moore's Revels." In *Race, Ethnicity, and Power in the Renaissance*, edited by Joyce Green MacDonald (Madison: Farleigh Dickinson University Press, 1997), 120–144.

Hall, Kim F. *Things of Darkness: Economies of Race and Gender in Early Modern England* (Ithaca: Cornell University Press, 1995).

Hall, Stuart. "Cultural Identity and Diaspora." In *Colonial Discourse and Post-colonial Theory: A Reader*, edited by Patrick Williams and Laura Crisman (London: Harvester Wheatsheaf, 1994), 392–403.

Halperin, David. *Saint Foucault: Towards a Gay Hagiography* (Oxford: Oxford University Press, 1997).

Hamilton, Edith, and Huntington Cairns, eds. *The Collected Dialogues of Plato* (Princeton: Princeton University Press, 1961).

Hammond, Paul. *Figuring Sex Between Men from Shakespeare to Rochester* (Oxford: Clarendon Press, 2002).

Hanson, Elizabeth. "Fellow Students: Hamlet, Horatio, and the Early Modern University." *Shakespeare Quarterly* 62.2 (2011): 205–229.

Harris, Cheryl I. "Whiteness as Property." *Harvard Law Review* 106.8 (1993): 1707–1791.

Harris, Jonathan Gil. "Surviving *Hamlet*." *Shakespeare Quarterly* 62.2 (2011): 145–147.

Harris, Mitchell M. "The Expense of Ink and Wastes of Shame: Poetic Generation, Black Ink, and Material Waste in Shakespeare's Sonnets." In *The Materiality of Color: The Production, Circulation, and Application of Dyes and Pigments, 1400–1800*, edited by Andrea Feeser, Maureen Daly Goggin, and Beth Fowkes Tobin (Burlington: Ashgate, 2012), 65–80.

Hartigan, John, Jr. , "Establishing the Fact of Whiteness." *American Anthropologist* 99.3 (1997): 495–505.

Hawkes, David. *The Culture of Usury in Renaissance England* (New York: Palgrave Macmillan, 2010).

Hawkes, Terence. "Swisser-Swatter: Making a Man of English Letters." In *Alternative Shakespeares*, edited by John Drakakis (New York: Methuen, 1985), 26–46.

Hendricks, Margo, and Patricia Parker, eds. *Women, "Race," and Writing in Early Modern England* (New York: Routledge, 1994).

Hendricks, Margo. "Coloring the Past, Rewriting Our Future: RaceB4Race." Race and Periodization Symposium, September 2019. www.folger.edu/institute/scholarly-programs/race-periodization/margo-hendricks.

Hendricks, Margo. "'I saw him in my visage': Problems with Race Studies in Early Modern English Literature." Paper delivered as part of the panel presentation "Black Studies in the English Renaissance" at the Shakespeare Association of America meeting, Bellevue, WA, April 2011.

Hendricks, Margo. *"Race: A Renaissance Category?" In A Companion to English Literature and Culture*, edited by Michael Hattaway (Malden: Blackwell Publishers, 2000).

Hendricks, Margo. "Surveying 'Race' in Shakespeare." In *Shakespeare and Race*, edited by Catherine M. S. Alexander and Stanley Wells (Cambridge: Cambridge University Press, 2000), 1–22.

Hernandez, Joe. "Hate Crimes Reach the Highest Level in More than a Decade." *NPR*, September 1, 2021. www.npr.org/2021/08/31/1032932257/hate-crimes-reach-the-highest-level-in-more-than-a-decade.

Hibbard, G. R., ed. *Hamlet* (Oxford: Oxford University Press, 1998).

Higginbotham, Derrick. "Women/Animals/Slaves: Race and Sexuality in Wycherley's The Country Wife." In *Early Modern Black Diaspora Studies: A Critical Anthology*, edited by Cassander L. Smith, Nicholas R. Jones, and Miles P. Grier (New York: Palgrave, 2018), 37–61.

Hill, Marc Lamont. *Nobody: Casualties of America's War on the Vulnerable, from Ferguson to Flint and Beyond* (New York: Atria Books, 2016).

Hirschfeld, Heather. "'We All Expect a Gentle Answer, Jew': *The Merchant of Venice* and the Psychotheology of Conversion." *ELH* 70.1 (2006): 61–81.

Homer. *The Odyssey*. Translated by Emily Watson (New York: Norton, 2018).

hooks, bell. *Black Looks: Race and Representation* (New York: Routledge, 2015).

Howard, Jean E. "The New Historicism in Renaissance Studies." *English Literary Renaissance* 16.1 (1986): 13–43.

Howard, Jean E. "Renaissance Studies in a Different Time." Special Issue: The State of Renaissance Studies II. *English Literary Renaissance* 50.1 (2019): 70–75.

Howard, Jean E. *Theater of a City: The Places of London Comedy, 1598–1642* (Philadelphia: University of Pennsylvania Press, 2007).

Howell, Martha C. "The Language of Property in Early Modern Europe." In *The Culture of Capital: Properties, Cities, and Knowledge in Early Modern England*, edited by Henry S. Turner (New York: Routledge, 2002), 17–25.

Hugenberg, Kurt, and Galen V. Bodenhausen. "Facing Prejudice: Implicit Prejudice and the Perception of Facial Threat." *Psychological Science* 14:6 (2003): 640–643.
Ignatiev, Noel. *How the Irish Became White* (New York: Routledge, 1995).
Illingworth, C. F. W. "The Gall-Bladder in Animals." *Edinburgh Medical Journal* 43.7 (1936): 458–461.
Iser, Wolfgang. *The Act of Reading: A Theory of Aesthetic Response* (Baltimore: Johns Hopkins University Press, 1978).
Iser, Wolfgang. *The Implied Reader: Patterns of Communication in Prose Fiction from Bunyan to Beckett* (Baltimore: Johns Hopkins University Press, 1974).
Issler, Klaus. "Lending and Interest in the OT: Examining Three Interpretations to Explain the Deuteronomy 23: 19–20 Distinction in Light of the Historical Usury Debate." *Journal of the Evangelical Theological Society* 59.4 (2016): 761–789.
Iyengar, Sujata. *Shades of Difference: Mythologies of Skin Color in Early Modern England* (Philadelphia: University of Pennsylvania Press, 2004).
Jacobson, Matthew Frye. *Whiteness of a Different Color: European Immigrants and the Alchemy of Race* (Cambridge, MA: Harvard University Press, 1998).
Jacobson, Roman. "Linguistics and Poetics." In *Style in Language*, edited by Thomas A. Sebeok (Cambridge, MA: Technology Press of Massachusetts Institute of Technology, 1960), 350–377.
Jameson, Fredric. *The Political Unconscious: Narrative as a Socially Symbolic Act* (Ithaca: Cornell University Press, 1981).
Japtok, Martin, and Winfried Schleiner. "Genetics and 'Race' in *The Merchant of Venice*." *Literature and Medicine* 18.2 (1999): 155–172.
Jardina, Ashley. *White Identity Politics* (Cambridge: Cambridge University Press, 2019).
Jarrett-Macauley, Delia, ed. *Shakespeare, Race, and Performance: The Diverse Bard* (New York: Routledge, 2017).
Jauss, Hans Robert. *Toward and Aesthetic of Reception*. Translated by Timothy Bahti (Minneapolis: University of Minnesota Press, 1982).
Jay, Martin. *Downcast Eyes: The Denigration of Vision in Twentieth-Century French Thought* (Berkeley: University of California Press, 1994).
Jefferson, Thomas. *Notes on the State of Virginia*. In *Race and the Enlightenment: A Reader*, edited by Emmanuel Chukwudi Eze (Oxford: Blackwell, 2000), 95–103.
Jenks, Chris, ed. *Visual Culture* (New York: Routledge, 1995).
Johnston, Arthur. "The Player's Speech in *Hamlet*." *Shakespeare Quarterly* 13.1 (1962): 21–30.
Jones, Eldred. *Othello's Countrymen: The African in English Renaissance Drama* (London: Oxford University Press, 1965).
Jones, Norman. *God and the Moneylenders: Usury and Law in Early Modern England* (Oxford: Basil Blackwell, 1989).
Jones, Robert P. "Self-Segregation: Why It's So Hard for Whites to Understand Ferguson." *The Atlantic*, August 21, 2014. www.theatlantic.com/national/arch

ive/2014/08/self-segregation-why-its-hard-for-whites-to-understand-ferguson/378928/.

Jung, Moon-Kie, et al., eds., *State of White Supremacy: Racism, Governance, and the United States* (Stanford: Stanford University Press, 2011).

Kapano, Baruti N. "Soul Thieves: White America and the Appropriation of Hip Hop and Black Culture." In *Soul Thieves: The Appropriation and Misrepresentation of African American Popular Culture*, edited by Tamara Lizette Brown and Baruti N. Kopano (New York: Palgrave Macmillan, 2014), 1–14.

Kaplan, M. Lindsay. "Jessica's Mother: Medieval Constructions of Jewish Race and Gender in *The Merchant of Venice*." *Shakespeare Quarterly* 58.1 (2007): 1–30.

Kaplan, M. Lindsay. "The Jewish Body in Black and White in Medieval and Early Modern England." *Philological Quarterly* 92.1 (2013): 41–65.

Kaplan, M. Lindsay, ed. *The Merchant of Venice: Texts and Contexts* (Boston: Bedford/St. Martin's, 2002).

Kaye/Kantrowitz, Melanie. *The Colors of Jews: Racial Politics and Radical Diasporism* (Bloomington: Indiana University Press, 2007).

Keating, AnnLouise. "Interrogating 'Whiteness,' (De)constructing 'Race.'" *College English* 57.8 (1995): 901–918.

Kendall, Frances E. *Understanding White Privilege: Creating Pathways to Authentic Relationships Across Race*. 2nd ed. (New York: Routledge, 2013).

Kendi, Ibram X. "Denial is the Heartbeat of America." *The Atlantic*, January 11, 2021. www.theatlantic.com/ideas/archive/2021/01/denial-heartbeat-america/617631/.

Kendi, Ibram X. *How To Be an Antiracist* (New York: One World, 2019).

Kendi, Ibram X. *Stamped from the Beginning: The Definitive History of Racist Ideas in America* (New York: Nation Books, 2017).

Kermode, Lloyd Edward, ed. *Three Renaissance Usury Plays* (Manchester: Manchester University Press, 2009).

Kietzman, Mary Jo. "*The Merchant of Venice*: Shylock and Covenantal Interplay." *ELH* 84.2 (2017): 423–452.

Kincaid, Jamaica. "On Seeing England for the First Time." *Transition* 51 (1991): 32–40.

Kinder, Donald R., and Lynn M. Sanders. *Divided by Color: Racial Politics and Democratic Ideals* (Chicago: University of Chicago Press, 1996).

King, Desmond. *Making Americans: Immigration, Race, and the Origins of the Diverse Democracy* (Cambridge, MA: Harvard University Press, 2000).

Kinney, Arthur F. *Shakespeare and Cognition: Aristotle's Legacy and Shakespeare's Drama* (New York: Routledge, 2006).

Kinney, Arthur F. *Shakespeare by Stages: An Historical Introduction* (Malden: Blackwell, 2003).

Kish-Goodling, Donna M. "*The Merchant of Venice* in Teaching Monetary Economics." *The Journal of Economic Education* 29.4 (1998): 330–339.

Kitch, Aaron. "The Character of Credit and the Problem of Belief in Middleton's City Comedies." *Studies in English Literature, 1500–1900* 47.2 (2007): 403–426.

Knowles, Eric D., and Christopher K. Marshburn. "Understanding White Identity Politics Will Be Crucial to Diversity Science." *Psychological Inquiry* 21 (2010): 134–139.

Knowles, Eric, and Kaiping Peng. "White Selves: Conceptualizing and Measuring a Dominant-Group Identity." *Journal of Personality and Social Psychology* 89.2 (2005): 233–241.

Knutson, Roslyn L. "Falconer to the Little Eyases: A New Date and Commercial Agenda for the 'Little Eyases' Passage in *Hamlet*." *Shakespeare Quarterly* 46.1 (1995): 1–31.

Knutson, Roslyn L. "The Repertory." In *A New History of Early English Drama*, edited by John D. Cox and David Scott Kastan (New York: Columbia University Press, 1997), 461–480.

Koelb, Clayton. "The Bonds of Flesh and Blood: Having it Both Ways in *The Merchant of Venice*." *Cardozo Studies in Law and Literature* 5.1 (1993): 107–113.

Kolchin, Peter. "Whiteness Studies: The New History of Race in America." *The Journal of American History* 89.1 (2002): 154–173.

Landreth, David. *The Face of Mammon: The Matter of Money in English Renaissance Literature* (Oxford: Oxford University Press, 2012).

Lanier, Douglas. *Shakespeare and Modern Popular Culture* (Oxford: Oxford University Press, 2002).

Laughland, Oliver. "US Police Have a History of Violence Against Black People. Will It Ever Stop?" *The Guardian*, June 4, 2020. www.theguardian.com/us-news/2020/jun/04/american-police-violence-against-black-people.

Lazare, Sarah. "Say Her Name: In Expression of Vulnerability and Power, Black Women Stage Direct Action with Chests Bared." *Common Dreams*, May 22, 2015. www.commondreams.org/news/2015/05/22/say-her-name-expression-vulnerability-and-power-black-women-stage-direct-action.

Leach, Mark M., John T. Behrens, and N. Kenneth LaFleur. "White Racial Identity and White Racial Consciousness: Similarities, Differences, and Recommendations." *Journal of Multicultural Counseling and Development* 30 (2002): 66–80.

Lechte, John. *Fifty Key Contemporary Thinkers: From Structuralism to Post-Humanism*. 2nd ed. (New York: Routledge, 2008).

Lee, Huey-ling. "The Social Meaning of Money in Dekker's *The Shoemaker's Holiday* and Shakespeare's *The Merchant of Venice*." *Comparative Drama* 49.3 (2015): 335–366.

Leinwand, Theodore B. *Theatre, Finance, and Society in Early Modern England*. Revised edition (Cambridge: Cambridge University Press, 2003).

Leonardo, Zeus. "Through the Multicultural Glass: Althusser, Ideology, and Race Relations in Post-Civil Rights America." *Policy Futures in Education* 3.4 (2005): 400–412.

Levine, Lawrence W. *Highbrow/Lowbrow: The Emergence of Cultural Hierarchy in America* (Cambridge, MA: Harvard University Press, 2002).

Lipsitz, George. *The Possessive Investment in Whiteness: How White People Profit from Identity Politics* (Philadelphia: Temple University Press, 2006).

Little, Arthur, Jr. , "Re-Historicizing Race, White Melancholia, and Shakespearean Property." *Shakespeare Quarterly* 67.1 (2016): 84–103.

Little, Arthur, Jr. , *Shakespeare Jungle Fever: National-Imperial Re-Visions of Race, Rape, and Sacrifice* (Stanford: Stanford University Press, 2000).

Little, Arthur, Jr., ed. *White People in Shakespeare: Essays on Race, Culture and the Elite* (New York: Bloomsbury, 2022).

Loomba, Ania. "'Delicious traffic': Racial and Religious Differences on Early Modern Stages." In *Shakespeare and Race*, edited by Catherine M. S. Alexander and Stanley Wells (Cambridge: Cambridge University Press, 2000), 203–224.

Loomba, Ania. *Shakespeare, Race, and Colonialism* (Oxford: Oxford University Press, 2002).

Loomba, Ania, and Jonathan Burton, eds. *Race in Early Modern England: A Documentary Companion* (New York: Palgrave Macmillan, 2007).

Loomba, Ania, and Martin Orkin, eds. *Post-Colonial Shakespeares* (New York: Routledge, 1998).

Lublin, Robert I. "'Apparel oft proclaims the man': Visualizing *Hamlet* on the Early Modern Stage." *Shakespeare Bulletin* 32.4 (2014): 629–647.

Lupton, Julia Reinhard. "Exegesis, Mimesis, and the Future of Humanism in *The Merchant of Venice*." *Religion and Literature* 32.2 (2000): 123–139.

Lynch, Deidre Shauna, and Evelyne Ender. "Introduction: A Time for Reading." Special Topic: Cultures of Reading. *PMLA* 133.5 (2018): 1073–1083.

MacDonald, Joyce Green, ed. *Race, Ethnicity, and Power in the Renaissance* (Madison: Farleigh Dickinson University Press, 1997).

MacDonald, Joyce Green. *Shakespearean Adaptation, Race, and Memory in the New World* (New York: Palgrave, 2020).

MacFaul, Tom. *Male Friendship in Shakespeare and His Contemporaries* (Cambridge: Cambridge University Press, 2009).

Mack, Maynard. "The World of Hamlet." *The Yale Review* 41 (1952): 502–523.

Marcus, Leah S. *How Shakespeare Became Colonial: Editorial Tradition and the British Empire* (New York: Routledge, 2017).

Marlowe, Christopher. *The Complete Plays*, edited by J. B. Steane (London: Penguin, 1986).

Maus, Katharine Eisaman, ed. *Four Revenge Tragedies* (Oxford: Oxford University Press, 1995).

Maus, Katharine Eisaman. *Inwardness and Theater in the English Renaissance* (Chicago: University of Chicago Press, 1995).

May, Vivian M. *Pursuing Intersectionality, Unsettling Dominant Imaginaries* (New York: Routledge, 2015).

Mbembe, Achille. *Critique of Black Reason*. Translated by Laurent Dubois (Durham: Duke University Press, 2017).

McDermott, Monica, and Frank L. Samson. "White Racial and Ethnic Identity in the United States." *Annual Reviews in Sociology* 31(2005): 245–261.

Meislin, Bernard J., and Morris L. Cohen. "Backgrounds of the Biblical Law against Usury." *Comparative Studies in Society and History* 6.3 (1964): 250–267.

Meissner, Christian A., and John C. Brigham. "Thirty Years of Investigating the Own-Race Bias in Memory for Faces: A Meta-Analytic Review." *Psychology, Public Policy, and Law* 7.1 (2001): 3–35.

Metzger, Mary Janell. "'Now by My Hood, a Gentle and No Jew': *The Merchant of Venice* and the Discourse of Early Modern Identity." *PMLA* 113.1 (1998): 52–65.

Middleton, Stephen, David R. Roediger, and Donald M Shaffer, eds. *The Construction of Whiteness: An Interdisciplinary Analysis of Race Formation and the Meaning of a White Identity* (Jackson: University Press of Mississippi, 2016).

Middleton, Thomas. *Thomas Middleton: The Collected Works*. Edited by Gary Taylor and John Lavagnino (Oxford: Oxford University Press, 2010).

Mignolo, Walter D., and Catherine E. Walsh. *On Decoloniality: Concepts, Analytics, Praxis* (Durham: Duke University Press, 2018).

Mills, Charles W. *Black Rights/White Wrongs: The Critique of Racial Liberalism* (Oxford: Oxford University Press, 2017).

Mills, Charles W. *The Racial Contract* (Ithaca: Cornell University Press, 1997).

Miola, Robert S., ed. *Hamlet*. 2nd ed (New York: Norton 2019).

Mitchell, W. J. T. *Seeing Through Race* (Cambridge, MA: Harvard University Press, 2012).

Monahan, Michael. *The Creolizing Subject: Race, Reason, and the Politics of Purity* (New York: Fordham University Press, 2011).

Montrose, Louis. *The Purpose of Playing: Shakespeare and the Cultural Politics of the Elizabethan Theatre* (Chicago: University of Chicago Press, 1996).

Morgan, Edmund S. *American Slavery, American Freedom: The Ordeal of Colonial Virginia* (New York: Norton, 2003).

Morrison, Toni. *Playing in the Dark: Whiteness and the Literary Imagination* (Cambridge, MA: Harvard University Press, 1992).

Mousley, Andy. *Re-Humanising Shakespeare: Literary Humanism, Wisdom and Modernity* (Edinburgh: Edinburgh University Press, 2007).

Mueller, Martin. "Hamlet and the World of Ancient Tragedy." *Arion: A Journal of Humanities and the Classics*, third series 5.1 (1997): 22–45.

Muhammad, Khalil Gibran. *The Condemnation of Blackness: Race, Crime, and the Making of Modern Urban America* (Cambridge, MA: Harvard University Press, 2011).

Muldrew, Craig. *The Economy of Obligation: The Culture of Credit and Social Relations in Early Modern England* (New York: St. Martin's Press, 1998).

Munster, Sebastian. *The Messias of the Christians and the Jews Held Forth in a Discourse between a Christian and a Jew*. In *Race in Early Modern England: A Documentary Companion*, edited by Ania Loomba and Jonathan Burton (New York: Palgrave Macmillan, 2007).

Muskal, Michael, and Lauren Raab. "Cleveland Blames Tamir Rice, 12, for His Own Death Then Apologizes." *Los Angeles Times*, March 2, 2015. https://www.latimes.com/nation/la-na-tamir-rice-lawsuit-blame-cleveland-20150302-story.html.

Myers, Ben. "Where are the Minority Professors?" *The Chronicle of Higher Education*, February 14, 2016. www.chronicle.com/interactives/where-are-the-minority-professors.

Myers, Ella. *Worldly Ethics: Democratic Politics and Care for the World* (Durham: Duke University Press, 2013).

Nakayama, Thomas K., and Robert L. Krizek. "Whiteness: A Strategic Rhetoric." *Quarterly Journal of Speech* 81 (1995): 291–309.

Neill, Michael, ed. *Othello* (Oxford: Clarendon, 2006).

Neill, Michael. "'He that thou knowest thine': Friendship and Service in *Hamlet*." In *A Companion to Shakespeare's Works: Volume I, The Tragedies*, edited by Richard Dutton and Jean E. Howard (Malden: Blackwell, 2003), 319–338.

Neill, Michael. "'Mullatos,' 'Blacks,' and 'Indian Moors': *Othello* and Early Modern Constructions of Human Difference." *Shakespeare Quarterly* 49.4 (1998): 361–374.

Nelson, Benjamin N. *The Idea of Usury: From Tribal Brotherhood to Universal Otherhood* (Princeton: Princeton University Press, 1949).

Nguyen, Cindy. "Interpellation." The Chicago School of Media Theory. https://lucian.uchicago.edu/blogs/mediatheory/keywords/interpellation/.

Nirenberg, David. "Shakespeare's Jewish Questions." *Renaissance Drama* n.s. 38 (2010): 77–113.

Novy, Marianne. *Shakespeare and Outsiders* (Oxford: Oxford University Press, 2013).

Oldenburg, Scott. "The Riddle of Blackness in England's National Family Romance." *Journal of Early Modern Cultural Studies* 1.1 (2001): 46–62.

Omi, Michael, and Howard Winant. *Racial Formation in the United States: From the 1960s to the 1990s*. 2nd ed. (New York: Routledge, 1994).

Opoien, Jessie. "At WI Convention, Ron Johnson Calls for GOP to 'take back our culture.'" *The Capital Times*, June 26, 2021. https://madison.com/ct/news/local/govt-and-politics/election-matters/at-wi-convention-ron-johnson-calls-for-gop-to-take-back-our-culture/article_46b93b52-ed0d-5f90-b0ed-d5347e12563a.html.

Orgel, Stephen. *The Reader in the Book: A Study of Spaces and Traces* (Oxford: Oxford University Press, 2015).

Orkin, Martin. "Othello and the 'plain face' of Racism." *Shakespeare Quarterly* 38.2 (1987): 166–188.

Ortega, Stephen. "Across Religious and Ethnic Boundaries: Ottoman Networks and Spaces in Early Modern Venice." *Mediterranean Studies* 18 (2009): 66–89.

Ovid. *Metamorphoses*. Translated by Charles Martin (New York: Norton, 2004).

Painter, Nell Irvin. *The History of White People* (New York: Norton, 2010).

Palliser, D. M. *The Age of Elizabeth Under the Later Tudors, 1547–1603* (New York: Longman, 1983).

Parker, Patricia. "Black *Hamlet*: Battening on the Moor." *Shakespeare Studies* 31 (2003): 127–164.

Paster, Gail Kern. *Humoring the Body: Emotions and the Shakespearean Stage* (Chicago: University of Chicago Press, 2004).

Patterson, Orlando. *Slavery and Social Death: A Comparative Study* (Cambridge, MA: Harvard University Press, 1982).

Patterson, Steve. "The Bankruptcy of Homoerotic Amity in Shakespeare's *Merchant of Venice*." *Shakespeare Quarterly* 50.1 (1999): 9–32.

Pavel, Thomas G. *The Poetics of Plot: The Case of English Renaissance Drama* (Minneapolis: University of Minnesota Press, 1985).

Peacham, Henry. *The Garden of Eloquence* (London: H. Jackson, 1593).

Peele, George. *The Battle of Alcazar. In The Stukeley Plays*, edited by Charles Edelman (Manchester: Manchester University Press, 2005).

Penn Medicine News. "Fatal Police Shootings Among Black Americans Remain High, Unchanged Since 2015." *Penn Medicine News*, October 28, 2020. www.pennmedicine.org/news/news-releases/2020/october/fatal-police-shootings-among-black-americans-remain-high-unchanged-since-2015.

Pennington, James W. C. *The Fugitive Blacksmith* (Gloucester: Dodo Press, 2009).

Pennington, James W. C. *A Narrative of Events of the Life of J. H. Banks, and Escaped Slave, from the Cotton State, Alabama, in America* (Gloucester: Dodo Press, 2009).

Plett, Heinrich F. *Enargeia in Classical Antiquity and the Early Modern Age: The Aesthetics of Evidence* (Leiden: Brill, 2012).

Poitevin, Kimberly. "Inventing Whiteness: Cosmetics, Race, and Women in Early Modern England." *Journal for Early Modern Cultural Studies* 11.1 (2011): 59–89.

Pollard, Tanya. "Tragedy and Revenge." In *Cambridge Companion to English Renaissance Tragedy*, edited by Emma Smith and Garret Sullivan Jr. (Cambridge: Cambridge University Press, 2010), 58–72.

Prescott, Paul. "Shakespeare and Popular Culture." In *The New Cambridge Companion to Shakespeare*, edited by Margreta de Grazia and Stanley Wells (Cambridge: Cambridge University Press, 2010), 269–284.

Price, Leah, and Seth Lerer. *The History of the Book and the Idea of Literature*. Special Topic. *PMLA* 121.1 (2006).

Prince, Gerald. "Introduction to the Study of the Narratee." In *Reader-Response Criticism: From Formalism to Post-Structuralism*, edited by Jane Tompkins (Baltimore: Johns Hopkins University Press, 1980), 7–25.

Pronin, Emily, et al. "You Don't Know Me, But I Know You: The Illusion of Asymmetric Insight." *Journal of Personal and Social Psychology* 81.4 (2001): 639–656.

Pronin, Emily, Thomas Gilovich, and Lee Ross. "Objectivity in the Eye of the Beholder: Divergent Perceptions of Bias in Self Versus Others." *Psychological Review* 111.3 (2004): 781–799.

Pronin, Emily, Daniel Y. Lin, and Lee Ross. "The Bias Blind Spot: Perceptions of Bias in Self Versus Others." *Personality and Social Psychology Bulletin* 28 (2002): 369–381.

Quintilian. *Institutio oratoria*. 4 vols. Translated by H. E. Butler. Loeb Classical Library (Cambridge, MA: Harvard University Press, 1986).

Rahmatian, Andreas. *Lord Kames: Legal and Social Theorist* (Edinburgh: University of Edinburgh Press, 2015).

Ramachandran, V. S. "Filling in Gaps in Perception: Part II. Scotomas and Phantom Limbs," *Current Directions in Psychological Science* 2.2 (1993): 56–65.

Rasmussen, Birgit Brander. "'Attended with Great Inconveniences': Slave Illiteracy and the 1740 South Carolina Negro Act." *PMLA* 125.1 (2010): 201–203.

Rees, Geraint, and Rimona Weil. "How Does the Brain Fill-in the Visual World?" *ACNR* 9.4 (2009): 12–15.

Rich, Adrienne. *On Lies, Secrets, and Silence: Selected Prose 1966–1978* (New York: Norton, 1979).

Richards, Jennifer, and Fred Schurink. "The Textuality and Materiality of Reading in Early Modern England." *Huntington Library Quarterly* 73.3 (2010): 345–361.

Roediger, David R. *The Wages of Whiteness: Race and the Making of the American Working Class* (New York: Verso, 1991).

Roediger, David R. *Working Towards Whiteness: How America's Immigrants Became White* (New York: Basic Books, 2006).

Romero, Simon, et al. "'It Feels Like Being Hunted': Latinos Across U.S. in Fear After El Paso Massacre." *New York Times*, August 6, 2019.

Rosaldo, Renato. *Culture and Truth: The Remaking of Social Analysis* (Boston: Beacon Press, 1993).

Rosenberg, Edgar. "The Jew in Western Drama: An Essay." In *The Jew in English Drama: An Annotated Bibliography*, edited by Edward Davidson Coleman (New York: New York Public Library and Ktav Publishing House, 1970), 1–50.

Ross-Kilroy, Aimée. "'The Very Ragged Bone': Dismantling Masculinity in Thomas Middleton's *The Revenger's Tragedy*." *Renaissance and Reformation/Renaissance et Réforme* 33.4 (2010): 51–71.

Rothenberg, Paula S., ed. *White Privilege: Essential Readings on the Other Side of Racism*. 4th ed. (New York: Worth Publishers, 2012).

Rothman, E. Nathalie. "Contested Subjecthood: Runaway Slaves in Early Modern Venice." *Quaderni storici* 47.140 (2012): 425–441.

Rowley, William. *All's Lost by Lust in All's Lost by Lust, and A Shoemaker, a Gentleman*. Edited by Charles Wharton Stork (Philadelphia: University of Pennsylvania, 1910).

Royster, Francesca T. "The 'End of Race' and the Future of Early Modern Cultural Studies." *Shakespeare Studies* 26 (1998): 59–69.

Royster, Francesca. "'Working Like a Dog': African Labor and Racing the Human-Animal Divide in Early Modern England." In *Writing Race Across the Atlantic World: Medieval to Modern*, edited by Philip Beidler and Gary Taylor (New York: Palgrave, 2005), 113–134.

Sack, Kevin, and Megan Thee-Brenan. "Poll Finds Most in U.S. Hold Dim View of Race Relations." *New York Times*, July 23, 2015.

Said, Edward. *Culture and Imperialism* (New York: Vintage, 1994).

Said, Edward W. *Orientalism* (New York: Vintage Books, 1979).

Sanchez, Melissa E. *Shakespeare and Queer Theory* (New York: Arden Shakespeare, 2019).

Schmidt, Michael S., and Matt Apuzzo. "South Carolina Officer is Charged with Murder of Walter Scott." *New York Times*, April 7, 2015.

Schreiner, Susan E. "Appearances and Reality in Luther, Montaigne, and Shakespeare." *Journal of Religion* 28.3 (2003): 345–380.

Schwartz, Matthew S. "Trump Tells Agencies to End Trainings on 'White Privilege' and 'Critical Race Theory.'" *NPR*, September 5, 2020. www.npr.org/2020/09/05/910053496/trump-tells-agencies-to-end-trainings-on-white-privilege-and-critical-race-theor.

Scott-Warren, Jason. "Reading Graffiti in the Early Modern Book." *Huntington Library Quarterly* 73.3 (2010): 363–381.

Sedgwick, Eve Kosofsky. *Touching Feeling: Affect, Pedagogy, Performativity* (Durham: Duke University Press, 2003).

Seipp, David J. "The Concept of Property in the Early Common Law." *Law and History Review* 12.1 (1994): 29–91.

Serwer, Adam. "The Coronavirus Was an Emergency Until Trump Found Out Who Was Dying." *The Atlantic*, May 8, 2020. www.theatlantic.com/ideas/archive/2020/05/americas-racial-contract-showing/611389/.

Shakespeare, William. *Hamlet: Prince of Denmark*. Edited by Philip Edwards (Cambridge: Cambridge University Press, 2003).

Shakespeare, William. *The Merchant of Venice*, edited by M. M. Mahood (Cambridge: Cambridge University Press, 2003).

Shakespeare, William *Mr. William Shakespeare's Comedies, Histories, & Tragedies* (London: Isaac Jaggard and Edward Blount, 1623).

Shakespeare, William. *Othello*. Edited by Norman Sanders (Cambridge: Cambridge University Press, 2003).

Shapiro, James. *Shakespeare and the Jews* (New York: Columbia University Press, 1996).

Shell, Marc. *Money, Language and Thought: Literary and Philosophic Economies from the Medieval to the Modern Era* (Baltimore: Johns Hopkins University Press, 1982).

Shepard, Alexandra. *Accounting for Oneself: Worth, Status, and the Social Order in Early Modern England* (Oxford: Oxford University Press, 2015).

Sherman, William H. *Used Books: Marking Readers in Renaissance England* (Philadelphia: University of Pennsylvania Press, 2008).

Simkin, Stevie, ed. *Revenge Tragedy* (New York: Palgrave, 2001).

Simpson, A. W. B. "The Penal Bond with Conditional Defeasance." *The Law Quarterly Review* 82 (1966): 393–395.

Smith, Bruce R. *Homosexual Desire in Shakespeare's England: A Cultural Poetics* (Chicago: Chicago University Press, 1994).

Smith, Cassander L., Nicholas R. Jones, and Miles P. Grier, eds. *Early Modern Black Diaspora Studies: A Critical Anthology* (New York: Palgrave, 2018).

Smith, Emma, ed. *Five Revenge Tragedies* (New York: Penguin, 2012).

Smith, Emma. *Shakespeare's First Folio: Four Centuries of an Iconic Book* (Oxford: Oxford University Press, 2016).

Smith, Ian. *Race and Rhetoric in the Renaissance: Barbarian Errors* (New York: Palgrave Macmillan, 2009).

Snook, Edith. "Recent Studies in Early Modern Reading." *English Literary Renaissance* 43.2 (2013): 343–378.

Snyder, Timothy. "The American Abyss." *The New York Times Magazine*, January 9, 2021.

Somashekhar, Sandhya, Wesley Lowery, Keith L. Alexander, Kimberly Kindy, and Julie Tate, . "Black and Unarmed." *Washington Post*, August 8, 2015. www.washingtonpost.com/sf/national/2015/08/08/black-and-unarmed/.

Spicer, Joaneath, ed. *Revealing the African Presence in Renaissance Europe* (Baltimore: The Walters Art Museum, 2012).

Spickard, Paul. *Almost All Aliens: Immigration, Race, and Colonialism in American History and Identity* (New York: Routledge, 2007).

Spiller, Elizabeth A. "From Imagination to Miscegenation: Race and Romance in Shakespeare's *The Merchant of Venice*." *Renaissance Drama* n.s. 29 (1998): 137–164.

Spiller, Elizabeth. *Reading and the History of Race in the Renaissance* (Cambridge: Cambridge University Press, 2011).

"Stark Racial Divisions in Reactions to Ferguson Police Shooting." Pew Research Center, Washington, DC, August 18, 2014. www.pewresearch.org/politics/2014/08/18/stark-racial-divisions-in-reactions-to-ferguson-police-shooting/.

Stockdill, Brett, and Mary Yu Danico. *Transforming the Ivory Tower: Challenging Racism, Sexism, and Homophobia in the Academy* (Honolulu: University of Hawai'i Press, 2012).

Stockton, Sharon. "'Blacks vs. Browns': Questioning the White Ground." *College English* 57.2 (1995): 166–181.

Stolberg, Sheryl Gay. "Baltimore Suspends 6 Police Officers in Inquiry in Death of Freddie Gray." *New York Times*, April 20, 2015.

Sullivan, Ceri. *The Rhetoric of Credit: Merchants in Early Modern Writing* (Madison: Fairleigh Dickenson University Press, 2002).

Sullivan, Shannon. *Revealing Whiteness: The Unconscious Habits of Racial Privilege* (Bloomington: Indiana University Press, 2006).

Summers, David. *The Judgment of Sense: Renaissance Naturalism and the Rise of Aesthetics* (Cambridge: Cambridge University Press, 1990).

Talbot, Margaret. "Getting Credit for Being White." *The New York Times Magazine*, November 20, 1997.

Tate, Greg, ed. *Everything but the Burden: What White People Are Taking from Black Culture* (New York: Harlem Moon, 2003).

Tawney, R. H. *Religion and the Rise of Capitalism: A Historical Study* (Gloucester: Peter Smith, 1962).

Taylor, Gary. *Buying Whiteness: Race, Culture and Identity from Columbus to Hip-Hop* (New York: Palgrave, 2005).

Taylor, Michael. "A Note on the 'Pyrrhus Episode' in *Hamlet*," *Shakespeare Quarterly* 21.1 (1970): 99–103.

The Executive Board, RaceB4Race. "It's Time to End the Publishing Gatekeeping!" June 11, 2020. https://medium.com/the-sundial-acmrs/its-time-to-end-the-publishing-gatekeeping-75207525f587.

The Geneva Bible. 1560 edition (Madison: University of Wisconsin Press, 1969).

"The Kerner Commission Report." *Social Service Review* 42.2 (1968): 261–263.

Thomas, Hugh. *The Slave Trade: The Story of the Atlantic Slave Trade 1440–1870* (New York: Simon & Schuster, 1997).

Thompson, Ann, and Neil Taylor, eds. *Hamlet*. The Arden Shakespeare (London: Bloomsbury, 2016).

Thompson, Ayanna, ed. *The Cambridge Companion to Shakespeare and Race* (Cambridge: Cambridge University Press, 2021).

Thompson, Ayanna. *Passing Strange: Shakespeare, Race, and Contemporary America* (Oxford: Oxford University Press, 2011).

Thompson, Ayanna. *Performing Race and Torture on the Early Modern Stage* (New York: Routledge, 2007).

Tigay, Jeffrey H. *Deuteronomy, The JPS Torah Commentary* (Philadelphia: Jewish Publication Society, 1996).

Tokson, Elliot H. *The Popular Image of the Black Man in English Drama, 1550–1688* (Boston: G. K. Hall, 1982).

Trepagnier, Barbara. *Silent Racism: How Well-Meaning White People Perpetuate the Racial Divide* (Boulder: Paradigm, 2007).

Tribble, Evelyn B. *Margins and Marginality: The Printed Page in Early Modern England* (Charlottesville: University Press of Virginia, 1993).

Turner, Henry S. "Recent Studies in Tudor and Stuart Drama." *Studies in English Literature, 1500–1900* 58.3 (2018): 473–537.

Virgil. *The Aeneid*. Translated by Robert Fagles (New York: Penguin, 2008).

Walker, Samuel, Cassia Spohn, and Miriam DeLone. *The Color of Justice: Race, Ethnicity and Crime in America*. 5th ed. (Belmont: Wadsworth, 2012).

Walter, John. *Crowds and Popular Politics in Early Modern England* (Manchester: Manchester University Press, 2006).

Walvin, James. *The Black Presence: A Documentary History of the Negro in England 1555–1860* (New York: Schocken Books, 1971).

Warley, Christopher. "Specters of Horatio." *ELH* 75.4 (2008): 1023–1050.

Watson, Veronica T. *The Souls of White Folk: African American Writers Theorize Whiteness* (Jackson: University Press of Mississippi, 2013).

Waxman, Olivia B. "'Critical Race Theory is Simply the Latest Bogeyman.' Inside the Fight Over What Kids Learn about American History." *Time*, July 16, 2021. https://time.com/6075193/critical-race-theory-debate/.

Weber, Max. *General Economic History*. Translated by Frank H. Knight (New York: Greenberg, 1927).

Weed, Elizabeth. "The Way We Read Now." *History of the Present* 2.1 (2012): 95–106.

Weheliye, Alexander G. *Habeas Viscus: Racializing Assemblages, Biopolitics, and Black Feminist Theories of the Human* (Durham: Duke University Press, 2014).

Weinstein, Brian. "Shakespeare's Forgivable Portrayal of Shylock." *Jewish Bible Quarterly* 35.3 (2007): 187–191.

Wells, Robin Headlam. *Shakespeare's Humanism* (Cambridge: Cambridge University Press, 2005).

Westlund, Joseph. "Ambivalence in the Player's Speech in *Hamlet*." *Studies in English Literature, 1500–1900* 18.2 (1978): 245–256.

Wheeler, John. *A Treatise of Commerce*. London: John Harrison, 1601.

Whitaker, Cord J. *Black Metaphors: How Modern Racism Emerged from Medieval Race-Thinking* (Philadelphia: University of Pennsylvania Press, 2019).

Willbern, David. *Poetic Will: Shakespeare and the Play of Language* (Philadelphia: University of Pennsylvania Press, 1997).

Williams, Jeffrey L. "The New Modesty in Literary Criticism." *Chronicle of Higher Education*, January 5, 2015. www.chronicle.com/article/The-New-Modesty-in-Literary/150993.

Williams, Patricia J. "In Living Black and White." *Washington Post*, March 29, 1998. www.washingtonpost.com/archive/lifestyle/magazine/1998/03/29/in-living-black-and-white/929dae95-7fd3-4680-ac7b-c957f8bcef14/.

Williams, Patricia J. *Seeing a Color-Blind Future: The Paradox of Race* (New York: Farrar, Straus, and Giroux, 1997).

Wise, Tim. "Membership Has Its Privileges: Thoughts on Acknowledging and Challenging Whiteness." In *White Privilege: Essential Readings on the Other Side of Racism*, edited by Paula S. Rothenberg (New York: Worth Publishers, 2012), 133–136.

Womack, Peter. "Imagining Communities: Theatres and the English Nation in the Sixteenth Century." In *Culture and History, 1350–1600: Essays on English Communities, Identities and Writing*, edited by David Aers (Detroit: Wayne State University Press, 1992), 91–145.

Wrightson, Keith. *English Society, 1580–1680* (New Brunswick: Rutgers University Press, 2003).

Yang, Jia Lynn. *One Mighty and Irresistible Tide: The Epic Struggle Over American Immigration, 1924–1965* (New York: Norton, 2020).

Yungblut, Laura Hunt. *Strangers Settled Here Among Us: Politics, Perceptions, & the Presence of Aliens in Elizabethan England* (New York: Routledge, 1996).

Zanker, Graham. "Enargeia in the Ancient Criticism of Poetry." *Rheinisches Museum für Philologie* 124 (1981): 297–311.

Zur, Dror, and Shimon Ullman. "Filling-in of Retinal Scotomas." *Vision Research* 43 (2003): 971–982.

Index

Page numbers in **bold** refer to content in footnotes.

Printed by Integrated Books International,
United States of America